GENDER IN HISTORY

Series editors:
Lynn Abrams, Cordelia Beattie, Pam Sharpe and Penny Summerfield

The expansion of research into the history of women and gender since the 1970s has changed the face of history. Using the insights of feminist theory and of historians of women, gender historians have explored the configuration in the past of gender identities and relations between the sexes. They have also investigated the history of sexuality and family relations, and analysed ideas and ideals of masculinity and femininity. Yet gender history has not abandoned the original, inspirational project of women's history: to recover and reveal the lived experience of women in the past and the present.

The series Gender in History provides a forum for these developments. Its historical coverage extends from the medieval to the modern period, and its geographical scope encompasses not only Europe and North America but all corners of the globe. The series aims to investigate the social and cultural constructions of gender in historical sources, as well as the gendering of historical discourse itself. It embraces both detailed case studies of specific regions or periods, and broader treatments of major themes. Gender in History titles are designed to meet the needs of both scholars and students working in this dynamic area of historical research.

The state as master

MANCHESTER
1824
Manchester University Press

OTHER RECENT BOOKS
IN THE SERIES

Love, intimacy and power: marriage and patriarchy in Scotland, 1650–1850 Katie Barclay (Winner of the 2012 Women's History Network Book Prize)

Modern women on trial: sexual transgression in the age of the flapper Lucy Bland

The Women's Liberation Movement in Scotland Sarah Browne

Modern motherhood: women and family in England, c. 1945–2000 Angela Davis

Gender, rhetoric and regulation: women's work in the civil service and the London County Council, 1900–55 Helen Glew

Jewish women in Europe in the Middle Ages: a quiet revolution Simha Goldin

Women of letters: gender, writing and the life of the mind in early modern England Leonie Hannan

Women and museums 1850–1914: Modernity and the gendering of knowledge Kate Hill

The shadow of marriage: singleness in England, 1914–60 Katherine Holden

Women, dowries and agency: marriage in fifteenth-century Valencia Dana Wessell Lightfoot

Women, travel and identity: journeys by rail and sea, 1870–1940 Emma Robinson-Tomsett

Imagining Caribbean womanhood: race, nation and beauty contests, 1929–70 Rochelle Rowe

Infidel feminism: secularism, religion and women's emancipation, England 1830–1914 Laura Schwartz

Women, credit and debt in early modern Scotland Cathryn Spence

Being boys: youth, leisure and identity in the inter-war years Melanie Tebbutt

Queen and country: same-sex desire in the British Armed Forces, 1939–45 Emma Vickers

The 'perpetual fair': gender, disorder and urban amusement in eighteenth-century London Anne Wohlcke

THE STATE AS MASTER

GENDER, STATE FORMATION AND COMMERCIALISATION IN URBAN SWEDEN, 1650–1780

Maria Ågren

Manchester University Press

Published by Manchester University Press
Altrincham Street, Manchester M1 7JA
www.manchesteruniversitypress.co.uk

British Library Cataloguing-in-Publication Data
A catalogue record for this book is available from the British Library

ISBN 978 1 5261 0064 1 hardback

First published 2017

Typeset by Out of House Publishing
Printed by Lightning Source

Contents

Tables

Preface

This book is one of several outcomes of the project Gender and Work in Early Modern Sweden, first carried out between 2010 and 2014 and now to be continued from 2017 to 2021. The over-arching purpose of the project was, and is, to gain a more precise picture of women's and men's work – what they actually did for a living – and to situate the results within a number of broader debates of interest to historians. One of these debates has to do with the transformative process known as European state formation. While a large historiography has been devoted to this process, and its causes, effects and national variants, comparatively little attention has been paid to the ways in which state formation affected people's working lives and what this, in turn, did to notions of gender. The present book is a contribution to this under-explored topic.

In writing this book, I have benefited greatly from the multifaceted expertise at my place of work: the Department of History at Uppsala University in Sweden. From the 1960s onwards, scholars at the department have made many contributions to the discussion about state formation and its Swedish peculiarities, not least the financial problems involved in a sparsely populated country on the periphery of Europe establishing itself as an empire of sorts. More recently, from the 1980s, gender history has gradually become an increasingly important field of speciality at the department. These two historiographic strands were brought together in the Gender and Work project, as this book, for instance, bears out. I wish to extend a warm thank you to all my colleagues for providing such a vibrant and friendly atmosphere. Special thanks are due to Jan Lindegren, who has a foot in both the older tradition, with its focus on state finance, and the newer one, with its interest in gender and work. Karin Hassan Jansson and Margaret Hunt have inspired me with many thoughtful comments, as have Theresa Johnsson, Marie Lennersand, Dag Lindström, Sofia Ling, Linda Oja and Christopher Pihl. Björn Asker suggested that I choose Örebro as my area of study, which was a good idea. Outside the department, Amy L. Erickson, Julie Hardwick, Petri Karonen, Sheilagh Ogilvie and Ariadne Schmidt have all contributed to my ideas, even though they may not be aware of this.

I had the good fortune in 2013 to be able to undertake a period of research at the Stellenbosch Institute of Advanced Study in Stellenbosch, South Africa. I wish to thank the director, Hendrik Geyer, the staff and all the fellows for a stimulating and wonderful time. When I say this, I am thinking in particular of Judith Baker, whom I unfortunately never met again after we said goodbye in May 2013, and Ian Hacking. In 2016, I benefited from a similarly fruitful research period at the Swedish Collegium for Advanced Study in Uppsala. I was happy to have this opportunity at precisely the time I was to finalise this book, and I am very grateful to the Collegium's principal, Björn Wittrock, and deputy principal emerita, Barbro Klein, the staff and all the fellows for lively discussions in a friendly setting.

I have been very lucky in having Martin Naylor at my side to correct and prune my language; I doubt that there is anyone else who is so meticulous and has such a vivid and unselfish interest in making someone else's work as good as it possibly can be. I also want to thank Thomas Lavelle for English tutorials and for being a long-time and very dear friend.

The Gender and Work project would never have become a reality in 2010 had it not been for the generous grant provided by the Knut and Alice Wallenberg Foundation. That the project can now continue for another five years is also due to the generosity of the Wallenberg Foundations. Thank you! I have received additional economic support for this book from Kungliga Vitterhets Historie och Antikvitets Akademien, Kungliga Humanistiska Vetenskaps Samfundet and Kungliga Gustaf Adolfs Akademien.

Finally, I wish to thank series editor Pamela Sharpe and editors Emma Brennan and Paul Clarke at Manchester University Press. It has been a pleasure to work with you. I also wish to thank Robert Whitelock for his meticulous and speedy copyediting of the manuscript; it has been a true pleasure to work together! Last but not least, I thank Michael, Hanna and Anders, my family, for being my supporters.

Introduction: Serving others – serving the state

Service to others was integral to medieval and early modern European culture. It played a prominent role in the Christian world view. The Gospels often draw on metaphors of service, and the master–servant relationship is at the core of several of their parables. One example is the story of the nobleman who left his servants money to be wisely invested while he was away; here, the servant who hid his pound in a napkin was upbraided and punished for not having acted in his master's interests.[1]

Stories like this suggest that there was a common understanding of what it meant to be a servant. Servants were not their master's equal; they could not expect gratitude for their work, and those who failed to put their master's interests first were to be severely chastised. There was thus a notion of a firm hierarchy between master and servant, which according to the Gospels was shared by Jews and Romans.[2] When some translations of the Bible used the word 'slave' or 'bondman' instead of 'servant', the idea of hierarchy became even more pronounced. It is also revealing that when Jesus takes leave of his disciples, he says (in the Gospel of John) 'Henceforth I call you not servants; for the servant knoweth not what his lord doeth: but I have called you friends; for all things that I have heard of my Father I have made known unto you.'[3] Here, the hierarchy between master and servant is suddenly and drastically turned on its head, in a way that cannot have been lost on the many people who would hear these words in centuries to come. It was a powerful way of demonstrating what acceptance of the Christian belief meant, and it became so powerful precisely because it drew on common assumptions about what service normally meant.

To medieval and early modern people, service to others was a natural but not necessarily attractive part of human life. On the one hand, a period as a servant in a household other than one's own was a phase in life and a step towards adulthood; it could offer opportunities to learn skills and save money.[4] On the other hand, service of this kind was invariably linked to subordination, as the Gospels made clear. European labour legislation often made service compulsory for young people,[5] and the everyday experience of service to others taught obedience and hierarchy in a tangible way. Together with the message conveyed every week in church sermons, these experiences probably shaped people's notions of what was desirable but not always attainable in life: to be one's own master or mistress.

In the early modern period, a new form of service was inserted into this cultural grid: service of the state. Admittedly, such service was not entirely new, since medieval kings had also had servants: domestic servants, military servants, and servants whose duties were similar to those of early modern and modern civil servants. Nevertheless, it is appropriate to stress the novel aspects of early modern state service. First, the impact and quantitative importance of this form of service increased dramatically. While most early modern people still supported themselves through agriculture, cattle rearing and small-scale crafts, the minuscule share of the population who availed themselves of the opportunity to work for the state was growing and involved other groups than the traditional elites. Second, early modern states were different from previous forms of polity: they were stronger, in terms of both resources and administrative efficiency. To be the servant of an early modern state was different from being the servant of a medieval prince.

Yet early modern state service was still based on the old ideas about what it meant to serve others. In his discussion of secretaries in *The Prince* (printed in 1532), Niccolò Machiavelli emphasised the importance of choosing good servants. By doing so, the prince showed that he himself had good judgement, thereby enhancing his reputation. To find out whether a servant was faithful or not, Machiavelli advocated the following test: 'when you see the servant thinking more of his own interests than of yours, and seeking inwardly his own profit in everything, such a man will never make a good servant, nor will you ever be able to trust him; because he who has the state of another in his hands ought *never to think of himself*.'[6]

Never to think of oneself means, of course, that one will always act in the interests of others. The words hark back to the Gospels' insistence that good and faithful servants should invest their master's money in the most profitable way, take care of the members of his household while he is away, give him food first before they sit down to eat, and never expect any thanks for what they do. Servants were instruments of their masters, according to both the Bible and Machiavelli, and these notions set their stamp on early modern European culture. In 1622, for instance, the English clergyman William Gouge emphasised that servants must obey their masters and keep close their secrets.[7] In 1665, a Swedish state servant swore to obey his superiors and not to divulge secrets entrusted to him if this might harm the interests of his master.[8] In 1685, another clergyman, Richard Lucas, reminded servants that whatever was in the interest of their masters and mistresses was also in their own interest.[9] Regardless of their tasks, servants were conceived of as instruments without self-interest, and nowhere was this more obvious than in a martial context. When the king ordered his men to go into battle and they obeyed, they put his interests before their own as they accepted the prospect of being killed. But *all* state servants were expected to act in a way that was not guided by concerns of self-interest. Self-interested behaviour in a state servant was tantamount to corruption. Even if soldiers did of course defect and corruption did happen, such practices nevertheless flew in the face of the image of the ideal servant.

In early modern state service, elements of continuity and change were thus combined. Such service was understood against the backdrop of extant cultural norms about the expected behaviour of servants, but it also denoted a radically new type of service. It was new because it involved more and new groups of people, and because it related to a much stronger and more aggressive form of state. Finally, it was pioneering in terms of its effects. State service and bureaucratic administration would, in the longer term, profoundly affect the lives of people and nations. Using the small mid-Swedish town of Örebro as its lens, this book discusses the meanings and practical realities of state service in the period 1650 to 1780. Showing what state service could mean to people's chances of supporting themselves, the book makes larger claims about how state formation was entangled in and dependent on people's everyday lives.

State formation on the ground

The more successful early modern states are usually conceptualised as strong. Power and a wealth of resources more or less define the new states that were established in many parts of Europe in this period. In the image of the Leviathan proposed by Hobbes (in 1651), overwhelming strength and a capacity to inspire fear are perhaps the most striking features associated with the monster that is the state.[10] The economic and human resources in the hands of early modern monarchs were indeed visibly larger than those of their medieval predecessors. In Spain, the army grew by a factor of fifteen between 1475 and 1635; in France, by a factor of ten between 1475 and 1705.[11] Consequently, the share of the population that was involved in military pursuits increased. Sweden and Prussia provide particularly salient examples of this.[12]

The notion of the strong early modern state has, however, been called into question. One line of argument has been that, by comparison with ancient China, many early modern European states showed signs of weakness.[13] Another has been that, even without a comparison with others, the strength of European states varied,[14] but was never total. There were, for instance, legal and social norms that sometimes restricted what state leaders could do to their own subjects. Machiavelli acknowledged such restrictions, pointing out that princes should respect their subjects' property and women.[15] Even if this was an ideal rather than real limitation on princes' scope to manoeuvre, it does say something about their need for legitimacy. Princes had to create legitimacy for themselves in order to prevent and curb dissatisfaction and revolt; this often put them in situations where they had to negotiate, rather than rule by fiat. They had to rely on and even co-opt older societal structures, such as guilds, to reach out into society and establish control.[16] They were dependent on credit and had to solicit it from men and women of flesh and blood, inside and outside their territories.[17] If by 'absolute' we mean complete independence and no restrictions, early modern monarchs did not have absolute power; indeed, they were strongly dependent on the acceptance and cooperation of their subjects.[18]

This dependence crystallised in a need for faithful servants: servants who went on campaigns for the state; servants who raised taxes and customs for the state; servants who saw to it that men, money and means were transported to where the state needed them; and servants who reasoned with dissatisfied subjects, wrote reports and implemented new rules, all with a view to furthering the common good and the interests of the state. While each individual servant may well have been dispensable to the state and its long-term plans, state servants as a group were indispensable.

The dependence was mutual. Just as the state depended on its servants, those servants and their families depended on the state. The state was a powerful actor, and being able to interact with it could bring great advantages. Both higher and lower state servants were in this position: state service offered many perquisites and opportunities. In a cash-poor society, it was, for example, no small advantage to have access to state money and to be able to use it for licit or illicit purposes. State servants also drew authority from their master, which could serve them well in their private lives. The whole family could benefit too: it was not uncommon, for instance, for a son or son-in-law to take over an office from his father or father-in-law. Female members of the family could be actively involved in state service, for instance by purchasing provisions for navy ships.[19] State service was often beneficial to the household as a whole.

But interaction with the state also involved risks. Office holders could easily fall from grace and face accusations of infidelity and treason. As creditors of the state they could be frustrated in their attempts to retrieve their money. The expansion of the military and civil sides of the state did offer many new income-earning opportunities to some subjects, but once taken, those opportunities often exposed the same subjects to popular dissatisfaction, violence and sometimes even death. When suspected of disloyal behaviour, French state servants ran the risk of being dragged by the hair through the streets by local mobs and subsequently drowned in the nearby river. In the German-speaking area, couples who accepted certain types of work for the state would be branded as dishonourable, which in turn curtailed the opportunities open to their children.[20] Even under less dramatic circumstances than these, being allied with the state could nevertheless carry the risk of being at the receiving end of complaints, scorn, hostility or ridicule from other subjects. There was good reason to stress, as Thomas Hobbes did, the horrifying aspect of the state.

In the southern Swedish town of Helsingborg, a customs official complained in the 1670s about how even the mayor had refused to let the official and his men inspect his house, in spite of this being part of their job. Instead, the mayor had expressed contempt for them and subjected them to violence. 'What we rightfully appropriate [i.e. in the form of excise] will sometimes be taken back [i.e. by the mayor] by force, sometimes taken out of our hands in situations when we [i.e. the customs officials] are not so numerous.' Apparently, the mayor did not hesitate either to use violence or to take advantage of their precarious situation. The official also claimed that the mayor had called the levy of excise 'theft and robbery'; this was tantamount to insulting the king and testified to the mayor's outrage. He and his supporters, for their part, claimed that the customs official had assaulted a woman, beating her so hard with a stick that her nose started to bleed. According to them, the townspeople feared these customs officials more than they did 'the enemy of the realm'.[21]

These stark realities suggest that it was probably much harder to be a servant of the state than to be a servant in general, simply because the tasks the master asked its servants to perform would inevitably involve them in socially complicated situations. The job was demanding, yet it also offered tempting opportunities both to the man employed and to his family, as has been shown in the case of both England and France. Margaret Hunt has shown, for instance, how in the late seventeenth century women with connections to sailors in the English navy were able to negotiate favourable terms with the Admiralty. As a result, they improved their own conditions, while at the same time shaping notions about the state's responsibility for (some of) its subjects.[22] In a similar vein, Sarah Hanley has argued that the early modern period witnessed a 'state–family compact' in France, linking a small group of men – often those in the legal professions – and their families to the state.[23]

The relationship between early modern states and their servants was a very particular one: it linked the monster – Leviathan – to ordinary men and women, creating mutual dependencies. The states needed the time and bodies of these people to extract resources and fight battles, but also to build legitimacy and trust. This is worth emphasising: we are no longer talking about absolutist states and their relationship to men, but about dependent and far from unconquerable states and their relationship to men *and* women. This calls for an approach that looks at state formation on the ground and acknowledges the relevance of working-class and gender perspectives. Lower state servants were workers, and so were their wives. What did their relationship to the state do to the ideals and practical realities of service to others? What did it do to the ideals of gender and the practical realities of work?

State formation as working-class and gender history

In their capacities as heads of households, both spouses could and did wield authority in early modern society. It is true, of course, that men's formal legal capacity was more robust and the sources of their authority more varied. The formal legal capacity of married women was circumscribed, sometimes to the point of total eclipse, and the sources of their authority were more limited. In several countries, however, the range of sustenance activities available to married and widowed women – what they could do to support themselves and their families – was more varied than that available to unmarried women, and wives and widows often had access to material and immaterial resources in a way that set them apart from their unmarried sisters. As heads of households, married women could use the labour of subordinate household members, many of whom were unmarried women. Power and authority were clearly associated with the male gender but also, and just as importantly, with age and household position. Consequently, while many men were excluded from positions of power and authority (typically those who were young and unmarried and did not have a household of their own), many women had at least some access to such positions.[24]

The process of state formation hit European societies at a time when the relatively independent household run by two spouses was the dominant model. This was the type of household that the new states had to harness to their project and, initially at least, this project neither presupposed nor entailed rigid notions about how work for the state was gendered. Swedish state servants, for instance, were sometimes described as assistants of the king, just as wives could be described as assistants of their husbands. But the analogy was taken a step further when the function of these royal assistants was described as 'suckling' subjects like a mother.[25] Here, the concrete tasks associated with state service were presented with strikingly female connotations. Moreover, like many new trades, jobs within the expanding state administration lacked strong guild traditions and could, at first, be allotted to anyone who seemed suitable. In Sweden, a tangible lack of men (due to recurrent warfare) necessitated an open attitude and a flexible gender division of labour.[26] In the late sixteenth century, for example, women held higher, well-paid positions on the country's royal demesnes, and in the seventeenth century lower state offices (such as those of postmasters, customs officials or constables) could be held by women.[27] Married men and women drew authority from their positions as heads of household, and they could also draw authority from their relationship with the state. Married men benefited more than married women, but they were both privileged compared with the unmarried.

Men who were heads of household, however, were under pressure to show that they were capable of handling the responsibility vested in them. They were expected to exercise self-control and to use their resources in ways that benefited their households, while at the same time disciplining 'their people', because, in the words of Paul, 'if a man know not how to rule his own house, how shall he take care of the church of

God?'[28] According to early modern ideals, wise stewardship of resources and behaviour befitting the occasion set the male head of household apart from many women, but also from many men. Men who misused resources and failed to conform to expected standards of comportment were everywhere, yet they were seen as decidedly problematic. With time, households with insufficient resources became more numerous, and more men were thus barred from being the sort of man that the ideals prescribed. This could have repercussions for the roles ascribed to husbands and wives. Husbands earning a living from waged work outside the household became more similar to other men with whom they worked, and less similar to their wives.[29]

Traditionally, the typical state servant was a nobleman, but with the dramatic expansion of state administration, other groups than the old elites were harnessed to the state. Just as non-commissioned officers were added to a group that originally comprised only high-ranking military officers, so lower state servants joined the civil administration, at the top of which noblemen were still to be found. Offering paid jobs on an unprecedented scale to men of modest backgrounds, state formation contributed to the process by which households with limited resources became more numerous. In many ways, these men were working-class men: they did subordinate, unpleasant and physically demanding work and were subject to harsh discipline. At the same time, however, they imposed order and discipline on others, and they did so on behalf of their mighty employer. They worked together with other men, but they also worked with their wives. They were servants, but servants of a new type.

This book looks at what state formation did to notions of service, gender and work. The point of departure is the claim that cultural meanings are produced, reproduced and changed by women and men through their interaction with each other. Some practices are understood as constituting honourable and important work, while others are not acknowledged as work at all. Some are associated with men, while others are identified with women. These connections are typically changeable, unstable and contingent. Male work can turn into female work, and vice versa. Many studies show that the meanings attached to sexual difference have not always, or everywhere, been constructed as binaries, nor has gender been a primary way of signifying relations of power in all contexts. Consequently, as Jeanne Boydston has stressed, we need to be wary of extrapolating from nineteenth-century Western European gender ideals to other cultures or time periods.[30] The emergence of state bureaucracies is a case in point. In the nineteenth century, civil service was seen as the archetypal male occupation, but if we assume that this was always so, we will miss a long preceding chapter about how states and households interacted and how women were an active part of the story.

The book

In this book, different historiographical strands are allowed to intersect. State formation and commercialisation are major themes in political and economic history; people's living conditions and gender relations are usually discussed in social and gender history. Here, they are all interwoven. Chapter 1 sets the scene by introducing the people, the period, the urban environments and the state administration under consideration. Chapter 2 analyses the role of violence and hostility in state servants' working lives and the expectations of servants to behave in certain ways. Chapter 3 analyses the tangible conditions under which lower state service was performed, showing why marriage and the contributions of wives were essential both to their husbands and to their husbands' master, the state. It also demonstrates the vital role of small-scale market relations and of cooperation and mutual help among women. Chapter 4 analyses the relationship among lower state servants' families, their employer, their peers and local authorities, discussing how social control and contact were parts of daily life and how society was knit together through these many practices. Chapter 5 looks at the roles of women and men, discussing why, in the longer term, early modern state formation created more opportunities for men than for women, when another outcome seems equally possible. Seen from the vantage point of the seventeenth century, both husbands and wives were, in fact, state servants of sorts.

In its use of sources and examples, the book takes a northern European view. In the early modern competition among states in Europe, Sweden (including modern Finland) and Denmark (including modern Norway and Iceland) were two major players, though their importance would wane in the course of the eighteenth century. We know that the seventeenth-century war effort put extraordinary pressure on Scandinavian societies, and that it affected the gender division of work in peasant households. In the words of Jan Lindegren, as 'bad times were always imminent, there had to be mechanisms for different sorts of catastrophes'.[31] A flexible gender division of labour was one such mechanism in peasant societies, also described as the 'two-supporter model'.[32] We know less, however, about how the process of state formation affected state servants' households and the ways in which work was divided between spouses in such households. Do we find the same kind of flexibility here, or was there something about state service that restricted the scope for spousal cooperation? The history of state formation throws new light on how different forms of service for others have been understood and gendered over time, while people's everyday activities in turn elucidate the mechanisms by which states were formed.

Notes

1 Luke 19:12–26.

2 Matt 8:9, 10:24, 24:45–51; Luke 17:9–10; John 13:14–16.

3 John 15:15. Cf. Luke 12:36–7.

4 S. Maza, *Servants and Masters in Eighteenth-Century France: The Uses of Loyalty* (Princeton: Princeton University Press, 1983); B. Harnesk, *Legofolk: Drängar, pigor och bönder i 1700- och 1800-talens Sverige* (Umeå: Umeå universitet, 1990); T. Meldrum, *Domestic Service and Gender, 1660–1750: Life and Work in the London Household* (Harlow: Longman, 2000); J. Whittle, 'Servants in rural England *c.*1450–1650: Hired work as a means of accumulating wealth and skills before marriage', in M. Ågren and A. L. Erickson (eds), *The Marital Economy in Scandinavia and Britain, 1400–1900* (Burlington, VT: Ashgate, 2005), 89–107; K. Ojala, 'Opportunity or compulsion? Domestic servants in urban communities in the eighteenth century', in P. Karonen (ed.), *Hopes and Fears for the Future in Early Modern Sweden, 1500–1800* (Helsinki: Finnish Literature Society, 2009), 206–22; H. Østhus, *Contested Authority: Master and Servant in Copenhagen and Christiania, 1750–1850* (Florence: European University Institute, 2013).

5 See discussion in D. Hay and P. Craven (eds), *Masters, Servants, and Magistrates in Britain and the Empire, 1562–1955* (Chapel Hill: University of North Carolina Press, 2004).

6 N. Machiavelli, *The Prince*, trans. W. K. Marriott (Ancona: Ancona Media, 2015), Chapter 22 (my italics).

7 L. Gowing, 'The manner of submission: Gender and demeanour in seventeenth-century London', *Cultural and Social History*, 10:1 (2013), 25–45 (31).

8 RA, Kammarkollegiet, Kansliet, H II:4, oath taken by Henrik Johansson, 1665.

9 R. Lucas, *The Duty of Servants* (London, 1685), 14, 123–4.

10 H. Bredekamp, 'Hobbes's visual strategy', in P. Springborg (ed.), *The Cambridge Companion to Hobbes's "Leviathan"* (Cambridge: Cambridge University Press, 2007), 29–60 (50–1). Thomas Hobbes described the Leviathan – i.e. the state – as 'an artificial man; though of greater stature and strength than the natural, for whose protection and defense it was intended'. Quoted in J. Tralau, 'Leviathan, the beast of myth: Medusa, Dionysos, and the riddle of Hobbes's sovereign monster', in Springborg, *Cambridge Companion to Hobbes's "Leviathan"*, 61.

11 G. Parker, 'Warfare', in P. Burke (ed.), *The New Cambridge Modern History*, Vol. XIII (Cambridge: Cambridge University Press, 1979), 201–19 (205).

12 C. Tilly, *Coercion, Capital, and European States, AD 990–1990* (Oxford: Blackwell, 1990), 67–95, esp. Table 3.2; J. Lindegren, 'Men, money and means', in P. Contamine (ed.), *War and Competition between States* (Oxford: Clarendon Press, 2000), 129–62

(137); B. R. Kroener, 'The modern state and military society in the eighteenth century', in Contamine, *War and Competition*, 195–220 (211–12).

13 V. Tin-bor Hui, *War and State Formation in Ancient China and Early Modern Europe* (Cambridge: Cambridge University Press, 2005), 41–2, 49, 224–31.

14 T. Ertman, *Birth of the Leviathan: Building States and Regimes in Medieval and Early Modern Europe* (Cambridge: Cambridge University Press, 1997).

15 Machiavelli, *Prince*, Chapter 19.

16 M. Raeff, *The Well-Ordered Police State: Social and Institutional Change through Law in the Germanies and Russia, 1600–1800* (New Haven: Yale University Press, 1983); D. Lindström, *Skrå, stad och stat: Stockholm, Malmö och Bergen ca 1350–1622* (Uppsala: Historiska institutionen, Uppsala universitet, 1991).

17 H. Landberg, *Det kontinentala krigets ekonomi: studier i krigsfinansiering under svensk stormaktstid* (Stockholm: Läromedelsförlagen, 1971); J. R. Bruijn, 'States and their navies from the late sixteenth to the end of the eighteenth century', in Contamine, *War and Competition*, 69–98.

18 P. Contamine, 'Introduction', in Contamine, *War and Competition*, 1–7 (5); J. Hardwick, *Family Business: Litigation and the Political Economies of Daily Life in Early Modern France* (Oxford: Oxford University Press, 2009), 3–9.

19 Bruijn, 'States and their navies', 80.

20 W. Beik, *Urban Protest in Seventeenth-Century France: The Culture of Retribution* (Cambridge: Cambridge University Press, 1997), 256–8; K. Stuart, *Defiled Trades and Social Outcasts: Honor and Ritual Pollution in Early Modern Germany* (Cambridge: Cambridge University Press, 1999), 235.

21 RA, Äldre Kommissioner 167. My translation.

22 M. Hunt, 'Women and the fiscal-imperial state in the late seventeenth and early eighteenth centuries', in K. Wilson (ed.), *A New Imperial History: Culture, Identity and Modernity in Britain and the Empire, 1660–1840* (New York: Cambridge University Press, 2004), 29–47.

23 S. Hanley, 'Engendering the state: Family formation and state building in early modern France', *French Historical Studies*, 16:1 (1989), 4–27.

24 M. Ågren (ed.), *Making a Living, Making a Difference: Gender and Work in Early Modern European Society* (New York, London: Oxford University Press, 2017), Chapters 3 and 5; A. Shepard, *Meanings of Manhood in Early Modern England* (Oxford: Oxford University Press, 2003), 1–9, 246–53; S. C. Ogilvie, *A Bitter Living: Women, Markets, and Social Capital in Early Modern Germany* (Oxford: Oxford University Press, 2003), 62–3, 69, 145, 172; L. Gowing, 'Ordering the body: Illegitimacy and female authority in seventeenth-century England', in M. J. Braddick and J. Walter (eds), *Negotiating Power in Early Modern Society: Order, Hierarchy and Subordination in Britain and Ireland* (Cambridge: Cambridge University Press, 2001), 44–62 (48, 51, 61).

25 K. Stadin, *Stånd och genus i stormaktstidens Sverige* (Lund: Nordic Academic Press, 2004), 71.

26 Lindegren, 'Men, money', 156.

27 See Chapter 1.

28 1 Tim. 3:5.

29 S. Dwyer Amussen, *An Ordered Society: Gender and Class in Early Modern England* (Oxford: Basil Blackwell, 1988); K. H. Jansson, *Kvinnofrid: synen på våldtäkt och konstruktionen av kön i Sverige 1600–1800* (Uppsala: Historiska institutionen, Uppsala universitet, 2002); Shepard, *Meanings of Manhood*, 252–4; Hardwick, *Family Business.*

30 J. Boydston, 'Gender as a question of historical analysis', *Gender and History*, 20:3 (2008), 558–83.

31 Lindegren, 'Men, money', 156.

32 Ågren, *Making a Living*, Chapter 3.

1

State formation and state administration

In early modern Sweden, state servants and municipal servants were all referred to as *betjänte*. The root of this word is *tjäna*, to serve, which also appears in related words such as *betjänt* (footman) and, more importantly, *tjänare* (servant). In the seventeenth century, *betjänte* was used both of those who served a private master and of those who served the king. In the words of an etymological dictionary, 'the semantic difference between these two types of servant was not pronounced at a time when holders of public office were regarded as private servants of the monarch'.[1] Linguistic practice thus speaks to the fact that state servants were perceived as similar, if not identical, to domestic servants. Sometimes, higher state servants were referred to as *ämbetsmän*, holders of an office (*ämbete*), a usage that stresses differences among state servants. The distinction was far from clear-cut, however. For instance, in the seventeenth century, *betjänte* could refer to both the highest- and the lowest-placed employees of the customs administration.[2]

Later on, the similarities within the state servant group and between them and domestic servants would be attenuated or completely lost from view as some state servants were labelled as civil servants (or bureaucrats) and some equipped with greater powers.[3] When, in 1809, state servants were referred to as 'statens drängar' (farmhands of the state), it was clearly intended as irony.[4] But the similarities between serving a person and serving an institution remain striking. In his discussion of the rise of bureaucracy, Max Weber pointed out that when bureaucratic institutions first arose, they were manned by the personal servants of the ruler.[5]

It is revealing that lower state servants would sometimes be taken for common servants. In 1746, two men passing through the town of Örebro refused to let three customs officials perform the regular inspection of their vehicle. Instead, the men ordered them to guard the vehicle overnight, until such time as it might please them to continue their journey. Dissatisfied with the way they had been treated, the officials reported the incident to the local excise court.[6] By refusing to have their wagon searched, the two men failed to acknowledge that the officials were acting on behalf of the state and had a duty to inspect travellers. Instead, they treated them as ordinary servants: as people one could send around on various errands or entrust with simple and possibly boring tasks, while oneself occupied with something more important. Clearly, the two men made a mistake when they tried to use the customs officials for their own purposes; the officials were not *their* servants, and were well aware of the fact.

This incident shows that, in the early modern period, the resemblance between state and 'ordinary' servants was probably obvious to everyone, particularly in the case of lower servants of the state. Like domestic servants, they were extensions of their master, expected to faithfully put the master's interests before their own. Like domestic servants, they often lacked control of their own work situation, as they were bossed around and expected to be in many places at the same time. And like domestic servants, they were entrusted with responsibility for vital but sometimes onerous missions involving their master's money. These similarities were not entirely coincidental. The role of the Swedish lower state servant was consciously modelled on that of the 'ordinary servant', just as several early modern organisations were modelled on the household.[7] Consequently, we should not look upon these men from the perspective of modern, rational bureaucracy, but as servants participating in a new project – state formation – the meaning and outcome of which still remained unknown to those involved.

State formation as a process of learning and negotiation

In his discussion of types of government, Max Weber contrasted the modern, rule-based bureaucratic model with traditional government, which he depicted as inferior on a number of counts. In traditional government, state servants are not recruited on the basis of relevant expertise, there is no hierarchy of offices or strict division of tasks, officials do not devote all their time to the office entrusted to them, and no clear distinction is made either between the official's private abode and the premises of the state or between his moneys and those of the state. While acknowledging that European bureaucracy first developed in a pre-modern setting, Weber devoted less attention to the gradual transition from one model to the other and completely ignored non-European developments.[8]

From a social-historical point of view, understanding this transition is crucial. How did states transform their ways of exercising power, and what obstacles stood in their way? One obstacle was finding people who could do the new jobs and inculcating in them certain standards of behaviour. New ways of making a living could arouse suspicion and contempt in society,[9] and state-initiated tasks even met with public disapproval.[10] Consequently, these were not easily resolved problems. A case in point is the occupation of the searcher (*besökare*, literally visitor). This was the lowest type of customs official, and the job consisted in searching people's wagons and kitchens to make sure that no evasion of customs and excise was taking place. The job probably did not exist on a large scale in Sweden before *c.*1620, and those who performed it were highly disliked and ridiculed. Such mundane problems were part of what state formation meant on the ground, problems that had to be resolved by the officials themselves. While there were rules governing their work, these were not exhaustive, and office holders had to come up with strategies and routines of their own making. No one knew from the start exactly how a searcher, or any other state servant for that matter, was to behave in every concrete situation.

For this reason, lower state servants talked to each other about their work and would sometimes seek the advice of their immediate superiors, so as to avoid making mistakes. Local superiors would, in turn, write to their superior in Stockholm to take counsel, and judges and magistrates did the same.[11] The people entrusted with these new jobs were simply not quite sure how to carry them out, and so they had to talk to each other. In local communities, state servants and their families sought support from and allied themselves with other families. They were learning to perform roles that were essential to the state, but the script for those roles was not yet set in stone. Ubiquitous notions about what service to others meant were a fundamental part of the script, but only went some way towards clarifying the kind of behaviour a state servant was expected to display.

There was thus a sense in which everybody involved in the administration of the early modern state was learning by doing during this transformational period. Late state builders could learn from early state builders.[12] Governments experimented with different systems for levying tax and manning armies; some experiments failed and others took their place.[13] Local officials tried to find ways of doing their work that annoyed neither their master nor its subjects. Governments, servants and subjects were all adapting to novel situations and trying to find ways to handle them. The process of state formation has been described both as a form of bargaining between states and subjects and as an open-ended and dynamic process of trial and error; as Michael Braddick has put it, there were no blueprints.[14] With hindsight, the process can be understood as leading up to Weberian rational bureaucracy,[15] but there was rarely such a design at the outset, as the adaptation of the traditional model of service shows.

The low level of formal training among many lower state servants probably encouraged experimentation and local solutions. Clergymen were quintessential state servants in early modern Swedish society, and they of course received a university education, as did members of the nobility who, by tradition and legal prerogative, were the ones who held state offices.[16] But early modern state administration grew much faster than the nobility, and, more importantly, noblemen were seldom interested in asserting their rights to lower positions within the state hierarchy, as these conferred neither wealth nor prestige.[17] Instead, members of the lower echelons of society had to be recruited for the many new tasks created in the process of state formation, and these men did not always have formal university training. The fact that there are examples of women working as lower public servants in the early modern period is indicative of the open and experimental approach at that stage. The scope for arrangements involving both spouses may have been larger than we often think.[18]

On the other hand, the strong emphasis in the Swedish administration on relevant and sufficient experience created a system that, paradoxically, more closely resembled rational bureaucracy in the Weberian sense than did the administrative systems of many other European countries. Through practice, lower state employees such as bailiffs acquired experience and knowledge both of the geographical district in which they worked and of the rules that obtained in their field. Attuned in this way to local circumstances and based on local rules, Swedish early modern state administration managed to be heterogeneous and at the same time competence-oriented. Heterogeneity was perhaps both functional and efficient, and the ways in which it was accepted – up to a point – suggest that historians should focus on the processes of trial and error through which state formation came about.[19]

State administration and customs administration

Between 1650 and 1780, the Swedish state administration did undergo change, but the continuities were stronger. Created mainly by the chancellor Axel Oxenstierna in the 1630s, the system was based on a combination of central state bodies known as collegiums and a regional administration headed by regional governors (*landshövding*). The explicit ambition of the chancellor had been to set up an administrative structure that would provide stability, regardless of who was king, and while the years of Caroline absolutism (1680–1718) did involve reforms, these did not affect the administration as much as the fiscal system. After the death of King Charles XII, novel forms of political interaction and identity formation were introduced during the period commonly referred to as the Age of Liberty (1718–72), but the system of central collegiums and a strong regional administration remained intact.[20]

The regional governors had a crucial position in the system. The English traveller John Robinson described their authority as comprehending 'that of Lord Lieutenant, and Sheriff together' (1694).[21] It was incumbent on them to keep a watchful eye on the judiciary, military and naval matters, the levying of tax and religious life. To assist them, they had an administrative body of their own (*länsstyrelse*), which was quite modest in size. In times of social unrest, governors were also expected to visit the local scene and talk sense into people; this was perceived to be an essential component of 'controlling' the realm.[22]

The regional administration was thus the backbone of the Swedish state, but the customs and excise administrations were also considered of particular importance, since, unlike most other state departments, they provided the state with ready money. Customs and copper were used as security when the seventeenth-century Swedish state set out to wage war, and in 1612 the chancellor declared that customs duty was the most reliable sort of income. Subsequently, many Crown-owned production units (large-scale farms as well as ironworks) were privatised in the hope that this would be a more efficient way of managing state resources. In 1724, customs and excise constituted the second largest source of state income, and in 1783 they were the largest source. It is telling that there was an ongoing battle in the seventeenth century over which part of the central administration the customs authorities were to report to; both the (older) *Kammarkollegium* and the (newer) *Kommerskollegium* wanted direct access to these monies.[23] Customs and excise were farmed out in some parts of the realm, for instance in the 1660s and 1670s, but the king then ruled that it was more profitable for the state to administer the levy of customs itself. For parts of the eighteenth century, many customs duties were again farmed out to interested parties, for instance in the 1710s, and later to a body known by several names; in the period 1726–65, it was called *Generaltullarrendesocieteten*.[24]

Customs were levied both on exported and imported goods and on domestic trade. The former type was known as the 'great customs' or 'maritime customs' (*stora tullen* or *sjötullen*), while the latter was referred to as the 'small customs' or 'inland customs' (*lilla tullen* or *landtullen*). They were administered by two different state departments. In addition to customs in the strict sense of the word, urban customs officials were also in charge of the excise. This was a tax on consumption of alcoholic beverages (spirits and beer), bread and meat. As in England, the excise was not imposed on consumers, but on producers. Unlike in England, however, commercial production of beer and spirits was rarely large-scale in Sweden; instead, it often took place in people's homes. Consequently, the work of Swedish 'excisemen' (there was no such term) differed quite significantly from that of their English counterparts. Rather than visiting brewers at clearly identifiable production sites, Swedish customs officials in charge of collecting excise had to monitor the doings of all the inhabitants of a town, in order to catch any evaders. They also had to differentiate between production for home use and production for sale, the former being subject to less excise than the latter.[25] These were no easy tasks and often caused disputes between officials and subjects.

As Table 1.1 shows, the largest category by far among customs officials consisted of searchers (*besökare*). They made up around 51 per cent of all such officials in the country in the mid-eighteenth century, and in Stockholm their share reached over 70 per cent. The total number of customs officials was just below 1,000: not a large group in a population of some 1.5 million, but still a significant one, represented in ninety-six places. *Besökare* and customs scribes in charge of inland customs and excise are, with their wives, the main protagonists of this book. The families of customs inspectors and some employees of the regional state administration appear as points of comparison.

To bind these customs officials to their master, several methods were used. They swore oaths of allegiance to the king, and until the mid-eighteenth century those who handled state money had to have someone who vouched for their economic capacity by standing surety (*borgen*) for them. Like anyone entrusted with acting as another person's legal representative, customs officials had to prove that they were authorised to act on behalf of their master; often, this was done by showing a power of attorney (*fullmakt*). In due course, customs officials started wearing, if not regular uniforms, then at least specific insignia, identifying them as holders of a specific occupation. And like other employees – a small group in early modern Scandinavia, where the overwhelming majority of the population were peasants – customs officials received a salary.[26]

Instruments such as oaths, sureties, powers of attorney, physical insignia and salaries were all ways of tightening the bonds between

Table 1.1 Customs officials in Sweden in the mid-eighteenth century

	In all Swedish towns (95) except Stockholm, by position (1748)	In Stockholm (1773/1775)
Customs inspectors	95	
Customs scribes	241	
Other customs officials	23	
Searchers	378 (51%)	132[a] (71%)
TOTAL	**737**	**186**

[a] The role distribution of these 132 is not known.
Source: RA, Personella berättelser, 1748, 1773, 1775.

master and servants, making them stronger and more formal than those between ordinary servants and their masters and mistresses. Such instruments were believed to enhance trust, predictability and accountability. A servant bound by oath and furnished with a power of attorney was supposed to act in a predictable way and to be accountable for his acts. Equally important, these instruments were ways of making the bonds publicly known. Ideally, they were to demonstrate to both the servant and other subjects that this was indeed a servant of the state. While this might not have been vital to top state servants such as regional governors, who were noblemen and thus distinguishable by their clothes and social manners, it was decisive for lower servants of the state, who would otherwise be indistinguishable from the crowd.

But while these instruments set customs officials and other lower state servants apart from ordinary maidservants and farmhands, the basic similarity remained the same. What characterised servants was their allegiance to their master, no matter whether the master was a peasant, a burgher or a king, and the impossibility of serving two masters at the same time was always at the heart of the relationship.[27] Few crimes were as heinous as stealing from one's master or betraying him. Of all the instruments, therefore, the oath was probably the most crucial one.

The regional state administration and the customs administration were not just important; they were also the parts of the state network with the lowest proportions of noblemen. Here, more than anywhere else, state servants were recruited from among men who had a modest social background and often lacked formal education.[28] Judging by the curricula vitae of thirty-one lower customs officials who worked in or

Table 1.2 Education and previous experience of customs officials in and near Örebro, 1748 and 1765

Attended school	8
Worked for 'other master'	10
Worked as state servant	25
Other jobs	9
No information	1

Note: several officials had more than one type of experience to report, hence the difference between the 31 officials I refer to in the text and the 53 instances of education/experience shown here.
Source: RA, Personella berättelser, 1748, 1765.

near Örebro in the mid-eighteenth century, only a minority had been to any form of school and no one had been to university. The two best-educated officials were, surprisingly, *besökare* Harald Roth and customs scribe J. M. Dahlberg, who were reported to have attended *gymnasium*, while customs inspector Petter Bergman claimed only to have 'attended school' in Söderköping. Officials reported to have had 'other jobs' are particularly revealing of the modest backgrounds of some state servants. Olof Nykvist had worked in a tobacco factory for nine years and then moved on to become a shop assistant before he ended up as a *besökare*. Daniel Wallman had worked with his father, who was a bricklayer, and Carl Borman had worked for a tailor; later, Daniel and Carl both became *besökare*. Petter Jurij had served in the army for eighteen years while Tomas Lybeck and Johan Höijer had done office work at ironworks; all three ended up as customs scribes. Several officials reported that they had been in private service, 'working for other masters', where they had 'earned their praise'.[29] Clearly, these state servants had been recruited among men who were used to working in subordinate positions.

Being 'ordinary subjects' themselves, customs officials and the staff of the regional administration were also among those who came into closest contact with subjects. Thus, the men in focus in this study were undoubtedly *lower* state servants, in terms of both their social origins and their distance from the central state administration. At the same time, they were probably particularly important to the overall performance and legitimacy of the state, because of their numbers and because of their proximity to the people who paid the taxes, customs and excise. The ways in which they and their families adapted their behaviour to the new role was crucial to the success of state formation.

Scandinavian small towns and state servants

Scandinavia was not highly urbanised in the early modern period. In the middle of the eighteenth century, some 20 per cent of the Danish population lived in cities and towns, while in Norway and Sweden the share was 10 per cent and in Finland no more than 4.5 per cent. By the end of the century, Copenhagen and Stockholm were relatively large cities, with 90,000 and 75,000 inhabitants, respectively. In total, Sweden had approximately 100 urban settlements in the eighteenth century, most of which were home to between 1,000 and 2,000 people. Some small towns had a population of no more than a couple of hundred.[30]

While many Swedish cities and towns were of medieval origin, several others were established in the sixteenth and seventeenth centuries on the initiative of the expanding state. Regardless of age, however, all towns and cities were drawn into the sphere of power of the state, and the state imposed rules and restrictions on economic life. Trade in 'merchant goods' (herring, salt, spices, certain forms of textile) was, for instance, deemed illegal if it took place in the countryside (*landsköp*). While this prohibition was far from new, seventeenth-century governments tried harder to forcibly locate such trade in the urban parts of the country. Townspeople were also forbidden to purchase food in the countryside as this was seen as a form of regrating (*förköp*). Instead, the peasants were supposed to bring their produce into town where it was sold at specific times and in specific places. It is unlikely that the latter rules could be enforced to the letter,[31] but they testify to the general ambition to base state finances on customs and excise and, more particularly, to make it easier to monitor those liable to pay such taxes. The profusion of customs regulations, especially in the period 1612 to 1718, is another indicator of the importance ascribed both to these forms of revenue and to the distinction between rural and urban pursuits.[32]

But it was not only trade that was forcibly located to towns. The same was true of some forms of craft, such as the domestic manufacture of arms. Production of light weapons for military use was central to seventeenth-century Sweden's imperial ambitions, and of all state-produced muskets (some 8,000 in the 1620s), one half were produced in the countryside of Närke according to a contemporary estimate. In 1640, more than 500 adult men were actively engaged in this spatially distributed production of rifles but the government did its utmost to have these men and their families move to Örebro. As many smiths resisted these plans, the effort was only partly successful. In contrast to the case of rural trade, the ambition to have all rifle smiths move to town had little to do with the levy of revenue and more with quality control. Muskets that exploded in the hands of the soldiers were of little use.[33] Nevertheless, both examples show how state formation put its imprint on people's everyday lives and underline the necessity of having state servants posted in urban areas to control people's activities and levy revenue.

With approximately 2,000 inhabitants in 1750, Örebro was a typical middle-sized urban community. The town had grown considerably since 1640, when its population can be estimated at between 1,000 and 1,200, and it continued to grow, reaching 3,267 inhabitants in 1800 according to official statistics. It is reasonable to assume that there were some 700 households in 1750, of which probably no more than half belonged to the burgher community.[34] The relocated smith families did not,[35] for instance, and the same was true of lower state servants. This was also typical; the share of the urban population made up of burghers, with burgher rights, seems to have declined in the eighteenth century.[36] Throughout the early modern period, there were tensions between urban communities and the state, with the former insisting on their right to self-governance, but there could also be powerful tensions within the urban communities themselves. Some towns, wishing to minimise economic competition, had a restrictive policy on the admission of new burghers, while other towns, and the central authorities, were in favour of an inclusive approach, as a larger population made for larger tax revenues.[37]

In spite of its modest size, Örebro was a nexus of economic life. The town's location on the road between Stockholm and Gothenburg, and between the food-producing areas of southern Sweden and the iron-producing region just north of the town (Bergslagen), made it of considerable economic importance.[38] The many ironworks of Bergslagen were far from self-sufficient and depended on a continuous inflow of grain and meat to feed the labourers. Most of these products came by way of Örebro, as the customs records make clear: grain was shipped to town on lake Mälaren, whence it was transported further north, and oxen and other animals were taken through Örebro on their way to Bergslagen. In 1643, for instance, customs duties for some 8,700 oxen and 2,400 sheep and lambs were paid.[39] Iron was transported in the opposite direction.

Örebro was also a centre for small-scale economic transactions, manifested, for instance, in its weekly markets. That food was easily available for purchase was, in 1627, believed to make the town an attractive location for a school, since schoolboys could buy comestibles in the marketplace, instead of having to rely on their parents to send them supplies.[40] The annual fairs (such as Henriksmäss in January and Larsmäss in August) added to the town's commercial importance. During these fairs, large numbers of people assembled to exchange products and money, at the same time creating other income opportunities for the inhabitants, from renting out rooms to serving food for payment, or helping police the town precincts. This opened up sources of income for many women and men, and the town saw a temporary increase in its population at such times. Such commerce also provided the opportunity for levying customs.

Swedish small towns often had a decidedly rural character and Örebro was no exception. The burghers were dependent on agricultural pursuits, and by renting Crown lands, they came to a position where they were able better to support themselves. According to the regional governor in 1680, this made the burghers neglect their 'ordinary' tasks in trade and crafts: 'being too active in farming, [the burghers] are prevented from engaging in their regular pursuits and thus hurt the peasants. Instead of producing an [agricultural] surplus, a burgher ought to buy the peasant's produce.' The ideal was to uphold the distinction between rural and urban sectors, but realities made this difficult.[41]

Finally, Örebro was a hub of state administration. The town was the seat of the regional governor and a centre of regional state administration. It was also the base for a regiment and, as already mentioned, the customs administration played a central role in town because of the proximity of Bergslagen and the long-distance trade it generated. While few in number, both higher and lower state servants were key figures in Örebro. Reading decrees from the central administration to the town assembly, counting oxen and collecting taxes at the central bridge, monitoring and inspecting market activities and cracking down on unruly behaviour, they embodied the state in the local context. Some were more mobile than others, of course. Bailiffs and (in the seventeenth century) governors travelled frequently, not only within towns, but throughout their regions.[42] Subjects also took the initiative, or were encouraged, to visit the offices of the regional state administration, whose staff were increasingly resident in the town from around 1700. This made for more dealings and encounters and turned some state servants into important local figures, who gradually became members of the middling sort.

Lower state servants and their families did not as a rule belong to any of the four socio-political estates (apart from the very few who were of noble parentage). Consequently, they were not represented in Parliament and lacked political rights. This contrasts with the stronger rights of the members of the four estates (nobility, clergy, burghers and peasantry). While the estates represented a declining share of the whole population, they nevertheless retained much of their traditional power long into the nineteenth century, making the difference significant between those who belonged to an estate and those who did not.[43] To be eligible for membership of a burgher community, and consequently of the burgher estate, one had to be of legitimate birth and good repute. In addition, a completed period of professional training and a promise to remain a member for at least six years were requirements.[44] We have examples of lower state servants such as customs officials trying but failing to become burghers.[45] It is not always clear why, but as this book will show, their mobility and unpopularity may provide answers.

Apart from being, in a sense, outsiders in the urban community, lower state servants also had in common that they had been chosen by their employer on some sort of meritocratic basis. This was in stark contrast to *betjänte* within the municipal administration, who were normally elected by the burgher community and held their offices on a more or less honorary and temporary basis.[46] It was also in stark contrast to European countries such as France, where many offices were venal.[47] Another characteristic of Swedish lower state servants was their occupational and geographical mobility. For instance, a man who had a job within the local customs administration could move to a post as clerk to the owner of an ironworks, before switching to a position within the regional state administration. This mobility is important, because it exposed the men and their families to unexpected encounters, new acquaintances and novel ideas. These combined experiences of being excluded, mobile, yet at the same time selected and invested with state authority were common to them and were eventually conducive to a shared identity.

The many similarities within the group do not, however, exclude differences and tensions. There were, for instance, considerable salary differentials. In the middle of the eighteenth century, a regional clerk could have a salary of 500 silver *daler* a year, and a customs inspector around 350–400. By contrast, a scribe working for the clerk could earn 100 silver *daler*, and a searcher 70.[48] A customs inspector may have been dissatisfied with his salary and level of consumption, but a *besökare* was clearly unable to survive on his salary alone. All their salaries were dwarfed by that of the regional governor, who was paid 1,500 plus various additional emoluments and expenses. These stratum-related differences cut through the professional hierarchy, making scribes and searchers perhaps more similar to some lower municipal servants, or even manual labourers and private soldiers, than to their local superiors. There was also a difference between state servants who were paid their salaries mainly in cash and those who received it mainly in kind. Various combinations of payment in cash and in kind were conspicuous, not least among military officers.[49]

Office holders in Stockholm generally belonged to the category who received cash, while servants of the regional state administration were among those who were paid in kind. The former were of course harder hit in times of inflation.[50]

Methods and sources

This book relies on information, culled from a large number of historical sources, on people's everyday activities and the expectations to which they were subject. Methodologically, it compares these findings with two different models of state service. The first model is the ideal type of rational bureaucracy proposed by Weber, in particular three components of that model: that rational bureaucracy is based on theoretical knowledge; that state servants are specialists, fully occupied by their offices and able to make a living from them; and that the private and professional spheres are strictly separated. The second model is based instead on the historiography of early modern domestic service and draws attention, for instance, to the subordination and vulnerability of servants, the catch-all character of their work, and the mutual dependencies between servant and master. At certain points, the book also uses insights from conceptual history to buttress, but also to problematise, the results. Thus, what people did and how they made sense of their actions by the use of language are analysed and explained with the two models as points of reference.

Chronologically, the book spans the period 1650 to 1780. In 1648 the Thirty Years War had come to an end, and not long after the peace the Swedish customs administration was expanded and reorganised. With the decision to set up special excise courts in 1672, a new body of source material was created that allows the historian to study the working lives and problems of customs officials. In the mid-eighteenth century, the customs administration once again received attention from a state interested in making it both more efficient and less disliked. These improving ambitions, too, generated source material, not least in the form of statutory law.

The case study of Örebro, which forms one of the main strands of this book, was based on the records of Örebro Rådhusrätt (the magistracy court), Örebro Kämnärsrätt (the lower municipal court), Länsstyrelsen (the regional state administration) and Örebro Stad (the municipal administration), all dating back to at least 1650. For the eighteenth century, a wider range of sources is available, including, in addition to those already mentioned, records from Örebro Accisrätt (the excise court), probate inventories, sources from the central customs administration and information on state pensions (culled from the records of Statskontoret, a body in overall charge of the state administration).

The customs administration has left rich source material, permitting a particularly detailed analysis of customs officials, their working conditions and their families. As for the court records, they all have their biases. Thus, the records of the magistrates' court over-represent the importance of crime and criminals, and of real estate and its owners, and say less about work and movable property. The records of the lower municipal and excise courts give a much more vivid picture of working people and their everyday lives, but over-represent forms of work that were understood to be transgressions of tax, customs and excise rules. A cursory glance at the latter sources would convey the impression that urban women did little else but produce and sell beer and liquor. While this was probably an important source of income for some of them, the fact that it looms so large in these sources should be attributed to efforts to enforce the prohibition of unauthorised sales of such beverages.

It is generally difficult to find information on women's work, and the wives of lower state servants are no exception. The problem is compounded by naming practices. Until the late nineteenth century, Swedish women did not in general change their names on marrying, but retained their maiden names. This complicates the tracing of female spouses in the sources. Sometimes women also used two different names in a seemingly non-systematic manner. It is not immediately obvious, for instance, that the person sometimes referred to as Sara Cajsa Broström was identical to the person known as Mrs Gezelius. This is why it was necessary to conduct a smaller case study of Örebro in which it was possible to keep track of the women.

The case study of Örebro is only one of the legs on which this investigation stands, however, the other two being data from other Scandinavian small towns (gleaned from both primary sources and the literature) and information found in the Gender and Work (GaW) database. With its information on around 16,000 early modern work activities, this database offers the possibility of finding evidence on lower state servants, and on married women in urban contexts, in Sweden in general.[51]

Notes

1 *SAOB*, 'betjänt'.

2 RA, Kammarkollegiet, Tull- och licentkontoret, F I, Vol. IX, Cautioners Beskaffenhet (1689); Vol. X, dödsattester för tulltjänstemän (1689–1733).

3 RA, Kammarkollegiet, Tull- och licentkontoret, F I, Vol. IX, Cautioners Beskaffenhet (1689); Vol. X, dödsattester för tulltjänstemän (1689–1733). By around 1800, there was a clear difference between private servants and state servants, and *betjänte* was used only of lower state servants, never of higher office holders. See also B. Asker, *I konungens stad och ställe: länsstyrelser i arbete 1635–1735* (Uppsala: Stiftelsen för utgivande av arkivvetenskapliga studier, 2004), 66; and E. Fahlbeck, 'Ämbets- och tjänstemän', in *Statsvetenskapliga studier till Statsvetenskapliga föreningens i Uppsala tjugufemårsdag 7/11 1944* (Uppsala, Stockholm: Almqvist & Wiksell, 1944).

4 *Journal för Litteraturen och Theatern*, 56 (18 November 1809). Thanks to Karin Hassan Jansson for drawing my attention to this source. *Dräng* does not just mean servant, but suggests that the servant is an unskilled performer of heavy work, primarily in a rural context.

5 M. Weber, *Wirtschaft und Gesellschaft: Grundriss der Verstehenden Soziologie*, 5th rev. edn (Tübingen: J. C. B. Mohr (Paul Siebeck), 1972), Vol. I, Part I, Chapter 3, §§6, 7.

6 ULA, Örebro Accisrätt, A, Vol. I, 329 (20 March 1746).

7 D. W. Sabean, *Property, Production, and Family in Neckarhausen, 1700–1870* (Cambridge: Cambridge University Press, 1990), 113; C. Pihl, *Arbete: skillnadsskapande och försörjning i 1500-talets Sverige* (Uppsala: Historiska institutionen, Uppsala universitet, 2012), 27–30.

8 Weber, *Wirtschaft und Gesellschaft*, Vol. I, Part I, Chapter 3, §§4, 5, 7.

9 P. J. Corfield, *Power and the Professions in Britain 1700–1850* (London: Routledge, 1995), 5, 27, 42–69, on lawyers and doctors; N. Korda, *Labors Lost: Women's Work and the Early Modern English Stage* (Philadelphia: University of Pennsylvania Press, 2011), on the establishment of acting as a new profession that often met with disapproval as an allegedly dishonest form of work.

10 Cf. Stuart, *Defiled Trades*, pp. 31, 52, 241–2, who mainly discusses the status of executioners, gravediggers, barber-surgeons etc. in German towns, but mentions that customs officials were sometimes described as dishonourable too.

11 See e.g. ULA, Örebro Accisrätt, A, Vol. I, 534–5; W. Smith, *Studier i svensk tulladministration,* Part II: *Tulltjänsten i landsorten på Kristinas tid,* Sveriges allmänna tulltjänstemannaförenings skriftserie, 4 (Stockholm: Sveriges allmänna tulltjänstemannaförenings skriftserie, 1955), 106, 126–8, 184; R. Thunander, *Hovrätt i funktion: Göta hovrätt och brottmålen, 1635–1699* (Stockholm: Institutet för rättshistorisk forskning, 1993), 264–7. On letters written by state servants to superiors, see also M. Hallenberg, 'Hapless heroes: Two discourses of royal service in sixteenth-century Sweden', in P. Karonen (ed.), *Hopes and Fears for the Future in Early Modern Sweden, 1500–1800* (Helsinki: Finnish Literature Society, 2009), 35–54.

12 Ertman, *Birth of the Leviathan*, 27. For an example, see C. Peterson, *Peter the Great's Administrative and Judicial Reforms: Swedish Antecedents and the Process of Reception* (Stockholm: Institutet för rättshistorisk forskning, 1979).

13 Å. Karlsson, *Den jämlike undersåten: Karl XII:s förmögenhetsbeskattning 1713* (Uppsala: Historiska institutionen, Uppsala universitet, 1994); M. Hallenberg, *Statsmakt till salu: arrendesystemet och privatiseringen av skatteuppbörden i det svenska riket 1618–1635* (Lund: Nordic Academic Press, 2008).

14 Tilly, *Coercion*, 67–95, 103; M. J. Braddick, *State Formation in Early Modern England, c. 1550–1700* (Cambridge: Cambridge University Press, 2000), 9–19, 427–37.

15 P. Frohnert, *Kronans skatter och bondens bröd: den lokala förvaltningen och bönderna i Sverige 1719–1775* (Stockholm: Institutet för rättshistorisk forskning, 1993), 285–95.

16 S. Norrhem, *Uppkomlingarna: kanslitjänstemännen i 1600-talets Sverige och Europa* (Umeå: Umeå universitet, 1993), 152–3; T. Söderberg, *Den namnlösa medelklassen: socialgrupp två i det gamla svenska samhället intill 1770-talet* (Stockholm: Bonnier, 1956), 125.

17 I. Elmroth, *För kung och fosterland: studier i den svenska adelns demografi och offentliga funktioner 1600–1900* (Lund: Liber Läromedel/Gleerup, 1981), 218–26; Stadin, *Stånd och genus*, 108, 132.

18 C. Vanja, 'Auf Geheiβ der Vögtin: Amtsfrauen in hessischen Hospitälern der Frühen Neuzeit', in H. Wunder and C. Vanja (eds), *Weiber, Menschen, Frauenzimmer: Frauen in der ländlichen Gesellschaft 1500–1800* (Göttingen: Vandenhoeck und Ruprecht, 1996), 77–95 (77). See also M. van der Heijden and A. Schmidt, 'Public services and women's work in early modern Dutch towns', *Journal of Urban History*, 36:3 (2010), 368–85 (377); J. Brewer, *The Sinews of Power: War, Money and the English State, 1688–1783* (London: Unwin Hyman, 1989), xvi, 68; B. Lundgren, 'Det äro många postmästaränkor som sitta vid tjänsterna efter männen …', *Historisk tidskrift*, 1 (1987), 23–34; E. Braut, *Frå spinnelin til lerret: kvinnearbeid i Stavanger ca 1700–1775* (Oslo: Tingbokprosjektet, 1994), 42; P. Karonen, *'Raastuvassa tavataan': suomen kaupunkien hallinto- ja oikeuslaitoksen toimintaa ja virkamiehiä suurvalta-aikana* (Jyväskylä: Jyväskylän yliopisto, 1995), 88.

19 B. Ericsson, 'Nordisk stadsadministration vid 1700-talets mitt i komparativt perspektiv', in B. Ericsson *et al.* (eds), *Stadsadministration i Norden på 1700-talet* (Oslo, Bergen, Tromsø: Universitetsforlaget, 1982), 374–5; Frohnert, *Kronans skatter*, 30–1, 285–6; Asker, *I konungens stad*, 329–34. See also M. Cavallin, *I kungens och folkets tjänst: synen på den svenske ämbetsmannen 1750–1780* (Göteborg: Historiska institutionen, Göteborgs universitet, 2003), 47; and Asker, *I konungens stad*, 350, who stress that for head clerks in the regional state administration, educational requirements were better defined. Brewer, *Sinews*, 68, argues that the English excise administration closely resembled the Weberian ideal type.

20 S. A. Nilsson, '1634 års regeringsform i det svenska statssystemet', in S. A. Nilsson, *De stora krigens tid: om Sverige som militärstat och bondesamhälle* (Uppsala: Historiska institutionen, Uppsala universitet, 1990), 199–225; A.-B. Lövgren, *Handläggning och inflytande: beredning, föredragning och kontrasignering under Karl XI:s envälde* (Lund: Historiska institutionen, Lunds universitet, 1980).

21 J. Robinson, *An Account of Sweden*; quoted in Asker, *I konungens stad*, 39.

22 Asker, *I konungens stad*, 93–6, 179–230; Nilsson, '1634 års regeringsform', 220.

23 K. Åmark, *Sveriges statsfinanser 1719–1809* (Stockholm: Norstedt, 1961), 410, 465–6, 468, 505; W. Smith, *Studier i svensk tulladministration,* Part I: *Från äldsta tid till omkring 1718*, Sveriges allmänna tulltjänstemannaförenings skriftserie, 3 (Stockholm: Sveriges allmänna tulltjänstemannaförenings skriftserie, 1956), 51–2, 110–17; Smith, *Studier i svensk tulladministration*, Part II, 128, 256, 306–7; S. A. Nilsson, 'Den karolinska militärstaten: fredens problem och krigets', in Nilsson, *De stora krigens tid*, 245–70.

24 Smith, *Studier i svensk tulladministration*, Part I, 110–17; K. Wikberg, *Alla dessa tullar – en arkivguide: vägledning till tullarkiv och tullhandlingar i Riksarkivet* (Stockholm: Riksarkivet, 2006), 29–36; RA, Kammarkollegiet, Tull- och licentkontoret, F III, Vol. I; F I, Vol. VII, fullmakt för Henrik Engelbrecht (1684).

25 Wikberg, *Alla dessa tullar*, 47–8.

26 Cavallin, *I kungens och folkets tjänst*, 69–73; Smith, *Studier i svensk tulladministration*, Part I, 273–4; Smith, *Studier i svensk tulladministration*, Part II, 64–5, 122, 126–7. In the eighteenth century, sureties were no longer required; see *Kongl. Maj:ts Reglemente för Landt-Tulls- och Accis-Kamrarne i Riket, 17 December 1756*, in R. G. Modée, *Utdrag utur alle ifrån den 7. decemb. 1718-1791 utkomne publique handlingar* (Stockholm, 1742–1829), Part VI, 4212–71, §1.

27 Cf. Luke 16.

28 S. Carlsson, *Ståndssamhälle och ståndspersoner 1700–1865: studier rörande det svenska ståndssamhällets upplösning*, 2nd rev. edn (Lund: Gleerup, 1973 [1949]), Table 12: noblemen made up 4 per cent of customs officials and 3 per cent of officials in the regional administration. See also K. Wirilander, *Herrskapsfolk: ståndspersoner i Finland 1721–1870* (Stockholm: Nordiska museet, 1982), 168–9; Smith, *Studier i svensk tulladministration*, Part I, 110.

29 RA, Överdirektörens för landtullen arkiv, Personella berättelser 1748, 1765 (Örebro, Lekhyttan, Hidinge).

30 A.-M. Fällström and I. Mäntylä, 'Stadsadministrationen i Sverige-Finland under frihetstiden', in *Stadsadministration i Norden på 1700-talet* (Oslo, Bergen, Tromsø: Universitetsforlaget, 1982), 173–286 (178–81); Ericsson, 'Nordisk stadsadministration', 345.

31 K. Bodell, *Stad, bondebygd och bergslag vid mitten av 1600-talet: varuutbytet i Örebro och dess omland enligt tullängdernas vittnesbörd* (Stockholm: Almqvist & Wiksell, 1970), 44–5, 176.

32 T. Kotkas, *Royal Police Ordinances in Early Modern Sweden: The Emergence of Voluntaristic Understanding of Law* (Leiden: Brill, 2013), 65–6, 143–6.

33 S. Klingnéus, *Bönder blir vapensmeder: protoindustriell tillverkning i Närke under 1600- och 1700-talen* (Uppsala: Historiska institutionen, Uppsala universitet, 1997), 69, 80–1, 97, 105.

34 The figure for 1640 is according to Mantalslängd 1641, in ULA, Örebro Rådhusrätt och magistrat, K 2 A:2, and Bodell, *Stad, bondebygd*, 31–2. In 1749, the population was 2,147 according to Tabellverket, the eighteenth-century precursor of what is today Statistics Sweden. The figure for 1800 is from *Historisk statistik för Sverige: D. 1, Befolkning 1720–1967*, 2nd edn (Örebro: Statistiska Centralbyrån (SCBO), 1969), Table 12. Sven Lilja estimates the population as slightly smaller in both 1750 and 1800: S. Lilja and L. Nilsson, *Historisk tätortsstatistik del 2: städernas folkmängd och tillväxt. Sverige (med Finland) ca 1570-tal till 1810-tal* (Stockholm: Stads- och kommunhistoriska institutet, 1996). It is likely that the seventeenth-century figures are underestimates; see C. Westling, *Småstadens dynamik: Skänninges och Vadstenas befolkning och kontaktfält ca 1630–1660* (Linköping: Historiska institutionen, Linköpings universitet, 2003), 84.

35 Klingnéus, *Bönder blir vapensmeder*, 112–13.

36 According to Tabellverket, there were 719 married couples in Örebro in 1749. By contrast, taxation records for 1763 suggest that there were 336 households with at least two members. ULA, Örebro Rådhusrätt och magistrat, K 2 A:2, mantalslängd 1763. On the declining share of the urban population that belonged to a burgher community, see Fällström and Mäntylä, 'Stadsadministrationen', 250–1.

37 Fällström and Mäntylä, 'Stadsadministrationen', 179–81, 186, 253, 271; K. Stadin, *Småstäder, småborgare och stora samhällsförändringar: borgarnas sociala struktur i Arboga, Enköping och Västervik under perioden efter 1680* (Uppsala: Historiska institutionen, Uppsala universitet, 1979), 31–2.

38 Bodell, *Stad, bondebygd*, Fig. 1.

39 *Ibid.*, 19–21, 50–1, 262.

40 K. F. Karlsson, *Blad ur Örebro skolas historia*, Part III (Örebro, 1875), x.

41 Klingnéus, *Bönder blir vapensmeder*, 112 (my translation); Bodell, *Stad, bondebygd*, 31.

42 Asker, *I konungens stad*, 178–9, 344–5; B. Asker, *Hur riket styrdes: förvaltning, politik och arkiv 1520–1920* (Stockholm: Riksarkivet, 2007), 106–7; O. Sörndal, *Den svenska länsstyrelsen: uppkomst, organisation och allmän maktställning* (Lund: Lunds universitet, 1937), 67.

43 J. Christensen, *Bönder och herrar: bondeståndet i 1840-talets liberala representationsdebatt. Exemplen Gustaf Hierta och J. P. Thorell* (Göteborg: Historiska institutionen, Göteborgs universitet, 1997), 95, 318 discusses an abortive proposal to extend the right to vote to 13 or even 24 per cent of the population. In Norway, 10 per cent had the vote.

44 Stadin, *Småstäder, småborgare*, 27–8; Westling, *Småstadens dynamik*, 47.

45 Örebro Rådhusrätt och magistrat, F 9 B.1, odaterad förteckning över herrar och innevånare i Örebro som icke vunnit burskap.

46 Fällström and Mäntylä, 'Stadsadministrationen', 193, 195.

47 Offices were not venal in Sweden in the sense of being sold by the state. However, it was hard to prevent one office holder from selling his office to someone else. In the military sector, for instance, offices could be purchased from the former holder. See F. Thisner, *Militärstatens arvegods: officerstjänstens socialreproduktiva funktion i Sverige och Danmark, ca 1720–1800* (Uppsala: Historiska institutionen, Uppsala universitet, 2007). Cf., for France, J. Hardwick, *The Practice of Patriarchy: Gender and the Politics of Household Authority in Early Modern France* (University Park: Pennsylvania State University Press, 1998), 27.

48 ULA, Örebro Rådhusrätt och magistrat, F 2, Vol. V, fo. 124 (1735); K 1 b, Vol. VI (1749); ULA, Länsstyrelsen i Örebro län, Landskontoret E 12 a, Vol. I (1761). Salaries varied from one place to another; Fällström and Mäntylä, 'Stadsadministrationen', 208.

49 F. Thisner, *Indelta inkomster: en studie av det militära löneindelningsverket 1721–1833* (Uppsala: Historiska institutionen, Uppsala universitet, 2014).

50 Asker, *I konungens stad*, 342–54; Cavallin, *I kungens och folkets tjänst*, 98 n. 114, 156, 206, 226.

51 R. Fiebranz, E. Lindberg, J. Lindström and M. Ågren, 'Making verbs count: The research project "Gender and Work" and its methodology', *Scandinavian Economic History Review*, 59 (2011), 273–93; Ågren, *Making a Living.*

2

Servants in the front line

The trade in oxen was crucial to the establishment of the early modern Swedish state. Dependent on liquid assets to pay for its ambitious warfare, the state had an interest in promoting economic activities that generated cash, and one of the few sectors that did this was iron production. Located in the central Swedish region of Bergslagen and producing for the international market, the ironworks north of Örebro were crucial to the state. What they needed to function well was ropes (for the mines), bellows (for the furnaces) and food (for the labourers), and the hides and meat of oxen could be used for all these purposes. Consequently, the southern Swedish trade in oxen, previously oriented towards Denmark, was forcibly redirected northwards to Bergslagen, where the cattle were slaughtered. As a result, both the iron industry and the iron trade flourished. But the oxen were important to the state in other ways as well. On their way to Bergslagen, they had to pass through Örebro, where many of them were sold and where the owners had to pay customs to the customs authorities.[1] All travellers had to pass over the bridge in the centre of the town.

On this bridge, customs official Erik Kraft was standing one summer's day in 1678, ready to protect the interests of the state. In the presence of a crowd, he and Pär Olofsson, an ox trader, engaged in a vociferous exchange of angry and derogatory words, sparked by their inability to agree on how much customs duty Pär should pay on two of his animals. In the course of the argument, both parties resorted to violence: Pär was said to have attacked Erik physically as well as verbally, and Erik, in turn, was said to have hit Pär in the mouth with a stick. Most serious, however, was Erik's allegation that Pär had tried to incite an uprising. His actions could easily have turned into an 'evil and rebellious example', Erik said.[2]

Judging from Erik Kraft's testimony when news of the altercation reached the local excise court, this was a case of attempted tax evasion, assault on a public official and even rebellion. According to Pär Olofsson, it was a matter of violent assault on one of the king's law-abiding and taxpaying subjects. Clearly, the incident was open to several interpretations. The case also shows that it could be disagreeable to encounter an official such as Kraft, but also that it could be disagreeable to have Kraft's job.

This chapter explores the ways in which animosity and violence were integral parts of many state servants' lives. It argues that, in order to handle these realities, state servants needed street-smartness, rather than theoretical knowledge. The chapter also shows how early modern states such as Sweden had to draw a fine but firm line between behaviour that their servants could legitimately engage in and behaviour that they must under no circumstances display. This was made all the more important by the fact that the work of a customs official, in particular, could easily be misinterpreted as a breach of the law. By defining boundaries, establishing definitions and curbing animosity, states sought to build legitimacy for themselves in the eyes of their subjects.

Fighting in public

The dispute between Erik Kraft and Pär Olofsson was not the only one of its kind. There were many local incidents of this sort in the period 1650–1780, and they often became personal. In March 1667, for example, a riot erupted in the large northern parish of Älvdalen, near the Norwegian border. The cause of the unrest was, it seems, the actions of a customs official by the name of Anders Kämpe. The peasantry accused him of having confiscated some tobacco brought to Älvdalen by a man from a place further north. The riot culminated in a violent attack on Kämpe, who not only suffered physical assault and had his wig and clothes torn to pieces, but was also deprived of his power of attorney (*fullmakt*).

In a subsequent letter to the parishioners, the regional governor Duvall severely admonished them. He had been informed, he wrote, of the ways in which the parishioners had shown disrespect for both His Majesty's Court of Chamber (*Kammarkollegium*) and Anders Kämpe's power of attorney. Duvall was appalled; how could the peasants of Älvdalen have resorted to such behaviour 'for no other reason than the mere fact that Kämpe had confiscated some tobacco from a man from Jämtland, entirely in accordance with his instructions and his power of attorney[;] tobacco being pernicious stuff, often and in strong words forbidden to you, not only by His Majesty but also by me'?[3]

It later transpired that the peasantry had questioned Kämpe's right to levy customs duty in Älvdalen. Customs had never been levied there before, they had argued, and, what is more, they doubted the validity of his power of attorney, suggesting that he had stolen it. The peasantry had also claimed that if the customs official had publicly announced his powers – something he could easily have done prior to the tumult, it being a Sunday, when many were assembled at the church – they would never have attacked him in the way they had done.[4] As in the case of Erik Kraft and Pär Olofsson, the defence balanced on the – very fine – distinction between asserting one's rights against a person who abused his position of authority and rising rebelliously against the state and its growing demands for resources. Duvall and, later, the councillors of the realm were not impressed, but at the same time they seem to have been aware that Kämpe had not handled the situation well.[5]

The cases of Erik Kraft and Anders Kämpe alert us to the public visibility of customs officials. They both worked in public (everybody could see them fighting on the bridge and confiscating tobacco), they interacted with the public (more than they would probably have preferred), and Kämpe was not accepted as a legitimate representative of his master because he had not publicly shown his power of attorney in the way subjects would have expected him to do, had they known that he wanted to be treated as the king's man. How were they to know that they were dealing with a servant of His Majesty and not a simple thief?

The work of customs officials was public in a number of ways, and it was often this public character of their duties that would involve them in difficult and conflict-ridden situations. In this respect, they were similar to domestic servants. Masters and mistresses sent their servants on errands that forced them to take to public streets and highways, where they were vulnerable to potential attack in their capacity as representatives of the heads of their households.[6] In a similar way, state servants were sent on 'errands' (for instance to Älvdalen) that compelled them to visit distant or disagreeable places, where they too were exposed to possible attack because they represented the state, and in spite of the fact that they were the king's men. This paradox was at the heart of the process of state formation. People disliked the many new state servants because they extracted resources in cash and kind, demanded that subjects perform corvée work at the numerous building sites of the early modern state, monitored and controlled trade, and sometimes poked their noses into other aspects of everyday life as well. Until such hostility towards state servants had been overcome, state formation was incomplete.

The Government was aware of these problems from early on. In the 1630s, officials in charge of the unpopular inland customs (*lilla tullen*) were attacked by angry peasants in many places. In Älvkarleby in 1637, for instance, a miller was said to have instigated an assault on the bailiff and the customs officials. In Hova in 1638, officials, including a customs scribe, were again attacked, and the customs fences were torn down. The Government concluded that a reason for these outbreaks was the lack of 'moderation' shown by some officials.[7] When the council of the realm (*riksrådet*) discussed the customs in 1641, Axel Oxenstierna expressed his fear that the national director of the customs administration would resign because of the great 'invidia' (hatred) that his job entailed. Apparently, even a customs official of much higher rank than Erik Kraft could find the situation difficult, and in fact he left office later the same year because of the many insulting pamphlets that had been written about him. On the other hand, office holders could get very angry too, say highly disparaging things about subjects and display behaviour not befitting a representative of the state. Brynte Cronsköld, another national director of the customs administration, was for instance said to have insulted the entire burgher estate by calling them a bunch of *hundsfottar*, arguably the worst conceivable term of abuse.[8]

There were many conflicts of this kind,[9] and they reveal some of the tensions inherent in the process of creating a new group of state officials. One tension arose from the unclear definition of 'home' and privacy. How far into the domestic sphere did the authority of state servants reach? While 'the private sphere' is not a concept historians feel comfortable about using for this period, it is clear that some of the conflicts that erupted had to do with differing understandings of spatial boundaries and the contested authority to transgress them. Another tension arose from the somewhat unclear distinction between some state servants, such as lower customs officials, and thieves. If customs officials and their families used confiscated goods for their own ends or, worse still, simply appropriated things from the vehicles they searched, what was in fact the difference between them and thieves? The practice – taking something from someone – appeared to be the same. Were customs officials nothing other than state-authorised thieves? In the following section, we will look at the cultural contexts that make the attacks that occurred comprehensible.

The right to live in peace

The right to live in peace was fundamental in medieval society, and remained so into the early modern period. The Swedish legal code, promulgated around 1350 and in force until 1736, laid down that it was a particular responsibility of the king to guard and protect the peace of the realm:

> It is incumbent upon [the king] to guard and to protect his people, in particular the peaceable who wish to live in peace and according to law[;] to protect them against violent and malevolent men from within the realm as well as against foreigners ... Peace will increase and absence of peace vanish, depending on the king.[10]

The general right to enjoy peace was elaborated and specified in other parts of the code. It was described as particularly pertinent in three places – the church, the courts and the home – where breaches of the peace were to be severely punished. It was also explicitly extended to women: violating or abducting a woman was considered a breach of the peace. This offence was not primarily seen as directed against the individual woman, but rather against her family and the institution of marriage; nevertheless, the effects of this clause were that women could receive support from the courts, for instance in cases of rape.[11]

A breach of the peace was thus particularly odious in church, in court, in the home and if it involved a woman. It implied the use of physical violence and armed fighting, a mode of behaviour commonly associated with warfare. A breach of domestic peace, for instance, was conceptualised as an armed attack on a person's house by a group of men.[12] An example can serve to illustrate how the essence of the crime was conceived of in late-seventeenth-century Sweden. In the 1690s, a man by the name of Nils Larsson was brought before the magistrates of Örebro on a charge of having breached the domestic peace of two unmarried sisters. These women lived in a house of their own, but close to or possibly on Nils's property. On the day of the incident, Nils had been fighting with his wife, and one of the sisters had tried to intervene. Apparently, this merely brought about an escalation of the hostilities. Nils entered the sisters' house, injurious words were exchanged, and both Nils and the sisters were wounded. Having considered the facts of the case, the court fined Nils and one of the sisters for the wounds they had inflicted on each other, but found Nils not guilty of a breach of domestic peace. As the magistrates saw it, Nils had not carried a weapon and he had not touched the sisters before they flung a log at him. This was contrary to some of the testimonies – one witness said that Nils had had a rapier in his hand and the sisters argued that he had entered their house in wrath – but the point here is not what actually happened, but the way in which the court defined the crime of breaching domestic peace: the perpetrator had to be armed and he had to attack first.[13] Although Nils was acquitted on this occasion, the case illustrates how any man who intruded into someone else's house would run the risk of being accused of breaching that person's domestic peace. Consequently, a state servant who intruded into another person's home ran the risk of being looked upon as a peace-breaker and, because of the military connotations of a breach of the peace, such an act was gendered as a man's crime. Thus, when customs officials sometimes had to enter people's houses to check whether they had produced bread or alcoholic beverages, this task associated them with both criminals and soldiers.

The right to live in peace was a powerful argument, as was the claim to be a peace-loving person. Pär Olofsson, who quarrelled with Erik Kraft on the bridge in 1678, explicitly invoked the right to live in peace when he told the court that he wanted to remain 'unmolested'[14] and that he wanted to return home with the help of God and in 'the king's peace'. In court, Pär also detailed his many attempts to resolve the conflict peacefully and avoid creating new ones. After the incident on the bridge, he had made several serious attempts to pay the customs duties; that nothing had come of them was not his fault, but rather a result of Kraft's stubborn refusal to accept payment. It was true, Pär conceded, that he had triggered the dispute, but subsequently he had made every effort to restore the peace amicably. While Kraft was described as a hot-tempered man who lacked self-control and had used a weapon (the stick), Pär portrayed himself as, after all, a peaceable man, keen to avoid conflict.[15] Although Pär never expressly accused Erik of having breached the peace, it is clear that the case has to be set in the conceptual framework of peace to be intelligible. Repeated offers of reconciliation by one party and a refusal to accept those offers by the other, for instance, were a recurring theme in accounts of breaches of the peace.[16]

The idea of peace was a cornerstone of Swedish and Scandinavian culture, as was the notion that the king had a special responsibility to ensure that his subjects could enjoy peace. The kind of peace that applied in the domestic sphere was no exception, but it could be difficult to square the right to it with the need to monitor some of the actions people engaged in at home, notably those concerned with the production of beer, bread and meat. The small-scale organisation of such food production and the construction of the excise made home inspections necessary, and while they cannot have happened every day, when they did they caused resentment. The fact that it was the king's men who were the peace breakers did not sit well with the king's special responsibility for upholding the peace.

The king's men – the servants of the state – were aware of the risk of being attacked and were not necessarily enthusiastic about entering people's homes. In 1743, for instance, two searchers inspected the brewing being carried on in one of Maria Dam's outhouses and accused her of having brewed more than she was permitted to. She contradicted them and went to the customs inspector to complain of their behaviour. Both searchers immediately left the outhouse and, when later asked by the court why one of them had not stayed to guard the incriminating evidence, one of the men answered that if either of them had been left alone there, he could easily have been beaten up. State servants, too, wanted to enjoy peace.[17]

Very likely, servants of the state preferred not to get too closely involved with certain aspects of other people's domestic lives. This seems to have been true, for instance, of bailiffs who had to levy execution when families were in arrears with their taxes. One eighteenth-century bailiff's assistant pointed out that poor people seldom had any movable property that he could seize. Instead, he would be confronted with 'a bunch of naked and hungry children whose howling makes matters even worse'. This assistant did not like to have to handle such situations, and he was not alone; his peers expressed similar reluctance.[18] Torn between compassion and their professional duty, lower office holders could at times feel frustration and despair. They also had to resolve other problems that pushed them into the mundane and even unsavoury parts of people's private lives. In 1655, for instance, the burghers of Örebro complained about an evil-smelling privy in the middle of town. A couple of municipal office holders were ordered to deal with the matter. Since the owner of the privy was the famous entrepreneur and merchant Casten Otter, their task was probably unappealing both because they had to confront him and because, if they failed to get him to remove the privy, they might end up having to do it themselves.[19] Across the spectrum of lower office holders – customs officials, bailiffs' assistants and municipal employees – the experience of confronting people in their homes and in intimate areas of life was one that was shared and disliked.

In the late eighteenth century, customs officials' intrusions into homes still caused animosity. The author of a pamphlet published in 1774 decried 'the abominable house visitations that breach the common *domestic peace*' and argued that they pitted 'citizens against each other' and could have 'terrible consequences' (what these were remained unclear).[20] Here, the resentment against searchers' 'visits' was still phrased in terms of infringements of domestic peace, but the inhabitants of the realm were no longer described as subjects but as citizens. A medieval concept describing the most protected sphere – house and home – was thus juxtaposed with the modern word for an acknowledged member of a polity. Through such collocations, the right to domestic peace was subtly transformed as it was invested with a meaning more germane to modern notions of privacy. Not only could one's armed enemies break into one's house, as medieval legislators had foreseen; so too could the servants of the state. It is telling that such collocations arose precisely in connection with the actions of customs officials.

Stealing

Tax or customs collectors often appear in the Gospels. Christ exhorted the publicans he encountered to stop taking more from people than they were entitled to, and they were routinely referred to as sinners. On the other hand, contrite collectors were upheld as role models, infinitely more lovable to God than the smug Pharisees.[21] There was thus some ambivalence in the way the Gospels depicted customs officials – as sinners who extorted too much tax but, at the same time, as prominent examples of repentance. This ambivalence probably reinforced people's notions that customs had to be collected according to certain rules. Give the emperor what is his – but no more. The striking similarities between the portrayal of tax collectors in the Bible and the way some customs officials acted in Swedish small towns may have been what emboldened people to criticise these officials, both when they intruded into the domestic sphere and when they extracted too much. In England, excisemen were described as a biblical plague, again because of the similarities between people's perceptions of them and the stories found in the Bible.[22]

In other early modern sources, customs officials who extorted more than was due were also described as dishonest and as thieves. Even royal statutes used the language of stealing to describe such state servants. If found guilty, the culprit had to repay what he had taken, and would be punished twice as severely as if he had been an ordinary thief stealing the same amount.[23] The rigour of the penalty suggests that while stealing was always an abomination, stealing from customs payers was particularly to be condemned.

In everyday encounters between customs officials and subjects, too, the language of stealing was sometimes explicitly used. In 1678, for instance, Gabriel Albrektsson and four other men visited a burgher's home to check that his brewing of beer conformed to the rules. The burgher went berserk, calling Gabriel a thief and accusing him and another man of taking bribes. He jibed at Gabriel for being a 'measurer of mash', saying that after measuring his mash Gabriel should eat it – a highly contemptuous thing to say, given its unpleasant smell. The man added with disdain that Gabriel was 'unable to support [him]self in any other way than by means of this dog's job'. In a gesture of utter contempt, he pulled down his trousers, exposing his buttocks to the men who had intruded into his house.[24]

A corrupt servant who did a despicable job and was little better than a thief and a dog: those were the epithets heaped on Gabriel Albrektsson's head. Similar exchanges of words occurred in other towns as well. In Uppsala in 1637, a municipal office holder and a customs scribe visited Mats Nilsson's house to claim some dues. As Mats was not at home, they took a pair of boots as security for his debt and left. When Mats returned home and was told what had happened, he was incensed and ran out into the street shouting: 'where is that traitor and thief, I will cut out his heart'.[25] In Örebro in the 1740s, customs scribe Anders Lybeck was described in similar terms by the widow Ingeborg Nilsdotter. The two of them were in dispute over the right to ferry people across a flooded area. Lybeck argued that his superiors had ordered him to help travellers across the water (for payment), but being the owner of the adjacent land, Ingeborg claimed first refusal on the task and the resulting income. In court, Anders said that Ingeborg had insulted him in various ways, including calling him a thief, a rascal and a knave. Witnesses attested that this was true, but pointed out that he had called her a thieving woman. She, they added, had shouted that he was a customs snooper who ought to remain at the customs house, 'tethered like a he-goat'.[26] In this exchange, the word 'thief' was probably the worst insult. Here, though, it did not refer to the act of taking property from a subject, but rather to depriving a subject of an income-earning opportunity. That was the sense in which Anders Lybeck was alleged to be a thief.[27]

Calling somebody a thief seems to have been the commonest form of invective in seventeenth-century urban settings. Moreover, it was perceived to be more than just a general insult; it was an accusation that had to be refuted, as otherwise it would be taken to be true. In fact, a common phrase in defamation cases was 'he made me into a thief', suggesting that simply by being called a thief a person risked becoming one in the eyes of the public.[28] Another word that conjured up the image of thieving was robbery. This was what some office holders in Örebro were accused of in the 1650s, when they had taken a chest from a man as security, presumably for unpaid taxes. The officials described to the magistrates how the man had torn their hair, accused them of robbing him, and threatened to come after them when their time in office had come to an end.[29] In Helsingborg in the 1670s, a customs official complained that one of the mayors had compared the work of a state servant to 'robbery and plunder' (*rån och rov*).[30] Other office holders were also called thieves and 'persecutors' (enemies),[31] suggesting that people thought they took too much and that they were over-zealous and partial.[32]

A third term of interest is 'thief of the Crown' or 'thief of the king', used of state servants who embezzled state income.[33] It is revealing that when the term was defined in 1724, the example of a customs official caught 'embezzling customs ... with connivance and unfaithfulness' was chosen to illustrate its meaning. The expression also turned up in legislation pertaining to customs and excise, suggesting that customs officials were regarded as particularly liable to commit this type of crime.[34] In his autobiography, regional governor Nils Reuterholm described how a customs inspector in Gothenburg had enriched himself by stealing from the Crown. After some years in office, this man had been raised to the nobility in spite of being no better than a thief; Reuterholm thought he should have been sent to the gallows instead.[35] Both subjects and state servants could act fraudulently against the Crown, of course, the former by evading tax and the latter by embezzling it, and governments feared that subjects and state servants would collude to rob the king and the Crown of their rightful revenue. However, the fact that only state servants could be branded as 'thieves of the king' created leverage for subjects who were dissatisfied with how they had been treated. They could accuse an office holder of being a 'thief of the king', but could not be such thieves themselves.

Both state law and the Gospels provided subjects with terminology and arguments that could be used to attack state servants in general and customs officials in particular. While there was animosity between subjects and state servants of many kinds,[36] it seems to have been particularly acrimonious in the case of customs officials. Lower customs officials inspected people's kitchens and vehicles, and were consequently perceived as snoopers and violators of domestic peace. People did not like to have 'visitors' (the literal meaning of *besökare*) in their homes. Moreover, both higher and lower customs officials were suspected of collecting too much and of putting some of what they received in their own pockets. This was comparable to the actions of simple thieves. For both reasons, customs officials were disapproved of, sometimes in vociferous and physically palpable ways.

Making noise

When state servants such as Erik Kraft fought in public places, they involuntarily associated themselves with disorder and unpleasant noise. Bridges, roads, mills, excise chambers and entry points to towns were evidently places where people could be heard shouting angrily at each other. It was not just the risk of encountering exacting state servants or being threatened by criminals that made these places unappealing. It was also the loud noises themselves. Indeed, it has been argued that raised and insistent voices were perceived as expressions of a lack of control in early modern society. In England around 1600, the cries of female street vendors were taken as a sign of defective guild control and malfunctioning market regulation. People who did 'honest work' did not have to cry out and create commotion, it was argued; they spoke in calm, gentle voices. There was also a gender aspect to loud sounds: men who were in control of the situation and of themselves, it was believed, did not resort to crying and shouting.[37]

In Sweden, too, loud noises were associated with unruly and emotional behaviour. Loud clapping of the hands, for example, was intended and interpreted as a sign of insubordination. A naval seaman accused of having attacked a municipal office holder in Örebro, for instance, uttered threatening words and clapped his hands at the town magistrates, which earned him a jail sentence. A soldier who had allegedly stolen a horse from a peasant used foul language, put on his hat (instead of doffing it) and clapped his hands in the presence of the regional governor Wrangel. This was viewed as a serious offence. On a third occasion, a group of soldiers who had attacked a resident of the town were explicitly ordered by the magistrates to remain 'silent and respectful'.[38] Thus, if coupled with a disrespectful attitude, loud sounds were understood to be signs of unruliness. This conjunction of noise and disorder is captured in the word *buller*, which today simply means a disturbing and unpleasant sound of some duration. In the early modern period, *buller* also referred to phenomena such as feuding, rebellion or a lack of peace. In 1525, for instance, King Gustav I mentioned '*buller* or other forms of insurrection' in one of his letters.[39]

Shouting could be interpreted as a form of intimidation. To shout at someone was tantamount to threatening them. In the mid-seventeenth century, a number of statutes addressed the problem of uncontrolled shouting and shooting in Stockholm. These ordinances expressed a concern with perceived threats to national borders and Parliament at this particular time, but they also suggest that shouting itself was an issue. Shouting and screaming were defined as punishable acts, regardless of whether anyone had come to any harm.[40] This implies that intimidation of others and contempt for the common peace, expressed through shouting, were seen as problems. The right to peace was obviously understood in a very concrete sense: it involved peacefulness.

Erik Kraft's physical attack on Pär Olofsson's *mouth* and his accusation of attempted rebellion should be seen in this light. Like a barking dog or an inebriated soldier, Pär had to be silenced. Pär, for his part, admitted that he had contributed to the commotion; he had been excited, had used very foul language and had threatened a state servant: 'I confess that at this point I said in excitement, the devil rises in rebellion, and [you should] hit scoundrels and dogs and not me, and then I challenged him and threatened to pay him for the way he had hit and insulted me.'[41]

Getting excited, invoking the devil and threatening a state servant in public was clearly not the way to behave, and Pär Olofsson knew it.[42] His main fault was of course in challenging a state servant, but people shouting at each other in public was obviously regarded as disagreeable in itself; Pär's repeated claims that he had tried to settle the dispute peacefully speak to this issue.

The problem for Kraft was that, in trying to silence Pär, he got himself embroiled in a noisy situation where he too had to resort to shouting. Even if the official was not always the one who shouted loudest, being associated with people who shouted and being shouted at were bad in themselves. Thus, in a conflict that erupted in 1779, when customs official Nils Jernberg tried to search the trunk of a Gothenburg merchant, the merchant was reported to have shouted at Jernberg: 'Go to hell, will you, I don't give a damn about your duties; if you had been polite I would have given you a tip but now you will not get one shit out of me.' Bad language and raised voices made this an unpleasant incident and the excise court consequently fined the merchant. Later, this conflict had developed into a full-scale street riot as the customs officials tried to disperse the agitated crowd, first by shouting at them and then by attacking them on horseback.[43]

If loud noises and angry voices were perceived as problematic in themselves, it probably mattered less whether the combatants were a state servant and a subject or two state servants quarrelling with each other. Yet fighting among state servants undermined their status and legitimacy, and statute law explicitly mentioned quarrelling between customs officials as something that had to be curbed. Local cases also bear witness to men from this professional group fighting each other in public. The searcher Nils Lundius, for example, attacked some customs scribes and was in turn attacked by his peer Zachris Wikman. Another searcher, Tillgren, attacked his colleague Keppel while he was on duty. It is telling that at the ensuing trial, the court explicitly praised Keppel for his 'patient and conciliatory behaviour', which was in stark contrast to that of his colleague.[44] Tillgren's behaviour did not improve the reputation of lower customs officials. But even when a customs official managed to curb his own wish to shout, spending time in places where other people shouted could be problematic if loud noises and raised voices were culturally construed as a lack of control. State servants were expected to control themselves and to exert control over others.[45]

When the peasant Jonas Persson attacked customs scribe Keppel in 1786, he did so because he thought Keppel was slow and lazy. Several witnesses testified that Persson, who had had to stand in line to have his papers cleared, had shouted things such as 'the bastard is asleep at his post', and 'don't sit and sleep, you bastard, sleep at night and work during the day, that's what I do, you son of a bitch'. At this, Keppel had sprung to his feet and boxed Persson's ears, and both men subsequently ended up in court. The misdemeanour of which Persson was found guilty consisted in his widely audible verbal assault on a state servant.[46] That it had taken place in the servant's office made the offence graver. Already in the seventeenth century, statutory law had laid down that attacks on state servants were particularly serious if they occurred in their offices or other buildings used by the state administration. In 1776, a new statute said that anyone who molested a customs official because of his job was to be fined ten *daler*, but that if the crime took place in the official's office, the fine was to be doubled.[47]

Erik Kraft's dispute with Pär Olofsson and Keppel's conflict with Jonas Persson were a century apart, but the theme of publicly and loudly displayed contempt for a state servant remained the same. The complex context in which people's dislike of lower state servants was publicly staged included aspects of both space and sound. It was not only a matter of wanting to pay less customs and excise, or of despising state servants for doing a 'dog's job'. It also involved resentment of unwelcome visits to one's home, as well as loud and angry sounds.

Protecting state servants and subjects from each other

The state found itself in an ambivalent situation. On the one hand, it was clearly keen to keep a watchful eye on its servants and their doings, so that they did not squander state funds and undermine the state's legitimacy. The state thus had an obvious interest in listening to and even eliciting complaints from subjects, since this was an invaluable source of information about its servants. On the other hand, it had to protect its servants, because otherwise no one would be willing to become a servant of the state.[48]

When the Swedish state instituted the excise courts in 1672, the professed purpose of the reform was to provide better protection for both customs officials and customs payers. Clearly, there had been a history of mutual animosity and outright fighting that the state wanted to put an end to. The statute therefore repeated what an earlier one had said in 1658: that it was absolutely forbidden to attack inspectors and lower customs officials. But, since customs officials had overstepped the limits too, it also pointed out that those officials were not to mistreat subjects. According to the statute, the relationship between subjects and servants was to be well balanced and based on fairness.[49]

Previously, admitting that both parties had erred had not been a prominent feature, although it did happen.[50] Instead, the focus had mainly been on protecting the 'customs servants' (*tullbetienterne*), as they were called. Subjects were exhorted not to scold the king's servants or disobey their orders. Scolding these men was tantamount to scolding and insulting the monarch, one of the statutes emphasised, and must cease. Physical attacks, particularly on searchers, were described as unacceptable. Henceforth, subjects were to show these state servants all due respect, and any failure to do so would be punished. The first two offences of this kind would incur a fine, but after a third offence the culprit would be sentenced to death as someone who had breached the king's peace.[51]

The focus on protecting both officials and payers of customs seems to have become more pronounced with time. According to instructions promulgated in 1675, customs and excise were a 'delicate matter' and a 'sensitive issue' that needed careful and circumspect handling.[52] The statute of 1672 had made this clear, and in 1678 it was repeated that customs officials were to behave politely and respectfully.[53] In 1684, a high-ranking customs official was told to make sure that subjects were treated well by those working under him.[54] There was obviously a growing awareness that some representatives of the state *were* crooked and that fraud *did* happen. Johan Buller and Anders Larsson, for instance, both claimed to be the rightful holder of the position of customs inspector in 1656, and they violently accused each other of being an impostor. As it turned out, however, neither of them had a valid power of attorney, and the local magistrates laconically concluded that both Buller and Larsson had simply acted as de facto customs inspectors.[55] In cases such as this, subjects were right to be suspicious of those who presented themselves as the king's servants, and to think of them as thieves. Another reason was that, even when in possession of a legal power of attorney, some state servants did not treat subjects well. Hitting them in the mouth with a stick, as Erik

Kraft had done, was not acceptable. Kraft and his like deprived the state of both income and legitimacy.

Consequently, late-seventeenth- and eighteenth-century statutes reveal a state trying to strike a fine balance between supporting and controlling its servants. On the one hand, it adjusted the procedural rules to make it easier for customs officials to prove that they had been attacked.[56] It also introduced more draconian sentences for those who attacked them. New statutes made clear that in cases where a group of people attacked customs officials with a view to taking back confiscated goods, the death sentence would apply immediately. Since the value of confiscated goods was very small from a fiscal point of view, the reason for this provision can only have been to set an example and to show support for the officials in their difficult job. The death sentence was to apply if someone physically attacked an individual official,[57] but it is clear that group assaults were considered particularly heinous. While the statutes did not go as far as Erik Kraft, who described Pär Olofsson as an inciter of rebellion, their characterisations of such assaults still show a certain similarity to the way plotting and conspiracy could be described: 'if men assemble to take goods past the customs gates with violence, or to retrieve confiscated goods'. The statutes went on to say that the instigator of such an enterprise would forfeit his life and goods and that, of his accomplices, every tenth man would lose his life.[58] As early as the 1720s, twenty men were sentenced to death for having attacked a group of customs officials. Another thirteen were sentenced to prison.[59]

On the other hand, the statute of 1756 repeatedly emphasised the importance of customs officials being polite and obliging to excise payers. Under no circumstances were they to insult those paying excise, the law warned. Instead, they were to be 'friendly and benevolent, attentive and fair', and to give speedy help to everyone. They must never dare to misconstrue or change the laws, or to attack anyone with abusive words or violent blows.[60] The emphasis on politeness was not entirely new; this was how the ideal customs official had been described in the seventeenth century too: as someone in possession of 'good moderation and the greatest courtesy'. If the state-employed customs officials were 'commonly spoken of as bad, odious and unbearable, this will have adverse effects on the [reputation of] His Majesty's Service', one writer observed.[61] When criticised, customs officials expressly claimed to have acted politely.[62] But the emphasis on politeness was even stronger in the eighteenth century, when customs scribes and searchers had to swear an oath to treat the king's subjects with respect.[63]

Words such as these bear witness to the state's intentions, to the way it wanted the customs administration to work. At the same time, they most certainly suggest that the behaviour of some customs officials had been and still was a problem. One of these officials was the searcher Lundius in Örebro. On one occasion, he was accused of drunkenness, carelessness and extorting too much in customs. After complaints from a customs payer, customs inspector Wigardt had ordered Lundius to repay her, which the searcher had apparently done. But once the matter came to court, other faults of his were also revealed, such as his treatment of his colleagues and of the postmaster Löthman. On one occasion, when Löthman had asked Lundius to open the customs gate, the latter had not bothered to come out of the customs house. Instead, he had simply thrown the key out of the window. This was against the statutes, but even worse was that when Löthman had pointed out that it was obviously the wrong key, Lundius had come running out of the house waving his iron spear at the postmaster in an intimidating manner and hurling abuse at him. Clearly, Lundius's behaviour was neither 'friendly and benevolent' nor 'attentive and fair'.[64] He had been remiss in throwing the key out of the window, and had used much more force than was called for under the circumstances.

Lundius was not alone. In eighteenth-century court records, we find many complaints about the behaviour of customs officials. These related not only to corruption and fraud – unquestionably instances of crime – but also to the unpleasant ways in which officials treated the public. Even when weapons and abusive language were not used, people took offence at lesser indications of a lack of respect. For instance, a woman objected to a customs scribe who, she claimed, had snapped at her when she was queuing up to pay her excise.[65] Snapping was not a crime, but it was a type of behaviour that did not sit well with the injunction to be friendly and polite. Searchers were also accused of being drunk and unpleasant to customs payers and colleagues. Sven Dimberg, for example, was reported to the excise court for having been so drunk that he had delayed the postal service. Dimberg had also been disobedient to the inspector and rude to customs payers and colleagues, and finally, he had tried to incite other officials to behave in the same way.[66]

Overuse of alcohol was often a factor when customs officials failed to be 'friendly and benevolent, attentive and fair'. Lundius drank too much, and so did many of his colleagues. It seems as if officials rarely had the time to take a proper lunch break. Instead, they purchased various alcoholic beverages to assuage their hunger. Trade in beer, liquor and food was an important source of income for many urban women, and the working conditions of customs officials explain the demand for such products.[67] Many people probably drank a lot, and searchers were mentioned as a group whose drinking habits were particularly problematic.[68] In eighteenth-century popular songs, over-indulgence in alcohol among lowly placed state servants was a recurring theme, not least in the work of Carl Michael Bellman.[69]

By the late eighteenth century, the central authorities had realised that overuse of alcohol among state servants was a problem not only for the men and their families, but also for the state. People took offence at the impoliteness displayed by drunken officials, and this could rub off on their employer. Consequently, Swedish customs inspectors were instructed to comment in their reports on the behaviour of their men, and these comments invariably included information on alcohol consumption. In 1748, the inspector in Växjö described all of his men in appreciative terms: one of them was 'sober and always at his post in the customs house'; another man had 'no specific qualifications yet but he is always sober'; a third was said to 'write reasonably well' and the inspector had not noticed any signs of 'unvirtuous inclinations'.[70] In Örebro in 1783, some of the men were described as 'sober and reliable', 'sober and faithful' or 'sober and virtuous', while others were said to be 'given to drinking but writes well', 'a drinker who needs continuous monitoring' or 'a drinker who leads an immoral life'.[71]

From the late eighteenth century, use of alcohol among customs officials was clearly a major concern for those with an over-arching responsibility for the collection of customs and excise. Officials who drank too much did a poor job, both because they made mistakes and because they mistreated colleagues and taxpayers. But there was more to it than that. People who drink too much also tend be rowdy and loud, and this was a problem in interactions between state servants and other subjects; their encounters tended to be noisy, and loud and angry sounds evoked negative feelings, not only in the eighteenth but in the previous century as well.

Causes of animosity

Why were Swedish customs officials so often exposed to animosity and even physical aggression? What was it about these men, and their work, that made people angry, and what do these reactions tell us about the lives of lower state servants and their households? This question goes to the heart of what state formation meant in people's everyday lives. The answer is complex.

Aggression against collectors of taxes and customs erupted in many other parts of the early modern world. In France, the farming out of customs to private companies is thought to have been an important reason for popular hostility to collectors. People believed that these men acted not so much for the common good, but rather out of personal interest and greed. Consequently, customs collectors were branded, for instance, as thieves, and *gabeleur* was used as a general word for someone who sought their own profit.[72] In seventeenth-century England, customs farmers aroused similar feelings, but gradually people got used to paying these taxes and accepted the system and its representatives. An important reason for this change in attitude, according to several historians, was the discreet ways in which excise on beer was levied. Beer was produced at large commercial units, whose owners paid the excisemen and then recouped the money by raising the price to the consumer. Consequently, Englishmen in general may not have been aware that they in fact paid excise on beer.[73] In the German-speaking area, finally, inhabitants of incorporated towns often displayed remarkable contempt for certain representatives of the state, such as executioners, because of the allegedly unclean and dishonourable character of their job. Some customs officials also seem to have been the target of such scorn.[74]

Just as in France, customs were farmed out in Sweden in, for instance, the 1660s and 1670s. Complaints about the system were rife in those decades, and the introduction of excise courts (in the 1670s) and the abolition of customs farming (in the 1680s) were the consequences of such discontent. Customs on international trade, which were the most profitable form, were again farmed out in the 1710s, between 1726 and 1765, and again between 1777 and 1782. The eighteenth-century customs company was only half-private, however, and the greed and self-interest of customs officials were not, it would seem, the primary focus of popular complaints. There is certainly reason to assume that the organisation of customs and excise mattered to popular opinion, but in eighteenth-century Sweden opposition to private interests still seems to have been more limited than in France.

The conspicuous way in which excise was levied may go some way towards explaining its unpopularity in Sweden, just as the unobtrusive method of collection could explain the acceptance of excise and excisemen in England. The excise on food and beverages produced for home consumption had to be paid before production could begin. If a person was in a hurry to make beer or bake bread for domestic use, it was probably easy to break the Swedish rules by mistake. And, even if people did remember to go to the excise chamber in advance, this was obviously seen as a nuisance and as something that robbed them of time; heads of households seem to have preferred to send their servants or children to pay the excise, rather than go themselves.[75] What is more, the excise on edibles intended for the market was paid separately by the consumer and it was unlawful to include it in the price. The collection of customs and excise was more visible in Sweden than in England.

It is hard to tell whether the work of Swedish customs officials was regarded as inherently 'unclean', dishonourable or taboo, as the work of some of their German counterparts was. Measuring mash (which searchers did) was described as a dog's job in one of the cases above, and pamphlets insulting customs officials were apparently in circulation in the seventeenth century.[76] It is suggestive that in one of the many statutes concerning customs officials it was said that, even if customs inspectors were not exactly comparable to noblemen, they nevertheless held 'honourable positions'.[77] Similar statutes in Germany mentioned customs officials in the same way,[78] and there would have been little point in making such remarks had it been obvious to everyone that these positions were indeed honourable. Talking about customs officials as performing a 'dog's job' does suggest a tinge of dishonour, although, unlike in the German-speaking world, that dishonour does not seem to have been regarded as contagious.

The extent of hostility towards Swedish customs officials is difficult to gauge, because the sources do not show us everyone's views, only those of the people who actually complained. In fact, we have reason to believe that some burghers were supportive of some of the customs officials, simply because the former had invested money in the latter. Before 1756, a customs inspector needed someone to stand surety for him, and the state was loath to accept a guarantor who was not a burgher. So, in every town with a customs inspector, there must have been at least two men, and sometimes many more, who had promised to pay if the inspector failed to deliver the customs. When Uppsala had been ravaged by a major fire in 1702, the central customs administration ordered an investigation into whether those who had lost property in the fire had stood surety for its officials.[79] This suggests that inspectors always had some local support, and in fact they rarely appear as the targets of animosity. The same was true of servants of the regional state administration; they do not figure prominently among those who were detested and attacked.

Moreover, many small towns enjoyed the right to keep the income from some or all of 'their' excise; the customs administration collected both the customs and the excise and then returned the latter to the town hall. In such cases, the burghers as a group had an obvious interest in the successful levy of excise. Örebro was not one of these towns. It is possible, therefore, that the townspeople took a somewhat less favourable view of the excise here than in places such as Norrköping, Karlskrona, Åbo (Turku) and Lovisa.[80] That hostility should have been confined to Örebro alone, however, is completely out of the question; examples from Uppsala and Helsingborg suggest a similar element of conflict, and the many royal statutes from the early seventeenth to the late eighteenth century testify to the national reach of animosity towards customs officials.

This animosity seems to have crystallised around those officials whose work brought them into close contact with ordinary payers of customs duty: all local officials in the seventeenth century, customs scribes and searchers in the eighteenth. People disliked them because they invaded the domestic sphere, because they confiscated people's property, because sometimes they probably did levy too much, and because some of them seem to have been strongly associated with the use of alcohol and with places and situations where loud and aggressive voices were heard. In many of these respects, the Swedish situation definitely resembled that of France.[81]

Unlike in France, however, the resentment against Swedish customs officials and other lower state servants was not fed by a 'culture of retribution', as William Beik has called it. In other words, there are few signs of a collective wish to punish these officials in public and humiliating ways. Swedish customs officials were not dragged by their hair to riverbanks and drowned. Subjects did complain about men who misbehaved or committed specific errors, and the central state instigated inspection campaigns, but that was all. The reason for the comparative lack of drama was probably the fact that municipal communities had their own stake in the collection of excise. This precluded actions of the sort described in France. The special character of the riot in Älvdalen in 1667 supports this analysis. Here, large parts of the peasant community attacked the customs official in his temporary abode, dragged him out into the open air, tore off his wig and threatened him. The coordinated action of many people and the symbolic elements (depriving the man of his wig) all suggest something in line with a culture of retribution.[82] But Älvdalen was different from Örebro and other towns: customs had not been levied here before the incident took place, and no members of the community had a stake in their successful collection.

Households in the front line

The conflicts between customs officials and the inhabitants of towns should not be imagined as conflicts between men. There are several indications that these disputes pitted entire households against each other, and that wives and servants were actively involved on both sides. The altercation between Erik Kraft and Pär Olofsson provides an example. According to Pär's testimony, his wife tried to pay the customs duty when Kraft refused to accept the money from Pär himself. Kraft was then so incensed that he tried to beat her, and it was only when Kraft's wife intervened by locking her husband in a room that Pär's wife was able to escape physically unscathed. Kraft did manage to shout 'she-dog' after her, though. His servants were also involved in the conflict; Kraft had them chase after Pär to a neighbouring town, and when he came back to Örebro, they vigilantly reported his return to their master.[83]

Kraft's wife prevented him from doing something he might later regret, and Pär's wife tried to set things to rights by paying the money her husband had initially refused to proffer. On both sides, the wives seem to have been actively involved in the business of customs and excise, probably because it affected their household economy. Other cases also show wives very actively administering a household's payment of excise. Lysbeta, married to Johan Israelsson, admitted in 1655 that their household had tried to evade paying the excise on beer and meat; on a later occasion, she wilfully took back customs money her husband had paid for some oxen. On that occasion she upbraided the customs officials, saying, 'Do you not remember that these oxen were sold in Arboga [i.e. not in Örebro, and therefore no duty was payable]?'.[84] Clearly, she saw herself as the person who knew what the household was obliged to pay. Sometimes spouses collaborated to fool and beat the customs officials. In Örebro in the 1740s, a searcher accused a couple of having smuggled alcohol into town and of later having violently taken it back after it had been confiscated by the customs. Apparently, what had happened was that the husband had held the searcher while the wife took the sack with the bottles and quickly disappeared with the contraband. This had caused some shouting and commotion. The witnesses to the event were clearly reluctant to give detailed accounts of what had happened.[85] Cases such as these suggest a low-intensity war between officials and townspeople.

The royal statutes do not elaborate on the involvement of customs officials' households, but they do occasionally mention that other people were to enjoy the same kind of royal protection as state servants themselves. In the statute of 1658, the king declared that he included all customs officials and 'their servants, people and household members' in his 'royal protection, peace and defence' – indicating that not only state servants but also those dependent on them had been subject to abuse.[86] The resentment towards customs officials spilled over onto their households, and this included physical and verbal abuse. Like their husbands, wives had to find ways of handling these forms of aggression.

Conclusion

Just like private soldiers on a battlefield, lower customs officials were in the front line and the first to be attacked by angry subjects. Violence was often part of their everyday experience of what it meant to work for the state. To handle these situations, they needed one thing more than anything else: street-smartness. Theoretical knowledge, hailed by Weber in his discussion of well-functioning government, was relevant to those office holders who were safely ensconced in their offices, but less relevant and certainly insufficient for these men. They and their households were the ones who had to persuade people to pay.

Street-smartness was not enough, however. The process of state formation forced these officials and the central state to adapt in a number of ways. The state adapted its rules and its attitudes to both servants and subjects, and the men adapted their behaviour. While the statute law of the mid-seventeenth century reminded subjects that they must under no circumstances resort to verbal and physical attacks on state servants, late-seventeenth- and eighteenth-century statutes not only repeated these injunctions, but also emphasised the servants' responsibility to behave in ways that did not cause people to take offence. It was a subtle but very important shift in focus and emphasis, and this shift was part of how the fine but firm line between licit and illicit behaviour was drawn. In order to make clear that home inspections by state servants did not fall under the heading of breaches of domestic peace, it was crucial that state servants should never display aggressive or military-like behaviour. And to make clear that confiscation of property by state servants did not fall under the heading of theft, it was equally crucial that those servants and their families should never avail themselves of the possibility of stealing. As experience showed that state servants might lapse in these respects when under the influence of alcohol, state law and the state administration evinced increasing concern about excessive use of such beverages.

Establishing a distinction between a man and his professional role was also part of the drawing of boundaries. When acting in his capacity as a state servant, a man had to be sober, self-controlled and law-abiding. When acting as a private person, he could behave differently, and also be treated differently. It is clear that this was a distinction that was made. When an inhabitant of Örebro threatened to take revenge on some office holders *when their term in office was over*, he showed that he would have liked to have his revenge immediately, but realised that he would then be punished. He grasped the distinction between being and not being in office, but it was only his fear of retribution that made him respect it. Likewise, the searcher who had attacked a colleague and claimed that the colleague was *off duty* at the time also showed that he was aware of the distinction: it was a serious crime to attack an official while he was exercising his office. Finally, when statutory law said that it was particularly reprehensible to attack an official *in his office*, it sent a signal to subjects that not only officials but also their work spaces were part of the state.

In the eighteenth century, attacking an official on duty remained a very serious crime and officials were still protected by the legal structures set up by their master, the state. But this protection was now extended to state servants on certain conditions, namely that they behave in ways that did not make subjects angry. Putting one's private self and private feelings to one side and adopting a professional role now became of paramount importance. It is in this light that the repeated references to soberness and politeness have to be seen. It was not sufficient to threaten subjects with punishment if they attacked a servant of the state; those servants had to prevent animosity ever arising by showing, as Keppel did, patient and conciliatory behaviour. This called for a process of learning, of fashioning oneself so that one could don the required professional persona.[87]

Notes

1 J. Myrdal, *Det svenska jordbrukets historia,* Vol. II: *Jordbruket under feodalismen: 1000–1700* (Stockholm: Natur och kultur, 1999), 256–7.

2 ULA, Örebro Accisrätt, box '1695–1810', Inkomna skrivelser 1695–1755.

3 ULA, Länsstyrelsen i Kopparbergs län, Landskansliet, A I a, Vol. V, letter from Duvall, 16 March 1667 (my translation). I wish to thank Linda Oja, who very kindly showed me this case and let me use it.

4 ULA, Länsstyrelsen i Kopparbergs län, Landskansliet, E I, Vol. I, rannsakning, 22 and 28 March 1667.

5 On the responsibility of governors to admonish the peasantry, see Chapter 1, and Nilsson, '1634 års regeringsform', 220.

6 S. Maza, *Servants and Masters*, 200, 223.

7 G. Wittrock, *Regering och allmoge under Kristinas egen styrelse: riksdagen 1650* (Uppsala: Skrifter utgivna av K. Humanistiska Vetenskapssamfundet i Uppsala, 1953), 116, 149–50, 213–19.

8 Smith, *Studier i svensk tulladministration*, Part I, 125–6, 149. *Hundsfott* is a reference to the genitals of a she-dog.

9 E.g. ULA, Örebro Rådhusrätt och magistrat, court record, 24 January 1653; Örebro Accisrätt, A, Vol. II, 12 September 1780. See also Örebro Rådhusrätt och magistrat, court record, 6 July 1653 (another dispute on the bridge about payment of customs); 13 March 1654 (a state servant was called an 'unfaithful servant of the Crown'); Örebro Rådhusrätt och magistrat, court record, 16 May 1681 (two linen weavers attacked a customs official, even though he was lying on the floor); Örebro Accisrätt, A, Vol. I, 768–70, Vol. II, 27 January 1779 (attack on customs officials, 1779). See also M. Ågren, 'Another process of state formation: Swedish customs officials, their work and households', *Cultural and Social History*, 11 (2014), 31–49.

10 Konungabalken, V, §7, in Å. Holmbäck and E. Wessén, *Magnus Erikssons landslag* (Stockholm: Nord. bokh. (distr.), 1962) (my translation). Peace is *fred* or *frid* in Swedish. The opposite is *ofrid*, which has been translated here as 'absence of peace'.

11 Jansson, *Kvinnofrid*.

12 K. H. Jansson, 'Våldsgärning, illgärning, ogärning: könskodat språkbruk och föreställningar om våld i den medeltida landslagen', in E. Österberg and M. Lindstedt Cronberg (eds), *Våld: representation och verklighet* (Lund: Nordic Academic Press, 2006), 145–65.

13 ULA, Örebro Rådhusrätt och magistrat, court record, 6 December 1691, 256–61.

14 The word used was *omolesterad*, an expression not in use in modern Swedish.

15 ULA, Örebro Accisrätt, box '1695–1810', Inkomna skrivelser 1695–1755, Skrivelse från Päder Olofson.

16 See K. H. Jansson, 'Våld som aggression eller kommunikation? Hemfridsbrott 1550–1650', *Historisk Tidskrift*, 126 (2006), 429–52; and K. H. Jansson, '(O)rättfärdigt våld: fejdkultur i 1500-talets rättsliga och militära gränsland', in M. Sjöberg (ed.), *Sammanflätat: civilt och militärt i det tidigmoderna Sverige* (Uppsala: Historiska institutionen, Uppsala universitet, 2009), 85–100.

17 ULA, Örebro Accisrätt, A, Vol. I, 25 October 1743, 60–1. See also other cases where the customs official explicitly said he was afraid of being treated as one of his colleagues had been: ULA, Örebro Accisrätt, box '1744–49', no dates, dispute between Petter Lindstedt and Anders Tyman and his wife.

18 Frohnert, *Kronans skatter*, 145–9.

19 ULA, Örebro Rådhusrätt och magistrat, court record, 21 May 1655, 121.

20 J. Höppener, *Bonde-Cur för den sjuka Riks-kroppen inom hus* (Stockholm, 1774) (my translation and italics). Thanks to Karin Hassan Jansson for drawing my attention to this source.

21 E.g. Matt. 9; Mark 2; Luke 3:12, 15, 18:10, 19.

22 Cf. Braddick, *State Formation*, 263.

23 *Kongl. Maj:ts Landt-Tulls och Accis-Ordning, 17 December 1756*, in Modée, *Utdrag utur alle ifrån den 7. decemb. 1718–1791 utkomne publique handlingar*, Part VI, Chapter 1, §1; *Sveriges rikes lag: gillad och antagen på riksdagen år 1734*. Facsimile of version printed in 1780 (Stockholm: Inst. för rättshistorisk forskning, 1984), Missgärningsbalken, Chapter 44, §1: 'stånde dubbel tjufsrätt'.

24 ULA, Örebro Accisrätt, box '1695–1810', Inkomna skrivelser 1695–1755, Skrivelse från Gabriel Albrichtzon. See also Smith, *Studier i svensk tulladministration*, Part I, 159.

25 E. Falk, *Verbala förolämpningar i 1630-talets Uppsala: en historisk talaktsanalys* (Uppsala: Institutionen för nordiska språk, Uppsala universitet, 2011), 83.

26 ULA, Örebro Accisrätt, A, Vol. I, 103–4. The case was handled by the *kämnärsrätt*.

27 See also Falk, *Verbala förolämpningar*, 186.

28 *Ibid.*, 182–9, 242–4.

29 ULA, Örebro Rådhusrätt och magistrat, court record, 6 June 1653.

30 RA, Äldre kommissioner, 167, letter from Johan Andersson, 11 March 1674.

31 Falk, *Verbala förolämpningar*, 173.

32 ULA, Örebro Rådhusrätt och magistrat, court records, 10 June and 12 December 1649.

33 See, for instance, ULA, Örebro Rådhusrätt och magistrat, court record, 14 April 1656, 180–3.

34 *SAOB*, 'kronans', or 'konungens tjuv', referring to somebody who has stolen from the Crown. Meaning now extinct. See also the example from *Utdrag utur alle ifrån den 7. decemb. 1718–1791 utkomne publique handlingar,* Part I, 598 (1724), used in *SAOB*, the same entry. In addition, see *Kongl. Maj:ts Landt-Tulls och Accis-Ordning, 17 December 1756*, Chapter 11, §3, p. 18.

35 N. Reuterholm, *Nils Reuterholms Journal* (Stockholm: P.A. Norstedt & Söner, 1957), 72–3.

36 M. Linde, 'Envåldskungens makt och ämbetsmännens: ämbetsmannakontroll och maktlegitimering i Karl XII:s Sverige', in *Karolinska förbundets årsbok* (Stockholm: Karolinska förbundet, 1997), 43–103.

37 Korda, *Labors Lost*, 163–73.

38 ULA, Örebro Rådhusrätt och magistrat, court records, 3 May 1654; 17 November 1656, 224; 14 July 1691. On the importance of loud noises, see also J. Eibach, 'Das offene Haus: kommunikative Praxis im sozialen Nahraum der europäischen Frühen Neuzeit', *Zeitschrift für historische Forschung*, 38 (2011), 621–64 (644).

39 *SAOB*, 'buller'. The word can also mean commotion or quarrel.

40 A. A. von Stiernman, *Samling Utaf Kongl. Bref, Stadgar och Förordningar &c. Angående Sweriges Rikes Commerce, Politie och Oeconomie Uti Gemen, Ifrån Åhr 1523. In til närwarande tid. Uppå Hans Kongl. Maj:ts Nådigesta Befallning*, Part II, 897–8; Part III, 5-6, 57–8, 191–7; Part IV, 199–200.

41 ULA, Örebro Accisrätt, box '1695–1810', Inkomna skrivelser 1695–1755, Skrivelse från Päder Olofson. The exact words were: 'då bekänner iagh i min ifrigzhet sade iagh, fahnen gör wproor, och stööt skälmar och hundar och icke migh, då mante iagh och honom uth, och hotade migh skola bethala dhet han stötte och skälte migh'. My translation into English is a free rendering.

42 Cf. Beik, *Urban Protest*, 32–3, who also points out that it was regarded as particularly reprehensible to challenge a state official in public.

43 ULA, Örebro Accisrätt, A, Vol. II, 27 January 1779. See also Ågren, 'Another process'.

44 ULA, Örebro Accisrätt, A, Vol. I, 324, 334, 340–1, 374, 822–3.

45 *Kongl. Maj:ts Landt-Tulls och Accis-Ordning, 17 December 1756*, Chapter 11, §4, p. 3; R. Hedlund, *Västerås befolkning vid slutet av 1600-talet: en socialhistorisk studie* (Västerås: Västerås kulturnämnd, 1980), 92, 120.

46 ULA, Örebro Accisrätt, A, Vol. II, 14 September 1786.

47 Stiernman, *Samling Utaf Kongl. Bref*, Part III, 196; Part IV, 180; *Kongl. Maj:ts förnyade Land-Tulls och Accis Stadga, 19 September 1776*, in Modée, *Utdrag utur alle ifrån den 7. decemb. 1718–1791 utkomne publique handlingar* (Stockholm, 1742–1829), Part X, Chapter 20, §1.

48 See also M. Lennersand, *Rättvisans och allmogens beskyddare: den absoluta staten, kommissionerna och tjänstemännen, ca 1680–1730* (Uppsala: Historiska institutionen, Uppsala universitet, 1999), esp. 256–8, on the risks involved for the state if it did not support its servants.

49 'Kongl. Maytz förordning och stadga öfwer acciis rätterne', 2 May 1672, in J. Schmedeman (ed.), *Kongl. stadgar, förordningar, bref och resolutioner* ..., Part I, Åhr 1706 (Stockholm, 1706), 628–33.

50 'Patent om tullbetienternes förswar', 12 May 1658, in Schmedeman, *Kongl. stadgar*, 313–14: customs officials must not exact too much. See also RA, Kammarkollegiet, Tull- och licentkontoret, F III, Vol. I, kommission 1668 angående klagomål över småtullsarrendet 1664.

51 'Patent om tullbetienternes förswar', 12 May 1658; 'Till alla hovrätter angående tullbetjentes tvistigheters avgörande', 23 September 1684; 'Protectorial för siötuls-betiente', 26 November 1695; 'Till Åbo hovrätt huru rannsakas och dömas skall om slagsmål emellan sjöfarande och tullbetjente samt besökare', 7 March 1696. All in Schmedeman, *Kongl. stadgar*, 313–14, 872–3, 1432–4, 1438, respectively. Similar prohibitions were laid down in a statute of 26 November 1632 and in the sixteenth century; see Kotkas, *Royal Police Ordinances*, 108, 117.

52 RA, Kammarkollegiet, Tull- och licentkontoret, F I, Vol. VIII, Instruktion för inspektorerna över småtullarna och acciserna 9 March 1675, particularly the preamble and item 27.

53 Kongl. Maijt:s Placat och Förordning angående handhafwandet af stora siötulls wäsendet, 28 February 1678, in Stiernman, *Samling Utaf Kongl. Bref*, Part IV, 179–82.

54 RA, Kammarkollegiet, Tull- och licentkontoret, F I, Vol. VIII, fullmakt för Henrik Engelbrecht (1684).

55 ULA, Örebro Rådhusrätt och magistrat, court record, 23 April 1656, 182–3.

56 *Kongl. Maj:ts förnyade Land-Tulls och Accis Stadga*, 19 September 1776, Chapter 20, §4.

57 *Kongl. Maj:ts Landt-Tulls och Accis-Ordning, 17 December 1756*, Chapter 10, §9; Chapter 13, §1; *Kongl. Maj:ts förnyade Land-Tulls och Accis Stadga, 19 September 1776*, Chapter 20, §1. On the fiscal value of confiscations, see Åmark, *Sveriges statsfinanser*, 566.

58 *Kongl. Maj:ts förnyade Land-Tulls och Accis Stadga, 19 September 1776*, Chapter 20, §2.

59 RA, Äldre kommissioner 178, utdrag ur den under assessor Herlin's praesidio, 29 March 1729.

60 *Kongl. Maj:ts Landt-Tulls och Accis-Ordning, 17 December 1756*, Chapter 13, §2.

61 RA, Äldre kommissioner 167, letter from Per Hammarskiöld, 24 February 1665.

62 RA, Äldre kommissioner 167, letters from Johan Andersson, 21 January and 11 March 1674.

63 *Kongl. Maj:ts Reglemente för Landt-Tulls- och Accis-Kamrarne i Riket, 17 December 1756*, 4260–1.

64 ULA, Örebro Accisrätt, A, Vol. I, 324, 334.

65 ULA, Örebro Accisrätt, A, Vol. I, 183–4.

66 ULA, Örebro Accisrätt, A, vol. I, 569–70 (2 August 1764). Similar examples at 811.

67 S. Ling, *Konsten att försörja sig: kvinnors arbete i Stockholm 1650–1750* (Stockholm: Stockholmia förlag, 2016). See also the results of the GaW project, presented in Ågren, *Making a Living*.

68 *Kongl. Maj:ts Reglemente för Landt-Tulls- och Accis-Kamrarne i Riket, 17 December 1756*, 4217.

69 P. Lind, *'Strunt alt hvad du orerar': Carl Michael Bellman, ordensretoriken och Bacchi Orden* (Uppsala; Litteraturvetenskapliga institutionen, Uppsala universitet, 2014).

70 RA, Överdirektörens för landtullen arkiv, Personella berättelser, 1748.

71 RA, Överdirektörens för landtullen arkiv, Personella berättelser, Förteckning på de nuvarande landtulls över- och underbetjänter vid Örebro Kungl. Landtullskammare år 1783.

72 Beik, *Urban Protest*, 63–72, 258.

73 Brewer, *Sinews*, 66–9, 102–9; Braddick, *State Formation*, 233–85; M. Ogborn, 'The capacities of the state: Charles Davenant and the management of the excise, 1683–1698', *Journal of Historical Geography*, 24:3 (1998), 289–312.

74 Stuart, *Defiled Trades*, 31, 52, 241–2.

75 ULA, Örebro Accisrätt, A, Vol. I, 23 June 1743; 2 November 1749; *Kongl. Maj:ts förnyade Land-Tulls och Accis Stadga, 19 September 1776*, Chapter 2, particularly §5. See also Chapter 4, §5: masters and mistresses cannot blame a failure to pay excise on their servants.

76 Such pamphlets are mentioned in 'Protectorial för siötuls-betiente', 26 November 1695. See also Smith, *Studier i svensk tulladministration*, Part I, 126.

77 'Till Åbo hovrätt om professorer', 4 April 1689, in Schmedeman, *Kongl. stadgar*, 1233.

78 Stuart, *Defiled Trades*, 31.

79 RA, Överdirektörens vid småtullarna och accisen arkiv, E 1 Kautioner, Vol. VII: the director of the customs administration made enquiries about Erik Scheningh's guarantors; the magistrates certified that the men belonged to the burgher community. See also Äldre kommissioner 167, 6 March 1674: it was mentioned that one of the mayors had stood surety for the customs official Johan Andersson; RA, Kammarkollegiet, Tull- och licentkontoret, F I, Vol. IX, 1 July 1702.

80 *Kongl. Maj:ts förnyade Land-Tulls och Accis Stadga, 19 September 1776*, Chapter 12, §4.

81 Beik, *Urban Protest*, 32, 35, 52.

82 See *ibid.*, 32–3, on the significance of tearing off wigs.

83 ULA, Örebro Accisrätt, box '1695–1810', Inkomna skrivelser 1695–1755.

84 ULA, Örebro Kämnärsrätt, Vol. A I, 27 September 1655.

85 ULA, Örebro Accisrätt, box '1744–49', no dates, conflict between Petter Lindstedt and Anders Tyman and his wife.

86 'Patent om tullbetienternes förswar', 12 May 1658: 'tjänare, folk och hjon'. The last term can be translated as household member, family member or servant; *SAOB*, 'hjon'.

87 See A. Florén, 'Nya roller, nya krav: några drag i den svenska nationalstatens formering', *Historisk tidskrift*, 107 (1987), 505–29; Braddick, *State Formation*, 261–2; Gowing, 'Manner of submission'.

3

Families in service

One morning in 1758, the searcher Lars Staf and his wife Brita Stina Berg left their home – a room rented from a local merchant – to start their daily work. Being a lower customs official, Lars probably first went down to one of the entry points to the town to check on travellers coming to Örebro; we know for certain that Brita Stina proceeded to a neighbouring house, where she spent the day baking bread for a household other than her own. The couple's finances were strained: they paid 100 copper *daler* a year for their abode, and with Lars's basic salary of 210 copper *daler* they could not survive without the extra income he sometimes secured by confiscating goods on which no excise had been paid. Brita Stina's contributions were also indispensable. She had managed to scrape together some 100 copper *daler*, savings that she kept in a locked chest in their room. Many years later, when the customs inspector reported to his superiors that Lars Staf had become a very poor man, he explicitly mentioned what he may have regarded as the main reason for the couple's poverty, namely that Lars's wife was by then bedridden and unable to contribute.[1]

Jointly responsible for the family economy, but working in diverse fields for two separate incomes, Lars and Brita Stina appear to share some characteristics with modern couples, who also get up every morning to be at work on time and who reconvene at home in the evening. During the day, Lars and Brita Stina were both away from home, which helps explain how a burglar was able to break into their room and steal Brita Stina's savings. When the thief was apprehended and taken to court, a description of the incident ended up in the court records, where it can be read today. But while the couple's everyday life resembles that of many modern couples, it was nevertheless inscribed in societal processes that were radically different from those of the twenty-first century.

Brita Stina's work – selling services to other households – was part of the increasing commercialisation of early modern society. Instead of baking their own bread, some households in Örebro paid women like Brita Stina to do the job for them. Some of these households belonged to the burgeoning middling sort; they could pay to have their bread baked for them, and in some cases had more resources than they could use themselves. There was a demand for domestic services of this kind, creating income opportunities of which many women availed themselves, and for commodities such as textiles. On the other hand, many forms of market relationship were controlled, restricted and sometimes even criminalised, in a way that is in stark contrast to modern society. Neither Lars nor Brita Stina could lawfully sell clothing of their own making, since this would infringe the monopolistic rights of the tailors' guild. Many jobs performed by women such as Brita Stina were poorly paid, not promptly paid, and sometimes not paid at all. Still, even such unpaid services were things people spent their days doing, both as expressions of mutual help and in the hope of being compensated somehow at a later point in time.

Lars's work as a customs official was to levy money from subjects, a crucial task in the administration of the early modern state. Because of its scale, this pan-European phenomenon often necessitated the employment of people who lacked both formal education and the habitus of gentlemen. Many of them worked from home, and while this did not apply to Lars Staf, he did not have a proper office either, since his work frequently required him to be on the move in the streets. His and his peers' jobs were not always well paid, or promptly paid. To secure a living, they needed both their wives' incomes and whatever additional income they themselves could obtain. Their everyday work experiences were thus very different from those posited by Weber in his discussion of rational bureaucracy: they did not and could not live by their state offices alone.

Nonetheless, state formation and commercialisation created new income opportunities,[2] and while very different, these two ways of making a living were both modelled on service, or understood, simply, as help. Men such as Lars Staf were in the service of the state, and women such as Brita Stina Berg were in the service of other families. Thus, Lars and Brita Stina embodied, served and helped both the expanding state and the burgeoning markets, as did many other couples in Sweden and elsewhere at this time.[3] This chapter explores the ways in which their work linked them to the state and to other households.

A makeshift economy

The economic hardship endured by the families of many lower state servants is difficult to map systematically. It can, however, be traced through indirect and incidental evidence. Most striking perhaps is the tendency for state servants to complain about their inadequate salaries. This was particularly relevant in inflationary years such as the 1760s. Thus, in 1759 the town scribe Johan Eric Bergström expressed dissatisfaction with his salary, and in 1762 he made up his mind to apply for a corresponding position in another town (Uddevalla), apparently in the hope of being able to boost his income.[4] Customs scribes Letin, Fernström and Wingström all voiced concern about the rising cost of living in the 1760s and 1770s. Letin announced that he wanted a pay rise, and Fernström pointed out that he had had to live off his inheritance because of his meagre pay. He had, he said, been completely ruined by serving in 'this terribly expensive place'. Wingström described his destitute condition and admitted that he had had to live off the customs duty he had levied.[5] While this was irregular, it was probably not unheard of. Such complaints should not always be taken at face value, though. In fact, Bergström's salary of 300 *daler* was not insignificant. Moreover, the issue of state servants' salaries was also a topic of public political debate in the late eighteenth century. While some participants in that debate claimed that state servants were so poorly paid that they often could not marry, others contended that what these complaints were really all about were a new taste for luxury and a higher standard of living.[6]

There is other evidence, however, that suggests a makeshift economy, in which many people relied on a precarious combination of incomes. In the general instructions for customs inspectors issued in 1675, there was a clause saying that inspectors had to make sure their subordinates did not engage in other income-earning activities.[7] This suggests, of course, that many lower customs officials did engage in such activities, and other evidence bears this out. For instance, although it was expressly forbidden, the illicit sale of beer at town entry points seems to have been a common source of extra income for customs officials in the late seventeenth century.[8] Access to extra earnings was indispensable.

Many lower state servants acted as informal lawyers, assisting or representing people in their dealings with the courts. For instance, a chief inspector in Gothenburg by the name of Hagert described how 'advocatyre' had been a step in his early career. Presumably, it was the writing skills and legal experience of these men that created a demand for their services.[9] Another source of income was teaching. Early modern Swedish schools (both the *trivialskola* and the *gymnasium*) devoted much of their time and energy to teaching the classical heritage in the form of Latin and Greek. Efforts were made to modernise school teaching, but there were complaints about a lack of good teachers in arithmetic and accounting (*ars rationaria*). Parents who could afford it seem to have opted for private alternatives, creating a demand for skilled instructors. Customs officials and men working closely with bailiffs seem to have been particularly popular as teachers of arithmetic and accounting, in Sweden and elsewhere.[10] For instance, Christopher Moback attended the *trivialskola* in Örebro for some time, but his father then sent him 'to those who teach accounting in the castle' (*c.* 1712), the castle being the headquarters of the regional state administration. Jacob Granhult had also attended the local school, but after studies in arithmetic he started working for Lars Kåhre, the previous regional treasurer, who was by this time (1715) castle governor.[11] Not surprisingly, we also find the bailiff's scribe Johan Örnbom teaching arithmetic, and customs inspector Törnqvist teaching accounting.[12] Teaching writing and arithmetic to children or 'local inhabitants' was something customs officials did throughout the country. They also offered their skills in these areas to, as one customs inspector put it, 'those who need my help'.[13] Thus, knowledge of accounting, in particular, was of value both because it could be sold in the services market and because it could open up a modest career in the state administration. It could also offer a splendid career. Salomon von Otter ended up as one of Sweden's top bureaucrats in the late seventeenth and early eighteenth centuries, playing a key role in the reorganisation of the navy. He started his career as an assistant in the regional state administration of Örebro, where his tasks included writing out fair copies of the accounts.[14]

Some customs officials, though, had sidelines that do not seem to have built at all on their professional skills. Thus, in the 1650s, Hans Moback was a 'bridge inspector' (a form of customs official), but also a tanner; in the 1690s, customs official Anders Månsson Lind was also a part-time butcher; in the 1740s, customs scribe Anders Lybeck earned extra income as a ferryman.[15] Another customs official (who was also a municipal official) ran a small spinning workshop in his home in the 1750s, and sought to increase his income even more by investing in the local tobacco factory.[16] A common pattern was for customs officials to cultivate tobacco, sell beer, fish, and engage in various crafts (tailoring, carpentry, shoemaking, painting etc.). One searcher was a violinist and also taught children to play the instrument.[17] Such occupational pluralism was far from uncommon in early modern Sweden, and can also be found elsewhere. By-employments were common among holders of public offices in the German-speaking area,[18] and even in England, where specialisation was arguably much more developed, there are examples of attorneys who were also brewers or wine-and-brandy merchants.[19] Occupational pluralism was probably widespread in most places.

When many Swedish customs inspectors reported, in 1748, that they and their subordinates had no by-employments, this was probably attributable to two factors: that they were unaccustomed to filling in the new form, and that they had an interest in stressing how badly off they were financially. Some inspectors, for instance, wrote 'nothing whatsoever' or 'absolutely nothing', as if to emphasise the precariousness of their situation. By contrast, the inspector in Strängnäs filled in sources of extra income for all customs officials' families except one. The inspector in Härnösand reported extra earnings for five wives out of seven. It is unlikely that the need for by-employment was considerably greater and the opportunities considerably better in these two towns than elsewhere. It is more likely that some inspectors were more meticulous than others in supplying the information.[20]

For the lowest type of customs officials (searchers), confiscating goods on which customs and excise had not been duly paid could be an important source of extra income.[21] The pursuit of such windfalls was not only accepted but, it seems, encouraged by the authorities, since officials were believed to be more zealous if they had something to gain from ferreting out excise evaders. Similar incentives have been observed for police work in other European countries; police officers had to be spurred on, it was argued, by the prospect of sharing in the profits from any fines imposed.[22] But these shares in confiscated goods and fines were more than tools to manipulate the behaviour of lower state servants. They were necessary extra incomes for families who, as their employer knew, were poorly paid. It is a token of this awareness that, when listing their employees, the Swedish eighteenth-century customs authorities included information not only on education, behaviour and marital status, but also on by-employments.[23] Rather than trying to prevent officials from bringing in extra earnings, as it had done in 1675, the state now realised that such practices were necessary and accepted them, as long as they were legal.

Nevertheless, despite these efforts, many seem to have had serious financial difficulties and, as a result, ended up with large debts. The estate of Erik Kraft, who was both a postmaster and a lower customs official, included sizable debts to the state, as did the estate of the man who married his widow, postmaster Lars Winge (1687).[24] *Landskamrer* Bohm, who worked in the regional state administration, died more or less destitute, leaving his wife to petition the king in 1759 for a state pension.[25] When the searcher Nils Elfsberg died, it was noted in his inventory from the 1730s that his widow was desperately poor; that she blamed her poverty on her husband; that she had done her utmost to pay his debts; and that she finally succeeded in doing so, but only because her mother assisted her.[26]

Indebtedness and a need for financial help were not only the effects of insufficient income or extravagant living. Men such as bailiffs, regional treasurers[27] and customs inspectors all had costs directly related to their work and needed buffers. They were often expected, or forced, to advance money to their employer, to people whose services they hired on behalf of the state, and to colleagues. For instance, customs inspector Bergman had to pay substantial amounts out of his own pocket for paper and writing material, and the excise court in Örebro supported his claim to be reimbursed. Even worse, though, Bergman had vouched for some of his subordinates. These debts were the reason why, in 1764, he was threatened with suspension. Faced with this crisis, Bergman summoned his subordinates and reminded them that all customs and excise moneys were to be submitted to the regional state administration once a week. While this was not a new rule, no one seems to have adhered to it, and consequently many scribes had deficits in their accounts. This was a major problem for Bergman. While claiming to be entirely innocent, he had nevertheless incurred his superiors' suspicions because he himself seemed to be in arrears.[28]

From the answers of his subordinates, the customs scribes, it is evident what the problem was. Their salaries were insufficient, particularly as these were years of inflation. What they did was live off the customs and excise they had levied. Only when they received their salaries did they deliver these moneys to the state. There would therefore be a certain time lag, which manifested itself as deficits in the accounts. If the accounts were checked on a weekly basis, there was little chance of hiding such manipulations. A growing deficit in the state accounts mirrored the increase in this kind of debt.[29]

Other state servants, too, had to have cash in hand to carry out their work. The regional treasurer Johan Broström had to pay excise on 90 barrels of grain levied as tax from the peasantry; he was later duly reimbursed for these costs, but they were costs nevertheless, requiring him to keep a ready supply of cash. Other state servants had to pay the immediate costs involved in the organisation of *durchmarschen* (movement of military troops); they too were reimbursed, but only after some time. Some municipal office holders (*kämnärer*) were apparently forced to pay the taxes of local ironmasters; when they complained to the magistracy court, it was decided that some of the iron should be sequestered until such time as the ironmaster repaid the office holders for their outlays.[30] Customs scribes were responsible for keeping the customs houses equipped, well maintained and in good order.[31] Such responsibilities also required them to keep cash in hand and, when they failed to do so, to resort to borrowing.

Probate inventories of lower state servants list their debts and claims, both of which could arise from the demands of their occupational lives rather than from extravagant living. For example, when Anders Strokirk died, he had still not been fully reimbursed for costs related to his previous position in the mining district around Nora; at the same time, he had incurred new debts linked to his post in Örebro.[32] Widows of state servants would regularly draw attention to costs their husbands had had to pay out of their own pockets: when Susanna Nordenadler, for instance, petitioned the Crown for financial support, she referred to the expense her late husband had incurred in having the fortress at Varberg repaired.[33] The result of professional obligations rather than private spending, these debts were called 'balances', in contrast to the ordinary words for debts (*skuld*, *gäld*).

The need for ready cash to carry out one's job has been described in the historiography on state servants.[34] Less attention has been paid to how wives' contributions helped fill the gap. Wives with economic resources could help their husbands keep their offices by continuously adding to the household's liquid capital. Casten Feif, who carved out a grand career for himself as one of Charles XII's top state servants, once perspicaciously noted in a letter that he would have been done for, had it not been for his wife's wealth and ample income.[35] It may have been less common to admit one's economic dependence on one's wife, but such dependence was probably widespread, especially among upstarts such as Feif. And many state servants, it must be remembered, were upstarts.[36] Few enjoyed such careers as Feif and von Otter, and not everyone needed as large a buffer as a regional treasurer, but even when the scale of operation was smaller, it must have been extremely useful to have access to the earned or inherited resources of a wife. This was true of Joel Gripenstierna and Brynte Cronsköld, who both held senior posts in the customs administration,[37] but it was also true of state servants at the bottom of the professional hierarchy.

At the same time, there was obviously a feeling that wives' inherited resources ought not to be used for these purposes. Thus, when Carl Johan Hellman announced his intention to apply for a position as a *häradsskrivare* (a rural bailiff's scribe) in 1762, he added that he had had no income whatsoever from his previous office and that he had been forced to use 'all his own and his wife's inherited property' to pay off the debts (the balance) he had incurred.[38] The remark added about his wife's inheritance was evidently meant to demonstrate the inequity of his situation. It was a long-standing principle of Swedish law that the inherited property of a wife was to be kept separate from that of her husband, but this principle was gradually undermined in the early modern period and particularly so in the eighteenth century.[39] Since prenuptial agreements were very uncommon in Sweden, the only records we have of husbands using wives' property are probate inventories, wills and, as in this case, incidental references made in court. It is impossible, therefore, to quantify the precise extent to which state servants had recourse to the separate property of their wives to cover costs arising from their offices, but for some types of office holder (such as bailiffs, regional treasurers and customs inspectors) it seems likely that it was a common phenomenon.

Women could also assist their male relatives and spouses in obtaining their offices in the first place by standing surety (*kaution* or *borgen*). Providing security for others was a widespread phenomenon in early modern society. Since the majority of people relied on credit, most people also sometimes relied on having someone who could stand surety. Families and friends could play an important role as guarantors. Candidates for state service who were to handle money on behalf of their employer had to find acceptable guarantors who could vouch for their character and wealth. Until 1756, this applied to all customs inspectors, for example. The state demanded guarantors who did not have debts of their own, who had not stood surety for anyone other than the official, and who preferably did not belong to the peasant estate.

Providing security for a state servant meant that one effectively entered into a contract with the state itself, and this was not without risk. When in one case a bailiff failed to pay what was due to the state, his guarantors had to pay 3,626 *daler* to his employer, and two of them even had to spend some time in jail. As a consequence, the bailiff had to compensate his guarantors by mortgaging his urban and rural estates.[40] Not surprisingly, finding a guarantor could prove very difficult; according to one customs official, none of his friends was willing to help because they had fared badly in the past after guaranteeing the trustworthiness of 'bailiffs, *räntmästare*, *proviantmästare* and other servants of the Crown'.[41] Systematic surveys carried out by the customs administration in the late seventeenth and early eighteenth centuries show that many of its officials lacked acceptable guarantors.[42]

It is interesting, therefore, to see that women, too, provided security, sometimes because they were forced to do so and other times on a more voluntary basis. Thus, in 1695, the state demanded that all customs officials *and their wives* pledge their private property as security for the customs they were in charge of. Thirty-one customs inspectors and their wives did so, with both husband and wife signing the deed of pledge. Only three officials seem to have been unmarried and relied instead on other men to stand surety for them. The importance of the wife's signature is illustrated in the case of Jacob Lindboum, the customs inspector in Luleå, who signed alone; in an appended letter, the magistracy court of Luleå certified that Lindboum's wife had just died and so could not sign. Since husband and wife were co-owners of any property they had acquired together, a deed that lacked the signature of the wife would be of little use to the state.[43]

Demanding such security from state servants and their spouses was not something the state did every year. In most cases, it was content to have people from the local burgher community vouch for customs officials. The records describe these guarantors as men or widowed women, suggesting that normally couples posted security, not individual men. In 1694, for instance, before Israel Lohmb was accepted as a customs official in Lindesberg, Erich Erichsson Berg and Susanna Sigfridsdotter, a widow, provided security for him. Signing the surety bond, they promised to compensate the state if Israel failed to deliver the moneys entrusted to him. Likewise, in a series of examples from the 1690s, Hindrich von Schwaitz presented three 'cautioners', one of whom was Anna Stiernhöök, and Anders Sahlin presented five, among them Ingrid Jönsdotter.[44] It is not always clear whether there was a kin relationship between the guarantors and the official, but often this seems likely. Thus, when Elof Skragge became customs inspector for Kopparberg in 1696, one of his guarantors was Elisabet Nyman, widow of the late Elof Skragge and presumably the mother or sister-in-law of young Skragge.[45] Anders Tretzel in Stockholm relied on the security posted by his mother-in-law Elisabet Hornej.[46] In Örebro, Catharina Palm vouched for her son-in-law, who wanted to become a *factor*, just as Per Andersson Väster vouched for his, who wanted to be a customs official.[47] In cases such as this, the whole family or even kin group would have a tangible interest in the state office and the way in which it was exercised. State offices were not for sale, as they were in France, but the state kept strict and continuous control of them by demanding security. From the point of view of the office holder and his family, however, there was a similarity in the sense that, in Sweden too, one had to come up with money both to acquire the position in the first place and to be able to discharge its duties successfully over the years.

The close involvement of a wife in the financial dealings of her husband became obvious if a state servant died without having first cleared his accounts with his employer. In such cases, the wife and other family members were seldom spared. There are examples of bailiffs' widows who were hit hard when their husbands fell seriously ill and failed to sort out their affairs with the state.[48] Likewise, the widows of customs and regimental scribes were held responsible for their late husbands' debts to the state, and so too were children, children's spouses and grandchildren.[49] In Örebro in 1698, for instance, Elisabeth Persdotter had to pay the debts of her late husband, who had worked both as a *slottsskrivare* (a castle scribe) and as a customs official.[50]

When all customs inspectors and their spouses were forced to pledge their property in 1695, the inspector in Uddevalla wrote to the central authorities asking to have his accounts checked and cleared once a year so that he could explain any 'balance'. 'My family have been hit hard by having to pledge their property to the state', he wrote, adding that he did not want them to suffer innocently in the future simply because 'he [his successor] who is unacquainted with the matter might not be able to clarify any obscurities in the accounts'.[51] The inspector's words illustrate both the tardiness with which auditing took place and the risks and dangers to which families were exposed by their close connections with the state.

With their money, women not only helped members of their households to survive; they also supported their husbands in their work as holders of state offices. And, since the state depended on these men to carry out their duties and to have the necessary cash in hand, such contributions by wives in effect subsidised the growth of the early modern state. The capital that women contributed could come from their families of origin, by inheritance, and in these cases it was not just the individual woman, but her wider kin network that subsidised the state. Sometimes, families were hit by the failure of the men they had invested in to meet their obligations, but families could also benefit from their connections with the state. This is very clear in the case of regional treasurers.

Regional treasurers (*lanträntmästare*) were in charge of the state's reserves of cash at the regional level and were among the few people who could be counted on to have cash in hand. Taxes and customs collected from subjects by bailiffs and customs officials were subsequently delivered to the treasurer. As a rule, the central state authorities in Stockholm refrained from paying out cash; instead, they issued their creditors with a type of promissory note known as an 'assignation', to be cashed with regional treasurers or, sometimes, customs inspectors. This resulted in complicated networks of credit and debt linking central to regional state authorities, and private credit to public credit. It also added greatly to the power and prestige of the regional treasurers and their wives. Together, they became hubs of financial life.

A relationship between two women of higher rank illustrates this well. Previously married to the man responsible for all the rifle factories in Sweden, Anna Gyllenharnesk was remarried to the regional treasurer in Örebro, Hans Klerck, some time before 1690. On several occasions Anna had extended services to Beata Klingenstierna, daughter of the late Casten Otter, who had run the local rifle factory in Örebro. Beata had been granted a state subsidy towards her brother's funeral expenses – a form of subsidy for which the word 'help' was used – and the central state authorities had given her an assignation to be cashed with the regional treasurer. But since there was no cash available at that particular point in time, Anna and her husband agreed that Beata could refer the bills she incurred to them, to be paid in due course. As security, Beata offered her rights to the customs revenue from the nearby town of Filipstad. In addition to this loan, Beata had cashed another assignation from the central state in 1681, but had immediately given the money to Anna for safekeeping. Over the years, Anna and her two husbands appear to have extended numerous loans to Beata. Disentangling this bundle of credit and debt was no easy task for the magistracy court when the two women fell out with each other and ended up in court.[52]

Linked to the state through their father or husbands, Beata and Anna both had access to considerable financial resources: to funeral help, to customs revenue, to taxes levied within the region for which the treasurer was responsible, and to income from the manufacture of weapons. Anna's role is particularly interesting, since, evidently, she was a local moneylender who could offer assistance both to her husband (and thus, indirectly, the state) and to people in the local community. It is not always clear when she and her husband used their own money and when the state's, but what is very clear is that Anna was actively involved in every transaction. Frequent references were made to her account books, and to decisions taken and agreements made by the moneylender herself and her customer: 'since this money [the funeral help] could not immediately be supplied, she [Beata] agreed with Mrs Gyllenharnesk that whenever she [Beata] needed them, she [Mrs Gyllenharnesk] would issue papers and receipts to be paid later by Mr Klerck'.[53]

Anna Gyllenharnesk was not the only spouse of a treasurer who was closely involved in her husband's professional duties. Married to Johan

Broström, who started out as an employee of the state mining administration and later became a regional treasurer, Anna Sara Frumerie was also a local moneylender. When she died (in 1759), her probate inventory bore witness to the extensive network of credit relations of which, even after her husband's death, she was still the centre. A striking feature of her estate was the large number of different currencies, suggesting that she had contact with a number of foreign travellers or traders. She had, for example, extended credit to another woman by the name of Frumerie and also provided security for her 'towards the payment of state grain' (state tax was often levied in the form of grain). For this, Anna Sara held a silver cup as security.[54] Very probably, this was a common occurrence in the homes of treasurers: the appearance on the doorstep of taxpayers unable to come up with the required tax on time and imploring the treasurer and his wife to advance them the money. Not surprisingly, the probate inventory of Anna Sara's daughter Sara Cajsa Broström, also married to a treasurer, listed large amounts of cash and no debts.[55] The situation was the same throughout the country. In Jönköping, for instance, treasurer Lohm provided short-term credit for Maria Palmqvist while she was waiting for an assignation from Stockholm.[56] Clearly, treasurers and their wives were often asked to help people who could not wait for their money to arrive, and it was their easy access to state funds that gave them the role of local bankers.

On a smaller scale, credit was extended by the wives of other state servants as well. Anna Catharina Robsahm had been married several times (at least once to a lower state servant) and was a prominent moneylender in Örebro.[57] Birgitta Wester had been married to *sekreterare* Lothigius and the couple had provided loans to help people pay the excise.[58] Birgitta Noreen was married to *häradsskrivare* Örnbom and extended credit, primarily to other married women.[59] Anna Cajsa Boman was only a searcher's widow, but she nevertheless lent out money: 6 *daler* to a burgher of Filipstad, with a winter coat as collateral.[60] In these cases, it is not always possible to trace exactly where the cash came from, but it is likely that state money was sometimes used. As lower customs officials sometimes admitted, they could on occasion 'borrow' customs money, though with the intention of repaying it as soon as possible.

Women married to regional treasurers differed radically from those married to scribes, searchers or municipal servants (*stadsbetjänte*). They had control of material and social resources that were completely beyond the reach of these other women, who, in turn, performed types of work that were probably inconceivable to Anna Sara Frumerie or Anna Gyllenharnesk. And yet, across the social divides these women had connections to each other and could make a living precisely because of those connections. Anna Sara Frumerie had for example lent money to Gustaf Holmberg, and when he died (in 1755) it was his widow who had to repay the loan. Her name was Helena Sandberg and she will be mentioned below as active in the meat trade.[61] Anna Sara also extended credit to a tailor's widow, a hatter's widow and the wife of a customs official. The networks channelling money, goods and services between families were hierarchical, but at the same time linked women from different echelons of society to each other, making them collaborators, although rarely on equal terms.[62]

The market in help

In a national survey conducted in 1748, Swedish customs officials' wives were reported to have income from making beer and liquor, baking, weaving, spinning, sewing, and midwifery. They also cultivated tobacco, ran public houses and rented out rooms. Some of them were involved in the credit market.[63] In Örebro, Brita Stina Berg and Malin Westman, both wives of searchers, baked bread in other people's homes and sold textiles on commission. Other women ran errands, acted as go-betweens and did odd jobs for more highly placed and well-off people. Their work was of a non-specific, catch-all character.

The types of work carried out by these women were not radically different from what is already known about urban women's work in the rest of early modern society. European women produced and sold comestibles, beverages and simple clothes. They spun, did laundry and cleaned. They tended the old and sick, washed the dead and assisted at childbirth. They were active as retailers and sometimes engaged in illegal networks in which stolen textiles circulated. When in possession of resources, they capitalised on them, renting out rooms or lending out cash at interest. Some women performed manual labour that was physically very demanding, such as rowing, carrying heavy objects or doing agricultural work.[64] Thus, the types of work urban women did seem to have been more or less the same everywhere. Often, such work was referred to as 'help', stressing the social rather than the economic relationship between the women and those they worked for. But even if the vocabulary played down the commercial dimension, there is no doubt that there was a market in services that created economic space that these women could enter, just as the expanding state's demand for faithful servants created similar space for their husbands. Theirs was a form of work that, even when offered on a market, would often be labelled as help or service.

While we know what types of work these women did, we know less about their social context and meaning. This is partly because work of these kinds was seldom systematically recorded in the historical sources, and partly because it did not take place so much within households as in the interstices between them. These two causal factors are interconnected: since households were the main units of taxation, activities that were clearly related to households tend to be more conspicuous in the historical sources, while activities loosely related to them tend to be obscure. What is more, the types of work women did are often difficult to classify. Some of their work was similar to domestic service. Some of it was a form of brokerage. Some can be described as micro-entrepreneurship, and some as clientship. These conceptual problems bear witness to the unfamiliar character of this work. These women were part of a growing market in services, but it was not a *free* market, but one steeped in relations of dependence. We can think of these networks and relations of dependence as uneven alliances: alliances between individuals who were not each other's equals in terms of resources, but who nevertheless depended on and were able to assist each other.[65]

An example of such an alliance comes from late-seventeenth-century Örebro. Here, a widow called Margareta used to run errands for other women. Some errands she ran for Anna Larsdotter, the wife of one of the municipal officials,who also rented out rooms and extended credit. On one occasion, an anonymous lady was staying temporarily with Anna, and since she needed someone to help her with a small matter, Anna called for Margareta. Margareta came and was asked to deliver the lady's pillowcases to yet another woman (the wife of a clerk) and return with the payment, in effect a commission to sell the pillowcases. On her return to Anna's house, Margareta was paid a small amount for her trouble, and the lady, Margareta later claimed, was satisfied with the transaction. But this was not true, according to Anna, the landlady, who took the matter to court; in her account, her guest had subsequently asked Anna to contact the clerk's wife to get the pillowcases back. Anna did as she was told, and purchased the cases herself. She then commissioned Margareta to sell them a second time, which Margareta succeeded in doing, but upon her return the story repeated itself, as Anna was unhappy with the price Margareta had obtained.[66]

Anna's reasons for bringing the suit are not entirely clear. It transpired that Margareta was upset because Anna had scolded her, so it is possible that Margareta had reciprocated by saying something less flattering about her taskmaster. At all events, this story tells us how three early modern women from different social strata earned income and how they collaborated in an uneven alliance. The anonymous lady temporarily in town did not run errands, and Anna only did so when it could not be avoided. Margareta, by contrast, often did so. Both the lady and Anna used her as their emissary and go-between. Through her, they carried out commercial transactions at times when they were otherwise occupied and in places where they preferred not to go. Even when dissatisfied with Margareta's performance, Anna did not stop making use of her. She used Margareta as if she were her servant. Legally, Margareta was not, but for many practical purposes she was.

The opportunity to carry out errands for more highly placed women was of course valuable, not to say indispensable, to Margareta. Being a widow and probably not particularly well off, she welcomed all forms of income, something she was not alone in. The service she performed for women such as Anna and the lady visiting her were, in fact, typical of a good deal of female work in the early modern period. Such work was predicated on difference, hierarchy and power, and, like that of lower state servants, it resembled the work of ordinary servants. Highly placed individuals used those who were lowly placed and acted 'through' them. There was a significant element of instrumentality involved. At the same time, though, both Margareta's and Anna's work suggest the presence of local female networks and collaborative practices. Anna, Margareta and the clerk's wife all benefited, though not all in the same way, from the fact that this particular lady was travelling through the town. Likewise, the lady benefited by having her textiles sold. These women were not equal partners, of course; it turned out that Anna had the capacity to buy back the pillowcases, while Margareta received merely a fraction of their value.[67] Nonetheless, they needed each other, and their transactions may be seen as testimonies of cooperation.

Anna's role was clearly different from Margareta's. It was based on her position as a landlady and tavern owner, and as the wife of a lower municipal servant, but she adroitly expanded her role, capitalising on the opportunities offered by a growing demand for services. People needed to find each other in the market in order to be able to strike deals (for instance involving pillowcases), and Anna obviously helped them in this respect. While Margareta's work was similar though not identical to traditional service, Anna's can be described as a form of brokerage.

It was common for women in seventeenth- and eighteenth-century Sweden to rely on the assistance of other women – to help each other by letting the other party 'help'. Whether such help was remunerated or not is often difficult to tell, since the sources are laconic. But even if money was not mentioned in direct relation to a specific task, the intention may nevertheless have been eventually to pay for it somehow. Annika Olofsdotter, for instance, relied on Catarina Jönsdotter to wash linen in 1698. The women were both married to men of the same profession, and Catarina's work was described in the court record as help.[68] It is conceivable, of course, that Annika repaid Catarina by performing the same or a similar service for her on some later occasion, but it is equally possible that she paid in cash or in kind.

The laundering had not taken place in Annika's house, but along the river running through the town, and one of the sheets had been washed away, a mishap Catarina had been unable to prevent. Annika later mentioned the incident in the house of Erik Larsson, referring to Catarina as a 'thieving woman'. Because of these words, and not the lost sheet, the matter ended up in court. There, Annika confessed to having uttered the words 'thieving woman', and was consequently fined 6 silver marks. Catarina was ordered to pay Annika the cost of the sheet. It is obvious that it was a matter of great importance to Catarina not to be referred to in town as a thief, since this would undermine her position in the local community and, among other things, stop people from employing her as a laundress. Similar reasons may have caused Margareta, mentioned above, to complain about the way in which Anna had scolded her. Being criticised in public was a serious matter, and if the criticism lacked substance it had to be challenged.[69]

Women called on the help of other women for more purposes than just washing clothing and linen; production of ale, liquor, bread and other edible wares could also be commissioned from someone outside the household.[70] So could childcare. This was a type of 'help' that was probably regarded as particularly suitable to combine with other chores and responsibilities. A married woman by the name of Marit, for example, provided multiple services for another household in 1654; her work consisted in taking care of a small boy, while at the same time grazing a horse.[71] Of course, combining childcare with other tasks increased the risk of a child suffering injury for want of attention. Better-off families could afford to have women employed just to watch their children.[72] The regional treasurer Lars Kåhre employed a wet nurse/nanny, for instance, evidence of his relatively high socio-economic position.[73] Even among the somewhat less wealthy, there was clearly a need for women who could be employed in various capacities, women who would come whenever they were needed.[74]

Standing in for others was another form of women's work. Sometimes, such vicarious acting for another was a way of circumventing the law. Elsa Månsdotter, for instance, who lived in town, claimed that her selling of a hen was commissioned by a rural maidservant. We can imagine the maidservant meeting Elsa at the town fence and handing over the hen; this would have been a way of avoiding paying the obligatory customs duty.[75] Other examples of vicarious action are less clear, but may also have had to do with circumventing the law. Magdalena Florin had slaughtered a cow and sold the meat to another woman without paying the (higher) excise due on commercial transactions. In response to accusations from customs officials, Magdalena claimed that she co-owned the cow with the other woman, Catharina Malmberg (1749). Maintaining that they owned the cow together and therefore were not liable to pay the higher rate of excise may have been a way of dodging the tax.[76] It may also have been true. A cow was not cheap, and co-ownership might have been an attractive solution. The wives of a burgher and a customs official respectively, Catharina and Magdalena may well have found it useful to cooperate in this way.

Commissioning and networks of help were probably not specific to urban women of lower social standing. Higher-ranking women living in the countryside also delegated tasks such as sewing, weaving and caring for the sick to married women of lower standing, thus creating income opportunities for them and their families.[77] Lower-placed rural women also delegated tasks. For example, Brita Persdotter sent Maria Christophersdotter to the nearby mill to purchase flour from the miller's wife. While the task was one associated with service, Maria was married and was not a servant of Brita (1736).[78] A married woman from Skänninge engaged in the illegal sale of tobacco, acting on the orders of her master (who was not her husband), but delegating the actual dealing to another woman.[79] Poor elderly women would run errands – although 'run' was perhaps not always the operative word – for other women, one instance being the widow Glantzberg, who laboriously carried a piece of meat to a tavern at the behest of the customs official's wife Magdalena Florin (*c.*1754).[80]

We find such networks in all parts and at all levels of society, and men were also involved in them. Transportation of goods and delivery of money and important documents were regularly organised through networks and understood in terms of 'commissions', 'errands' or 'help'. Some men worked full-time performing commissions for their peers, relaying information and commodities between Stockholm and smaller towns. One example is the merchant Johan Reinhold Kohl, who carried out commissions in Stockholm for many people of standing in Örebro.[81] At a global level too, the phenomenon of sending people on 'errands' is striking, for instance during the eighteenth-century craze for natural history and the collection of rare plants; Linnaeus sent his former pupils around the world to bring back exotic flowers and herbs, and other patrons did the same.[82] Both men and women carried out simple errands for their superiors. Count Grevesmöhlen, for example, sent two peasant women and two men to town with some animals he wanted selling, having first provided the women with cash so that they could pay the customs (1777). The women do not seem to have been his servants.[83]

Such practices of mutual help, commissioning and delegation were probably common – much more common than their incidence in the sources suggests. When they do surface, it is often because they caused disputes at the time.[84] It seems as if these practices were and remain hard to classify, for contemporaries and for the historian. They were not master/mistress–servant relations, but they were similar to such relationships. Thus, when a person commissioned someone else's servant to purchase something or run an errand, there was a risk that the servant would erroneously be believed to be acting on behalf of her or his own master. This was what happened when the wife of the bishop of Karlstad commissioned Nils Ullbom to purchase some cloth for her in Stockholm (1749). Ullbom did so and sent the cloth back to Karlstad with a merchant. But since Ullbom was the secretary of a highly placed judge, the merchant misunderstood his task and had the cloth delivered to the wrong person, failing to pay inland customs into the bargain.[85] Had it not been for this breach of tax rules, we would probably not have discovered the convoluted route by which the cloth travelled from Stockholm to Karlstad via Örebro, nor how the bishop's wife effectively acted through another person's servant. She used him as if he were her own servant, just as the two travellers (in Chapter 1) tried to use the customs officials as ordinary servants. Commissioning could easily cause misunderstandings.[86]

Another reason some of these practices turned up in court records was that the people collaborating were accused of stealing or of receiving stolen goods. As Garthine Walker, Natasha Korda and Anne Montenach have noted for England and France, urban women seem to have been particularly heavily engaged in networks trading in textiles. Some of these networks were, no doubt, illicit, and they often attracted the attention and provoked the suspicion of neighbours and the courts.[87] The same pattern can be found in Sweden. Textiles in all forms were valuable – even used clothes, since these could be remade to fit new users.[88] There was a second-hand market in which various networks operated, some of them involving men as well as women. Two men broke into the house of Casten Otter, for example, and stole a wide array of bed linen; later, the wife of one of the men sold some of the textiles to the mayor, claiming rather unconvincingly that she had bought the items in another town (1653).[89] Quite often, however, these networks seem to have been female-only, with women in subordinate positions – such as servants or vagrants – stealing in their temporary abode and then passing on the stolen items to more established women. Thus, Malin Hansdotter had lived for some time in Pedher Monsson's house, during which time she had stolen clothing, yarn and a knife, which she had subsequently sold to the wife of Lars, a shoemaker, in return for liquor and some money. She had also stolen some malt and sold it to the wife of a cordwainer (1656).[90] Similarly, Petter Rosendahl, a burgher of Örebro, accused Agneta Jönsdotter of having bought an apron from a beggar girl, claiming that the girl had purloined it while staying in his house (1698). Agneta denied ever having done this, but a wet nurse working in another family testified that the same girl had been staying in their house for some time and that thefts had occurred during that period too. The girl was also said to have sold stolen items to the wife of Jöns Håkansson.[91] In 1759, Kerstin Bengtsdotter was accused by her own husband of having embezzled some of their marital property, some of which they did not even own but held as security for loans. Eleven women testified that Kerstin had offered them various goods, allegedly as security, and many of these items were clothes or other forms of textiles.[92]

But not all textiles sold were second-hand; some were new and reached the market through other channels. Silk, satin and other valuable fabrics were clandestinely sold through illegal networks.[93] The pillowcases brought into Örebro by the anonymous lady, to be sold with the help of Anna and Margareta, may have been part of such a network. Clothing could be smuggled into towns hidden, for instance, under consignments of tea.[94] In this way, even small Swedish towns were involved in the global economy in the eighteenth century; customs officials would sometimes come across 'goods from Bengal' as they searched travellers.[95] In these contexts, customs officials and female trading networks would of course run into each other.

Selling – and possibly stealing and receiving – goods through legal or illegal networks was probably a source of income for many, even if the exact degree of illegality cannot always be gauged.[96] These networks were characterised by the frequent but not exclusive involvement of women, and by uneven alliances between women in low positions and those who, being married and resident in the local community, held somewhat higher positions. While not unknown in the countryside, such commercial networks probably thrived in urban areas. Crowded housing created opportunities for stealing. People lived close together without always knowing each other well and sometimes kept valuable property in their homes, such as clothes, linen, jewellery and weapons. They also kept food. It is clear that many people were hungry, not least in the 1650s, and it was probably hard to resist the temptation to steal what was there in front of one's eyes. Housing, too, was a challenge, and there were people who did not have a proper home, especially in the late eighteenth century. For instance, the wife of a boatswain lived as the housekeeper of a widowed carpenter while her husband was away, probably because the only home the couple had was his ship. Her wages consisted in room and board (1765).[97]

Despite their absence in the historiography, wives of lower state servants played their part in these complex networks of exchange and dependence. As the Appendix to this book makes clear, women associated with public servants in Örebro carried out a wide range of sustenance activities among which tasks that can be labelled as trade and managerial work were particularly conspicuous. Another common type of work consisted in providing food and accommodation. Wives of public servants also carried out various administrative tasks, on behalf of either the household or the husband and his employer.[98] Anna Trång, Malin Westman and Helena Sandberg, for example, were all married to lower state or municipal servants. Anna and Malin were married to customs officials, and Helena was married first to a *stadsvaktmästare* and subsequently to a *vice häradsskrivare*. Anna and Helena were both engaged in the production and sale of comestibles: liquor in Anna's case and meat in Helena's. Helena supplied meat to women of higher social standing, and she also sold clothing and rented out fields. Malin sold textiles on commission for more highly placed married women. Anna owned some land near town, but seems to have used it herself. After the death of her husband, the municipal authorities granted Anna a temporary right to bake and sell bread so as to support herself.[99] Wives of other lower state servants made funeral arrangements, providing sweet edibles and pipes of tobacco for the funeral guests and decking the room in black cloth.[100] Judging from her probate inventory, which mentioned a good deal of yarn, a spinning wheel and a small handloom, the wife of the bailiff Lars Hellström spun yarn, wove it, and sold ribbons and mittens. The same source suggests that her daughter (married to one of the town councillors) ran a public house.[101] The wife of *räntmästare* Wykland was described as 'gathering in four loads of hay'; whether she actually did this work herself or had someone else do it for her is not clear from the sources. In the latter case, her role was to manage someone else's work.[102]

While the families of customs scribes and searchers did not have easy access to as much cash as those of some higher state servants did, other opportunities were open to them. Confiscated goods were either resold to the owner after valuation, or offered for the same price to the official who seized them. Thus, the official's household not only benefited from the confiscation premium; confiscations were also a source of property that could be consumed or resold. Seized property typically consisted in food, textiles, hides and animals. While it is difficult to prove, it is likely that wives and other household members were involved in looking after, using and trading in such goods.[103]

Like other townspeople, state servants' families could sometimes capitalise on the fact that they lived in a place with recurring fairs. On such occasions, musicians employed by the municipal authorities blew trumpets and beat their drums as local merchants, travelling vendors and various customers congregated in the streets. There was a temporary increase in the population, creating a demand for coffee, food and accommodation.[104] But even in periods when there was no fair, there was a constant need for rooms and meals, not least among some of the lower state servants themselves. Lower customs officials would sometimes rent rooms together, while other state servants rented them individually from burghers.[105] Women such as Anna Larsdotter and Swen Schening's wife (in the seventeenth century), and Catharina Martleur, Anna Dreilich and Catharina Lenbom (in the eighteenth), took in lodgers, and Elisabeth Hamn ran a restaurant. Their husbands all held various lower state or municipal offices.[106] It is probably no coincidence that Anna Larsdotter and Catharina Lenbom were also involved in female networks through which textiles were sold. People who rented out rooms, or even ran guesthouses, made many acquaintances and were asked by guests and townspeople alike to facilitate all sorts of dealmaking.

Contacts were established in other ways as well, sometimes bordering on the illegal. Ella Albrechtsdotter, for instance, who was married to a *kämnär* (one of the town judges), was said to have received stolen rye from a married couple. The wife in question worked as a wet nurse in the house of a local office holder and was accused of having helped herself to some rye when she was sent to have it processed (1698).[107] Ella argued, however, that she had bought the proffered grain in good faith and was acquitted. Margaretha Ström was not so lucky. Married to a lower customs official, she took an active part in work at the customs house, but she also availed herself of the opportunity to steal some valuable textiles from a wagon while the owner was inside the customs house. These and many other stolen items were later resold through a criminal network (1764). Margaretha slipped out of the hands of Swedish justice, though, and was later reported to be living in Norway.[108]

These many-sided practices of exchange, delegation and collaboration turned households into permeable and dependent, rather than closed and self-contained, units. They linked households together in networks that were both social and economic in character. It was through such networks that many women supported themselves and those close to them, by 'delegating' or offering tasks to others, or by making use of the opportunity to take on tasks thus offered. Often, these tasks were carried out in public, in places that cannot be described as being inside specific households or belonging to specific families. Laundering took place on the riverbank, grazing of horses and receiving of hens on the outskirts of the town, and running errands in the streets. The best way of conceptualising these early modern households is to think of them as 'open houses', to use Joachim Eibach's expression; this allows us better to describe women's ways of supporting themselves and their families, and also gives a clearer sense of how early service markets arose and functioned.[109]

The ways in which urban women's work was organised in the early modern period bear a strong resemblance to patterns and practices described (in modern research) as informal economies. Such economies are not visible in official statistics, are often based on family and community, do not always result in immediate remuneration, and are frequently understood in terms of mutual aid.[110] Women are probably over-represented in the modern informal economy.[111] All of this fits well with what we have found for early modern Örebro, where women engaged in such diverse activities as selling a variety of services to others and stealing and receiving goods. These activities had a wide spatial distribution, transcending the boundaries of home and household, and are seldom directly and systematically visible in the historical sources.[112] Paradoxically, this may explain why women's work is often believed to have taken place inside the home.

Survival strategies should not be romanticised. Like other types of 'informal' work, these strategies sometimes required both women and men to turn to petty crime. When Margaretha Ström had stolen cloth from a customs payer, and her husband, a customs official, visited her in jail, he wailed: 'because of this, I will suffer and lose my office'. She tried to comfort him by promising that she would find him a new job as a forest keeper in the part of the country she came from.[113] Clearly, they were in dire straits and they knew it. Moreover, even when lawful, wives' economic contributions were seldom sufficient, and many households ran into debt, particularly if the husband's job involved handling money on behalf of the state. Relations of credit and debt criss-crossed the social space.

Despite the description of these activities as mutual aid (in modern research) or as 'help' (in early modern records), it is clear that informal networks were seldom built on equality. They could involve individuals with varying resources, some of whom gained much more from the collaboration than others. But the opposite is also true: both parties could gain. The informal economy of early modern towns was based on uneven alliances, building awkwardly on both hierarchy and cooperation. In spite of their avowedly hierarchical character, early modern societies accommodated people who were at the same time both equal and unequal, both socially distant and very close.

Conclusion

According to Weber, the modern bureaucrat is a specialist, fully occupied with the demands of her or his office. Swedish customs officials, along with many other state and municipal servants, did not conform to this model in the early modern period. Instead, they were forced into occupational pluralism by low salaries and an often urgent need for ready cash. A customs official could, for instance, combine his job for the state with butchering, teaching or (illegal) selling of beer. But such by-employments were not enough.

Wives made numerous economic contributions to lower state servants' households, contributions that were probably unremarkable at the time, left few traces in the sources and are now easy to overlook. These contributions had much in common with what is today thought of as an informal economy: they were based on both horizontal and vertical relations within the local community, were often understood as 'mutual help', and did not always result in immediate pecuniary benefits. In a broader perspective, however, work of this nature was invaluable as a source both of income and of social contact and support.[114] Moreover, as long as it did not cross the line into lawbreaking, the work of these women does not seem to have been conceptualised as something that undermined their honour and respectability. Rather, a woman like Brita Stina Berg, who was married to customs official Lars Staf and earned a living baking bread for other households, was expressly described as 'a person of good repute'. As Kirsi Ojala has argued, this was how maidservants' work was often described: as honourable.[115] Brita Stina was like a servant in that she helped others for payment, and such work was honourable. On the other hand, being denounced as a thief was a serious threat to the survival of a wife such as Catarina Jönsdotter, who did laundry for other women. Access to lawful and honourable work was indispensable to urban women, and wives of lower state servants were no exception. Indeed, reputation may have been particularly important to these women, as their husbands' work made them targets of aggression in the local community.

The necessary work of wives should be brought into the discussion about the early modern state and its expectations of its servants. Wives could and did make economic contributions to their households, and this alleviated some of the pressure on the household finances of state servants, just as the wives' social connections established through their work must have created opportunities and goodwill for the whole household. It is no exaggeration to say that state servants' wives subsidised and buttressed the process of state formation by adding their incomes to those of their husbands, thus reducing the temptation to resort to irregular methods (such as bribe-taking or living off money that belonged to the state). The contribution of wives' inheritances and family connections could even be the decisive factor in enabling men such as regional treasurers and customs inspectors to acquire their state offices in the first place.

State formation required some state servants and their families to produce more value for the state than the state could afford to pay for. This forced them to hold down several jobs in parallel, but also to work in a 'shadow economy': the grey area between the lawful and the criminal, the decent and the sordid. In this respect too, state servants resembled ordinary domestic servants, who would sometimes be their employers' creditors.[116] However, just as the state tacitly exploited its servants and their families, so the servants and their wives exploited the state – or at least its cash flow – by borrowing state money and making it available to others through intricate networks of credit and exchange. While early modern history has recorded some of the unsavoury aspects of lower state servants' working lives, the picture remains incomplete until it also integrates the contributions of their wives (and probably children too) across the entire spectrum of economic activities, ranging both from formalised to informal exchanges and from legal to illegal activities. Just as many of these families were linked in everyday life through uneven alliances, they were also, for better or for worse, linked to the state through another form of uneven alliance.

Notes

1 ULA, Örebro Kämnärsrätt, 1758 and 1764; RA, Överdirektörens för landtullen arkiv, Personella berättelser 1773.

2 M. R. Hunt, *The Middling Sort: Commerce, Gender, and the Family in England 1680–1780* (Berkeley: University of California Press, 1996), 130.

3 See e.g. Hardwick, *Practice of Patriarchy* for a study of a similarly placed group: French notaries.

4 ULA, Örebro Rådhusrätt och magistrat, court records, 28 May 1759 and 17 November 1762.

5 ULA, Örebro Rådhusrätt och magistrat, court record, 28 April 1762; Örebro Accisrätt, A, Vol. I, 536–7, 557–8, A, Vol. II, 28 June 1779. On salary complaints, see also R. Bengtsson, *Bland smugglare, kapare och obstinata köpmän: Göteborg genom tiderna ur ett tullperspektiv* (Stockholm: Carlsson, 2006), 65–6.

6 J. F. Kryger, *Tankar wid lediga stunder*, Part I (Stockholm, 1761), 168–9.; anon., *Tankar om husbönders och tjenstehjons borgerliga rätt* (Stockholm, 1779), 358–9; J. Möller, *Oförgripliga tankar om barnamord, til desz orsaker och anledningar, samt de medel och utwägar, som böra anwändas til desz förekommande* (Stockholm, 1796), 32–3. Thanks to Karin Hassan Jansson for drawing my attention to these debates.

7 RA, Kammarkollegiet, Tull- och licentkontoret, F I, Vol. VIII, instruktion för inspektorerna över småtullarna och acciserna, 9 March 1675, item 37.

8 The rationale for this prohibition was probably the conflict of interest that might arise if somebody who was in charge of excise collection produced beer himself: *Kongl. Maj:ts Landt-Tulls och Accis-Ordning, 17 December 1756*, chapter 11, §4; *Kongl. Maj:ts förnyade Land-Tulls och Accis Stadga, 19 September 1776*, Chapter 2, §9. See also Hedlund, *Västerås*, 92, 120, 196.

9 See e.g. ULA, Örebro Rådhusrätt och magistrat, court record, 10 January 1649; RA, Överdirektörens för landtullen arkiv, Personella berättelser 1748.

10 See e.g. Brewer, *Sinews*, 225.

11 K. F. Karlsson, *Blad ur Örebro skolas historia*, Part II (Örebro, 1872), 21–2; K. F. Karlsson, *Blad ur Örebro skolas historia*, Part IV (Örebro, 1899), clxxxv, cxciv, ccxvi, cclxxxix.

12 ULA, Örebro Rådhusrätt och magistrat, F 2, probate inventories, Vol. IV, nos 39, 256; Vol. XV, no. 45.

13 RA, Överdirektörens vid landtullen arkiv, Personella berättelser 1748, 'Näring bredvid tjänsten'.

14 S. von Otter, 'Landshöfdingen Salomon von Otters Lefwernes Beskrifning', in C. C. Gjörwell, *Det swenska biblioteket*, Part III (Stockholm: Nyström & Stolpe, 1759), 118.

15 ULA, Örebro Kämnärsrätt, A 1, no. 6, 7 December 1654; A 1, no. 7, August 1698; Örebro Accisrätt, A, Vol. I, 103–4. Cf. S. Gustafsson, *Leverantörer och profitörer: olika geografiska områdens och sociala gruppers handel med fästningsbygget Sveaborg under den första byggnadsperioden 1748–1756* (Helsingfors: Finska Vetenskaps-Societeten, 2015), who also mentions a customs official who combined his office with butchering.

16 ULA, Örebro Accisrätt, A, Vol. 1, 879, 894–5, 904 (documents from Örebro Hallrätt); Örebro Rådhusrätt och magistrat, court record, 11 February 1756.

17 RA, Överdirektörens för landtullen arkiv, Personella berättelser 1748, 'Näring bredvid tjänsten'.

18 Vanja, 'Auf Geheiß der Vögtin', 87.

19 Corfield, *Power and the Professions*, 26.

20 RA, Överdirektörens för landtullen arkiv, Personella berättelser 1748, 'Näring bredvid tjänsten'.

21 See also Smith, *Studier i svensk tulladministration*, Part I, 279.

22 C. Denys, 'The development of police forces in urban Europe in the eighteenth century', *Journal of Urban History*, 36:3 (2010), 332–44 (335).

23 Wikberg, *Alla dessa tullar*, 22–3.

24 ULA, Örebro Rådhusrätt och magistrat, F 2, probate inventories, Vol. II, 420.

25 ULA, Örebro Rådhusrätt och magistrat, court record, 7 November 1759.

26 ULA, Örebro Rådhusrätt och magistrat, F 2, probate inventories, Vol. IV, no. 90.

27 The position of regional treasurer (*lanträntmästare*) was created in the late seventeenth century. Regional treasurers worked under the regional governors.

28 ULA, Örebro Accisrätt, A, Vol. I, 557–8.

29 *Ibid.*

30 ULA, Örebro Accisrätt, A, Vol. I, 408–9. (1746?), 582–3. (1764). See also Örebro länsstyrelse, Landskontoret, Lantränteri- och specialräkningar, F 6, Vol. XVIII (1759); Örebro Rådhusrätt och magistrat, court record, 21 August 1654. Other examples of customs officials who had advanced money to their employer: Örebro Rådhusrätt och magistrat, court record, 10 January 1649. See also R. Bengtsson, 'Eric Ohlsson Pelbergh i Malmö: en accismästares vedermödor under de första svenskåren', *Argus* (1990); and Smith, *Studier i svensk tulladministration*, Part II, 149, 182–3. (outlays), 156 (credit to customs payers).

31 *Kongl. Maj:ts Reglemente för Landt-Tulls- och Accis-Kamrarne i Riket, 17 December 1756*, §18.

32 See e.g. ULA, Örebro Rådhusrätt och magistrat, F 2, probate inventories, Vol. V, no. 65 (inventory of Anders Strokirk's widow, *c.* 1737).

33 E.g. RA, Statskontoret, Kansliet, E 1 D, Vol. XVI, Nordenadler.

34 M. Hallenberg, *Kungen, fogdarna och riket: lokalförvaltning och statsbyggande under tidig Vasatid* (Eslöv: Symposion, 2001).

35 *Svenskt Biografiskt Lexikon* (Stockholm: *Svenskt biografiskt lexikon*, 1918–), 'Casten Feif'.

36 See Chapter 1.

37 Smith, *Studier i svensk tulladministration*, Part I, 149, argues that Gripenstierna and Cronsköld owed their large fortunes to their wives.

38 ULA, Örebro Rådhusrätt och magistrat, court record, 24 February 1762.

39 M. Ågren, *Domestic Secrets: Women and Property in Sweden, 1600–1857* (Chapel Hill: University of North Carolina Press, 2009), 100–39.

40 ULA, Örebro Rådhusrätt och magistrat, court records, 22 September and 20 October 1656, 211, 218.

41 Smith, *Studier i svensk tulladministration*, Part II, 64–5., 122, 126, 127 (quotation), 307.

42 RA, Kammarkollegiet, Tull- och licentkontoret, F I, Vol. IX.
43 RA, Överdirektörens vid småtullarna och accisen arkiv, E 1, Kautioner, Vol. VII; Ågren, *Domestic Secrets*.
44 RA, Överdirektörens vid småtullarna och accisen arkiv, E 1, Kautioner, Vol. VI, 182–3, 77–8, 153–4.
45 RA, Överdirektörens vid småtullarna och accisen arkiv, E 1, Kautioner, Vol. VII.
46 RA, Kammarkollegiet, Tull- och licentkontoret, F I, Vol. IX.
47 ULA, Örebro Rådhusrätt och magistrat, court record, 30 July 1690; RA, Överdirektörens vid småtullarna och accisen arkiv, E 1, Kautioner, Vol. VI, 14 October 1694.
48 Frohnert, *Kronans skatter*, 152, 154, 232.
49 RA, Äldre kommissioner 139, Vol. II, Handlingar från Jönköpings län 1759, investigations into the debts of regional treasurer Barckman, *regementsskrivare* Hagelstein, *regementsskrivare* Hallonqvist and customs scribe Berg. See also ULA, Örebro Rådhusrätt och magistrat, court record, 7 November 1759: the son-in-law of *landskamrer* Bohm was held responsible for his father-in-law's debts to the state.
50 ULA, Örebro Kämnärsrätt, A 1, no. 7, June 1698. It is not entirely clear from this case what had given rise to the debt.
51 RA, Överdirektörens vid småtullarna och accisen arkiv, E 1, Kautioner, Vol. VII, letter from Lars Larsson.
52 ULA, Örebro Rådhusrätt och magistrat, court record, 12 May 1690. Beata Klingenstierna had been married to bishop Zacharias Klingenstierna, but must have been a widow at this time. Her father Casten Otter was director of the rifle factory at Örebro. Anna Gyllenharnesk's first husband was Bengt Simonsson Gyllenharnesk, previously *överinspektor* of all rifle factories in the realm. Source: *Svenskt Biografiskt Lexikon*; and G. Elgenstierna, *Den introducerade svenska adelns ättartavlor, med tillägg och rättelser* (Stockholm: Norstedt, 1925–36).
53 ULA, Örebro Rådhusrätt och magistrat, court record, 12 May 1690, 437.
54 ULA, Örebro Rådhusrätt och magistrat, F 2, probate inventories, Vol. IX.
55 ULA, Örebro Rådhusrätt och magistrat, F 2, probate inventories, Vol. XII.
56 RA, Äldre Kommissioner 139, Vol. II, Handlingar från Jönköping 1759, 48.
57 ULA, Örebro Rådhusrätt och magistrat, F 2, probate inventories, Vol. XII, no. 22.
58 ULA, Örebro Kämnärsrätt, A 1, no. 7, March 1698.
59 ULA, Örebro Rådhusrätt och magistrat, F 2, probate inventories, Vol. VII, no. 13.
60 ULA, Örebro Kämnärsrätt, A 1, no. 14, 1763.
61 ULA, Örebro Rådhusrätt och magistrat, F 2, probate inventories, Vol. IX, no. 113.
62 See also Hardwick, *Family Business*, 144–5.
63 RA, Överdirektörens för landtullen arkiv, Personella berättelser 1748, 'Näring bredvid tjänsten'.
64 A. Clark, *Working Life of Women in the Seventeenth Century* (London: Routledge, 1992 [1919]); J. Bennett, '"History that stands still": Women's work in the European past', *Feminist Studies*, 14 (1988), 269–83; P. Earle, 'The female labour market in London in the late seventeenth and early eighteenth centuries', *The Economic History Review*, 42 (1989), 328–53; D. Simonton, *A History of European Women's Work: 1700 to the Present* (London: Routledge, 1998); C. Vanja, 'Zwischen Verdrängung

und Expansion, Kontrolle und Befreiung: Frauenarbeit im 18. Jahrhundert im deutschsprachigen Raum', *Vierteljahrschrift für Sozial- und Wirtschaftsgeschichte*, 79.4 (1992), 457–82, Hunt, *Middling Sort*, 132–4, Hedlund, *Västerås*, K. Vainio-Korhonen, 'Handicrafts as professions and sources of income in late eighteenth- and early nineteenth-century Turku (Åbo): A gender viewpoint to economic history', *Scandinavian Economic History Review*, 48:1 (2000), 40–63; Ogilvie, *Bitter Living*; G. Walker, *Crime, Gender and Social Order in Early Modern England* (Cambridge: Cambridge University Press, 2008); A. L. Erickson, 'Married women's occupations in eighteenth-century London', *Continuity and Change*, 23 (2008), 267–307; M. R. Hunt, *Women in Eighteenth-Century Europe* (New York: Pearson Longman, 2009), 168–208.

65 M. Ågren, 'Emissaries, allies, accomplices and enemies: Married women's work in eighteenth-century urban Sweden', *Urban History*, 41 (2014), 394–414.

66 ULA, Örebro Kämnärsrätt A 1, no. 6, 27 November 1684.

67 ULA, Örebro Kämnärsrätt A 1, no. 6, 27 November, 4 and 11 December 1684.

68 ULA, Örebro Kämnärsrätt, A 1, no. 7, March 1698.

69 On the importance of reputation and rumour, see S. Howard, 'Investigating responses to theft in early modern Wales: Communities, thieves and the courts', *Continuity and Change*, 19:3 (2004), 409–30; M. Neale, 'Making crime pay in late eighteenth-century Bristol: Stolen goods, the informal economy and the negotiation of risk', *Continuity and Change*, 26:3 (2011), 439–59.

70 ULA, Örebro Accisrätt, A, Vol. I, 606 (1765), 671 (1766), 791 (1779).

71 ULA, Örebro Rådhusrätt och magistrat, court record, 25 September 1654, 85.

72 L. Oja, 'Childcare and gender in Sweden *c.* 1600–1800', *Gender and History*, 27 (2015), 77–111.

73 ULA, Örebro Nicolai, Husförhörslängder A I, Vol. II (1707–47).

74 Cf. Vanja, 'Zwischen Verdrängung und Expansion', 471, on women working as 'Zugehfrauen'.

75 ULA, Örebro Kämnärsrätt, A 1, no. 7, July 1698.

76 ULA, Örebro Accisrätt, A, Vol. I, 516–17.

77 J. Karlsson, '"God! Let me not waste a moment of this year": An intersectional perspective on the practices of time-use in gentry women's households in Sweden 1793 to 1839', master's thesis (Uppsala University, 2013), 27–8, 32–5, 67. The results refer to the late eighteenth and early nineteenth centuries.

78 GaW database, Uppsala University, case 4053 (original source: Uppsala landsarkiv, Stora Malms kyrkoarkiv, K I, 1).

79 GaW database, Uppsala University, case 5491 (original source: Vadstena landsarkiv, Östra häradsrättsarkiv, A 1 A, 18).

80 ULA, Örebro Accisrätt, box '1752–1819'.

81 ULA, Örebro Rådhusrätt och magistrat, F 2, probate inventories, Vol. V, no. 71 (Kohl's probate inventory), and F 9 c 5, Handlingar angående näringsverksamhet.

82 M.-C. Skuncke, *Carl Peter Thunberg: Botanist and Physician. Career-Building across the Oceans in the Eighteenth Century* (Uppsala: Swedish Collegium for Advanced Study, 2014).

83 ULA, Örebro Accisrätt, A, Vol. II, 12 November and 17 December 1777.

84 Cf. L. MacKay, 'Why they stole: Women in the Old Bailey, 1779–1789', *Journal of Social History*, 32:3 (1999), 623–39, on mutual help and the risk of the nature of such help being misunderstood.
85 ULA, Örebro Accisrätt, A, Vol. I, 483–9.
86 See also C. Spence, *Women, Credit, and Debt in Early Modern Scotland* (Manchester: Manchester University Press, 2016), 176–7. on such by-employments.
87 Walker, *Crime, Gender*, 164–7; A. Montenach, 'Legal trade and black markets: Food trades in Lyon in the late seventeenth and early eighteenth centuries', in D. Simonton and A. Montenach (eds), *Female Agency in the Urban Economy: Gender in European Towns, 1640–1830* (New York: Routledge, 2013), 17–34; Korda, *Labors Lost*, 93–143. See also J. Styles, 'Clothing the north: The supply of non-élite clothing in the eighteenth-century north of England', *Textile History*, 25:2 (1994), 139–66 (150–9); and MacKay, 'Why they stole', 625–6.
88 See, for instance, ULA, Örebro Rådhusrätt och magistrat, F 2, probate inventories, Vol. IV, 18: the estate did not even include the deceased man's everyday clothes because, as the widow pointed out, these had been altered to fit the children, or sold to raise cash.
89 ULA, Örebro Rådhusrätt och magistrat, court record, 4 May 1653, 18–19.
90 ULA, Örebro Rådhusrätt och magistrat, court record, 3 November 1656, 220–1.
91 ULA, Örebro Kämnärsrätt, A 1 no. 7, March 1698.
92 ULA, Örebro Rådhusrätt och magistrat, court records, 19 and 26 September 1759.
93 ULA, Örebro Rådhusrätt och magistrat, court records, 30 January 1650, 6–7, 9; 28 March 1653, 11; 21 September 1653, 47; 13 March 1654, 64, 66; 27 August 1656, 206–9. For examples from the eighteenth century, see Ågren, 'Emissaries'.
94 ULA, Örebro Accisrätt, A, Vol. I, 658.
95 See e.g. ULA, Örebro Accisrätt, A, Vol. I, 443, 447, 652–4; A, Vol. II, 20 February 1783; box '1695–1810', 1744.
96 Cf. Neale, 'Making crime pay'.
97 ULA, Örebro Accisrätt, A, Vol. I, 606.
98 See Appendix.
99 ULA, Örebro Accisrätt, '1752–1819', 9 October 1755. Helena Sandberg sold meat to Mrs Fries and Mrs Hedenbohm. The former's husband later became mayor, the latter's was a town councillor; Örebro Accisrätt, A, Vol. I, 362, 490; Örebro Kämnärsrätt, A 1, Vol. XIV, 1759, 1760; Örebro Rådhusrätt och magistrat, court records, 20 September and 29 December 1756.
100 ULA, Örebro Rådhusrätt och magistrat, F 2, probate inventories, Vol. V, nos 66, 81, 82, 87; Vol. XII, nos 25, 40; Vol. VI, no. 30; Vol. IX, no. 25.
101 ULA, Örebro Rådhusrätt och magistrat, F 2, probate inventories, Vol. XII, no. 4; Örebro Rådhusrätt och magistrat, court record, 31 December 1759.
102 ULA, Örebro Kämnärsrätt A I, Vol. VII, November 1698.
103 ULA, Örebro Accisrätt A, Vol. I, 767.
104 Many burgher households rented out rooms, particularly during the fairs, and it is likely that the wives were in charge. Two examples are the households of town councillors Abraham Udd and Anders Hedenbom: ULA, Örebro Rådhusrätt och

magistrat, court record, 31 March 1690; Örebro Kämnärsrätt, A 1, Vol. XIV, 1764. Women selling coffee: Örebro Rådhusrätt och magistrat, court records, 1756, 1759. See also Hedlund, *Västerås*, 100, 121–2.

105 See, for instance, how the baker Olof Wahrenberg took in a judge and a regimental scribe as lodgers: ULA, Örebro Rådhusrätt och magistrat, F 2, probate inventories, Vol. XV, no. 119.

106 Anna Larsdotter's husband Jonas Nyman served as a *stadstjänare*; Swen Schening was a postmaster; Catharina Martleur was married first to Magnus Hansson senior, a mayor, and then to Samuel Fransson, castle clerk (*slottsbokhållare*); Anna Dreilich's husband served as *auditör*, customs official and regimental scribe; Catharina Lenbom had been married to the town scribe. Elisabeth Hamn's first husband was employed within the mining administration and her second husband was a regimental scribe.

107 ULA, Örebro Kämnärsrätt, A 1, Vol. VII, April 1698.

108 ULA, Örebro Kämnärsrätt, A 1, no. 14, February 1764.

109 Eibach, 'Das offene Haus', 629–32. See also Montenach, 'Legal trade', 25.

110 J. P. Gaughan and L. A. Ferman, 'Toward an understanding of the informal economy', *The Annals of the American Academy of Political and Social Science*, 493:1 (1987), 15–25 (22).

111 M. Hoyman, 'Female participation in the informal economy: A neglected issue', *The Annals of the American Academy of Political and Social Science*, 493:1 (1987), 64–82 (67).

112 Korda, *Labors Lost*, 21–5 points to the importance of women's activities in the informal economy of late-sixteenth- and early-seventeenth-century London; Gaughan and Ferman, 'Toward an understanding'; Hoyman, 'Female participation'; Ogilvie, *Bitter Living*, 146–9. See also J. C. Scott, *Seeing like a State: How Certain Schemes to Improve the Human Condition Have Failed* (New Haven: Yale University Press, 1998); and J. C. Scott, *The Art of Not Being Governed: An Anarchist History of Upland Southeast Asia* (New Haven: Yale University Press, 2009) for a discussion of the state's quest for legibility and citizens' conscious efforts to evade the gaze of the state. Cf. L. Runefelt, 'Att springa bort sin dag för en hare: lättja, egennytta och rörlighet i retorik om allmogen 1750–1850', in M. Wallenberg Bondesson, O. Husz, J. Myrdal and M. Tydén (eds), *Människans kunskap och kunskapen om människan: en gränslös historia* (Lund: Sekel Bokförlag, 2012), 96–112.

113 ULA, Örebro Kämnärsrätt, 1764.

114 S. Norrhem, *Kvinnor vid maktens sida: 1632–1772* (Lund: Nordic Academic Press, 2007), stresses how Swedish elite women created and nurtured the social capital and social connections of their families.

115 ULA, Örebro Kämnärsrätt 1758. See also Ojala, 'Opportunity or compulsion?', 215, 221.

116 T. Stretton, *Women Waging Law in Elizabethan England* (Cambridge: Cambridge University Press, 1998), 173–8; Spence, *Women, Credit, and Debt*, 106–7.

4

The struggling master

On a cold day in January 1747, the customs officials of Örebro were hard at work. Two men were mending a customs fence that had been knocked down by the people assembled in the town during the recent fair. A third was searching a peasant's cart, while a fourth had gone to fetch something to eat. A fifth man was stamping parcels of tobacco, while a sixth was too inebriated to do anything at all. At this point, a horse-drawn coach approached the entry point to the town at high speed, passing through the customs gate without being properly searched first by the officials. They later claimed to have run after the coach, shouting for it to stop, but their voices were drowned out by the deafening clatter of wheels and hoofs on the street.[1]

Unfortunately, it turned out that the man travelling in the coach was a merchant and a member of the customs-farming company. He later reported the incident to a customs official in Stockholm. This man, in turn, brought the matter to the attention of the excise court in Örebro. As a result, the customs officials were criticised by their superior, inspector Wigart, for having been remiss, but they defended themselves by saying that they (or at least four of them) had been occupied with other tasks that their job involved. While it could be argued that they could have handled the situation if they had all been at their posts, it is still easy to see the situation from their point of view. The merchant had clearly taken advantage of the fact that they were busy and understaffed.

This case illustrates the difficulties involved in customs officials' work. It was their job to be at their posts and, like soldiers, defend the interests of the state. But it also hints at some of the difficulties their employer had to overcome. The key concern was to extract as much customs and excise as possible. To do that, control of people's movements was essential. Officials, fences, gates and informers were some of the instruments used to achieve that objective. Making the control system work was complicated and the state had to struggle to attain its goal. As a side effect of these efforts, the meanings of service started to shift from a personal to a slightly more impersonal relationship.

This chapter focuses on three aspects of the system of control: first, the tangible ways in which the levy of customs and excise was organised; second, the role played by customs inspectors in controlling their subordinates; and third, the use of courts to control both officials and customs payers. Yet, in spite of high ambitions, the system did not manage – or try – to uphold something Weber regarded as crucial to a well-functioning bureaucracy: a strict separation of the private and professional spheres. The lack of such a separation explains how wives could play important roles in the state administration. This will be discussed in the fourth part of the chapter.

Controlling space, controlling officials

In seventeenth- and eighteenth-century illustrations, Swedish towns were regularly depicted as being encircled by fences. These could be quite awe-inspiring, but they could also be similar to the types of enclosures peasants used to keep their cattle from straying. Such fences did not prevent people from smuggling things into and out of towns, and complaints about their inadequacy were not unheard of. In eighteenth-century Örebro, the customs inspector complained to the magistracy court about the many unlocked 'back doors' through which goods could be smuggled, and in Vänersborg the customs authorities marked on their maps two 'secret doors' they knew were used for smuggling.[2] The need to have customs fences repaired and monitored is a recurring theme in statute law and court records from the period. In 1638, for instance, fences were torn down by angry subjects, and this was not an isolated incident, as the general instructions for customs inspectors issued in 1675 make clear.[3] In the case from 1747 mentioned above, officials were at work repairing the fences. In 1776, at the end of the period under discussion, one statute still mentioned the problem of people climbing over customs fences or throwing goods over them; at that time, the statutory height of these barriers was no more than 1.5 metres.

For all their shortcomings, fences did nonetheless define the urban area, and laws and regulations differed inside and outside them. Consequently, there was a need to patrol the boundary that they formed. Legal entry points were clearly defined, and those passing through them were checked by state officials, who inspected passports and searched carts and wagons for goods liable to customs duty.[4] Illicit entry points were closed as soon as they were discovered. In Piteå, the endeavour to prevent smuggling even went so far as to keep the fire exits locked.[5] In addition, a distinction was made between main roads and byroads; travelling on a road of the latter sort with items on which customs or excise was due laid one open to suspicion of underhand activities. The very act of taking the byroad could be interpreted as suggesting an intention to cheat the customs authorities.[6] So, both roads and town entry points were sites of state control, places where subjects keenly felt the presence of the exacting and extracting state.[7]

At the same time, entry points to towns were sites of social contact, places where encounters, disturbances and petty crime seem to have occurred particularly frequently. Townspeople assembled at the gates to purchase grain (illegally) directly from the peasantry,[8] and when officials tried to prevent such regrating, minor riots would sometimes occur. Rural people came to the town fairs and got drunk; on their way home they became angry with each other or with officials, flew into a temper and started fighting, often at the town gates. Customs houses sometimes turned into illicit pubs. People with loose connections to the local community often seem to have lingered near the entry points, hoping for whatever opportunities might arise. Rightly or wrongly, such people were looked upon with suspicion and reported to the courts. For various reasons, the entry points were not only points of control – they were also points of disorderliness and sociability.[9]

For the 'master' – the Swedish early modern state – controlling these spaces was vital, yet difficult. Partly for this reason, the administration of customs and excise was farmed out during certain periods, as in many other European countries. The tax-farming company was in charge of the levy of customs and paid a fixed sum of money to the fiscal administration, relieving the state of the day-to-day responsibility. The rules governing the levy of customs and excise, however, were set out in royal statutory legislation, and customs officials were still regarded as state employees. Thus, only in a restricted sense of the word was customs administration 'private'. As a consequence, we can get an idea of what the state's intentions were by studying its legislation. Moreover, by looking at how the rules were understood and contested, we can grasp how those intentions translated into everyday practices.

The work of many state servants was organised so as to minimise the risk of fraud and embezzlement. While this was true of everyone who handled the state's money, it was particularly striking in the case of customs officials. For them, an intricate control system had been devised, based on material structures such as documents, locks and stamps. This system was further buttressed by the willingness of subjects to inform on officials, and officials' willingness to inform on each other. Key components in it were customs receipts, customs ledgers and customs chests. Intended to create a watertight system of control, these elements of material culture could of course be manipulated. Nevertheless, it is clear how the system was supposed to work. On arrival at a town entry point, individuals required to pay customs would (if honest and upright) declare what goods they had, and the customs scribe would make a note in the customs ledger. They would then pay the customs duty and receive a receipt. Customs payers were entitled to check in the ledger that the same amount had been entered there as on the receipt, and they could also demand two receipts, one of which would be marked 'duplicate'. When they left town, presumably after selling their goods in the market square, they would put the main receipt into one of the locked customs chests that were kept at the entry points. They could keep the duplicate for themselves.

The chests, to which only three people had the key, were to be opened a couple of times a year. The receipts were taken out, counted and sewn together with a strong thread. A note with the number was also sewn together with the receipts and the thread was then sealed. Finally, the whole package was sent to the central customs administration, where it was checked against the ledgers that had also been submitted. As the statute laws put it, the king and his subjects had a common interest in preventing underhand behaviour on the part of state servants, and the chest and the receipts were the means of achieving this objective.[10]

This system – the ledgers, receipts and chests – structured the working life of customs scribes. To a large extent, their job consisted in using the ledger and dispensing the receipts in the prescribed manner. In doing so, they controlled subjects while at the same time being controlled themselves. Consequently, it was impossible to do the work of a customs scribe without oneself being subject to the control system. If a scribe tried to put some of the payments into his own pocket, this would be noticed when the number of receipts did not match the number in the ledger, or already when customs payers checked their receipts against the ledger. Control was built into the mundane artefacts of work and predicated on the assumed common interests of customs payers and the king.

The attention the state devoted to these and other artefacts of customs collection lends further support to this interpretation. The various ledgers and diaries used by local customs officials were usually printed in Stockholm. Before they were distributed at the local level, they were sewn through and the thread was sealed so as to prevent any subsequent manipulation of the number of pages. If the seal was damaged in transit, this had to be reported immediately the consignment arrived at its destination; otherwise the local customs administration would come under suspicion. Similarly, official stamps and seals were carefully monitored, and were marked with a cross before they were discarded and sent back to the central administration.[11] Clearly, there was a belief that easy access to cash would tempt officials, and an expectation that some would succumb to that temptation.

The use of written certificates for goods under transport added yet another dimension to the system of control. So-called 'passports' (*förpassning*) certified that all customs duties had been paid for the object in question, and while peasants' own produce was exempt from customs, they still had to carry a type of certificate when transporting their goods from one place to another. Thus, if someone wanted to travel with a cheese from, say, Arboga to Örebro, a 'passport' had to be taken out for the goods. Failure to do so was considered a crime. By checking the passport ledger of Arboga against the customs ledger in Örebro, state authorities could – at least in theory – monitor how goods travelled around the country. Of course, the thrust of the system was to identify major smugglers, not to catch people who wanted to give a cheese to a relative in a nearby town. Still, the combined use of 'passports', receipts, ledgers and customs chests created a far-reaching and tightly knit net in which people could get caught – both state servants and other subjects.[12]

Everyday control was not only put in place, however, through a requirement to use certain objects in certain ways. It also operated through the system of officials informing on each other. Such mutual control was expected, encouraged and practised in the seventeenth century,[13] and remained in place in the eighteenth. Thus, it was explicitly stipulated in statute law that higher and lower officials were to 'pay attention to each other'. Any official who neglected to inform on a colleague who was remiss was to be punished as if he himself had been remiss,[14] and any member of the general public who informed on negligent or criminal customs officials was allowed to remain anonymous and would in theory be rewarded.[15] To raise public awareness of the standards expected of customs officials, parts of the relevant statutes were read from church pulpits.[16]

These were not just empty words. Lower customs officials certainly did inform on each other, although it is difficult to say how frequently this happened. In Örebro in 1746, for instance, the searchers Petter Lindstedt and Carl Wallgren informed the excise court that another searcher, Zachris Wikman, had failed to demand customs on a batch of firewood. The court asked the customs inspector to have Wikman dismissed, which is probably what happened; at a later point, he was referred to as a soldier.[17] In other cases, officials reported that their peers had been too drunk to perform their work in an acceptable way.[18] Use of alcohol was obviously widespread, sometimes as a substitute for food, and officials did not hesitate to inform the authorities about their colleagues' lapses.

Officials could also be accused by their peers of having kept extra ledgers alongside the official one. This could be construed as a way of circumventing the control system and was therefore considered a serious form of misconduct. To be successful, however, such a strategy presupposed that customs payers colluded by not putting their receipts in the customs chest. In one case, it seems likely that the accused customs scribe had had no intention of cheating, but had simply run out of stamped paper. He claimed to have sent a searcher to the customs inspector to fetch a new ledger, but the inspector was not at home and the searcher did not have the time to go looking for him as he was on patrol duty. Pressed by an impatient group of townspeople who wanted to pay their customs immediately, the scribe had simply noted the sums on a scrap of paper, intending to transfer his notes to the new ledger later on. He got away with a warning; the court impressed on him the importance of always having proper ledgers in the future.[19]

Work was organised and regulated in ways that encouraged customs officials to observe and talk about each other's activities. Searchers normally worked in pairs, since they were afraid of being attacked,[20] and the same was probably true of customs scribes and other lower officials as well. This made it easier for the officials to monitor each other, but it also encouraged talk. Officials chatted and argued about their work performance and the rules that applied, sometimes in anger, but sometimes simply out of curiosity. On one occasion, for instance, searcher Tillgren accompanied his peer Keppel when the latter was out on inspection. The colleagues discussed 'their jobs as customs and excise officials' and whether they were entitled to carry loaded rifles while on duty. Unable to resolve the matter, they went down to the customs house and checked the relevant statutes. Later, the discussion developed into a fight (which is why we know about it), but what merits attention is the fact that they talked about their work and the limits of their powers.[21] Conversations such as this raised awareness of what rules applied and how they were to be understood.

The system designed by the state was guided by the idea of controlling people's movements through various spatial arrangements. Nobody was supposed to slip into or out of town without having paid what was due, and it was the job of the customs officials to prevent this from happening. Only those roads that could be monitored were to be used. At the same time, officials were ostensibly prevented from cheating the state by putting money in their own pockets. However, the core problem remained: people had to meet and interact – at the town's entry points, for instance – and it was difficult to control what they said and thought during such interactions. The fact that we find only a few signs of explicit criticism of the control system does not mean that customs officials never nurtured such thoughts.

The role of inspectors

Many lower state servants and their families had not grown up in the town where they worked, nor could they partake of the legal and political rights that citizenship conferred. They were strangers, outsiders in the local community, sometimes no more than itinerant workers. Their geographical mobility could be the result of their own dissatisfaction with their situations and their hope for something better if they moved elsewhere. In the case of customs officials, however, it was often the result of a policy consciously crafted by their employer: officers were moved around in order to prevent them from fraternising with customs- and excise-paying subjects.[22] For instance, customs inspector Hans Wigart was born in Västervik and had worked in Gävle and Stockholm before taking up a position in Örebro, which he subsequently left to move to Ystad.[23] His colleague Hagström made a career in Stockholm, but was born in Södermanland and had been posted both on the Norwegian border and in Karlskrona in the far south before ending up in the capital.[24] The role of mobility is highlighted, almost incidentally, in a legal provision reminding customs officials that they must not take collections of statutes and written orders with them when they moved from one position to another.[25] This must have been a recurrent problem if it was deemed necessary to mention it in statute law.

The state's wish to keep track of these officials makes it possible to establish quantitative patterns for the mid-eighteenth century (Table 4.1). Across the country, fewer than 10 per cent of all officials of the customs administration worked and lived in their places of birth. On the one hand, this meant that customs officials were exposed to new places, people and ideas in a way that few other subjects were at this time, but on the other hand it also suggests that they were more rootless than most.

Table 4.1 Place of birth of customs officials in twenty Swedish towns, 1748

	Number	Per cent
Born in the town where they currently worked	22	9
Born in the surrounding region	75	30
Born outside the surrounding region	156	62

Source: RA, Överdirektörens för landtullen arkiv, Personella berättelser 1748. Kansliet, E 3:1.

Towns included: Åbo, Arboga, Borås, Falun, Gävle, Gothenburg, Helsingborg, Jakobstad, Kalmar, Karlskrona, Lund, Malmö, Norrköping, Örebro, Piteå, Skövde, Sundsvall, Söderhamn, Uppsala and Västerås. For Gothenburg, 'surrounding region' means Halland and Bohuslän.

Against this backdrop, it is not surprising that customs officials stuck together. Sometimes, they even lived in clusters of their own. According to a tax list from 1761, twelve customs officials appear to have lived in rented rooms in a building near the town mill in Örebro. Nine of them were married and had families. Only three customs officials' families lived in other buildings at this point in time. It is possible that this was partly a fiscal fiction; other sources suggest that some officials lived in the customs houses, at least at times. But if it was a fiscal fiction, at least that fiction tells us that the customs inspector (who definitely lived in the building) paid the tax in question for his subordinates.[26]

Regardless of whether all twelve families actually lived together under the patriarchal protection of the inspector, or whether he just paid their taxes, the Örebro situation certainly suggests that customs officials were closely dependent on each other. For instance, two other Örebro customs officers, Öman and Ammurin, lived together with their wives in the same attic rooms.[27] The living arrangements of customs officials in other small Swedish towns support this impression. In Ulricehamn in 1690, for instance, two officials lived together in the northern customs house, together with a tailor and an old woman and her daughter.[28] The sources also suggest that the inspector was an important person everywhere. In Dalarö, his large house was in close proximity to the church, with the abodes of his subordinates nearby.[29]

Customs scribe Carl Fernström and his family belonged to this category of outsiders who were dependent on the benevolence of their superiors. Fernström worked under customs inspector Petter Bergman who, for a long time, had turned a blind eye to the debt, or 'balance', that had piled up during Fernström's time in office. Finally, however, he had to report the matter to the court. At the hearing, Fernström explained that he had done his utmost to clear the debt, but had failed. He asked the court to intercede for him 'at the highest level' (that is, in Stockholm), claiming that his troublesome and meagrely paid job as a customs scribe 'exposes me to ruin and destroys me every day'. He expressed his gratitude to Bergman, who had a Christian heart and had realised how impossible it was for a 'stranger' (*främling å orten*) such as Fernström to support himself on his small salary.[30]

Fernström's position as an outsider made him particularly vulnerable and dependent on Bergman's goodwill. Bergman was, he thought, a good boss. At the same time, like other customs inspectors, he kept his subordinates under strict surveillance. The inspectors, the local excise court, payers of customs duty and those 'at the highest level' all had an interest in how Fernström performed his work, and although Bergman seems to have hesitated before reporting the debt to the court, not everyone was as tolerant and, in the words of eighteenth-century people, 'Christianly mild' (*kristmild*). Fernström was subject to patriarchal care, but also patriarchal control.

Other state servants, too, benefited from material and moral support from their superiors, and other inspectors acted like Bergman. For instance, customs inspector Wigart defended some of his subordinates in court and drew attention to their many qualities. He argued that even though the searcher Petter Lindstedt had a record of being drunk at work, he was nevertheless one of the most knowledgeable customs officials in Örebro. But Wigart could also criticise his subordinates. When one of them had failed to watch the customs house so that a traveller was able to sneak into town without paying customs, Wigart gave an admonitory speech to all his searchers before the excise court, impressing on them the necessity of never leaving the entry points to the town unsupervised.[31]

The lower officials, in turn, showed respect for Wigart, for instance by seeking his professional advice. But they may also have feared him. One searcher, for example, was caught 'correcting' the ledger in which all excise receipts were listed. This was a serious offence, and the searcher claimed to have committed it out of fear of Wigart. Apparently, one of the officials had forgotten to make a note of a receipt directly when it was given to the excise payer. Consequently, there was no record of the sum ever having been paid. The customs officials seem to have discussed the problem between them, but the person in charge of the ledger (the scribe) was unwilling to enter the information afterwards. While these discussions were taking place, Wigart had found out that the receipt was not mentioned in the ledger and become suspicious, since this might have indicated that an official had pocketed the excise money himself. According to Forsberg, the searcher, he had then been so afraid of what Wigart might do that he had illicitly added the information afterwards and behind the scribe's back.[32]

But while searchers and scribes may at least occasionally have been afraid of the inspectors, they were also heavily dependent on them for protection and material support. In a similar fashion, eighteenth-century inspectors and their seventeenth-century predecessors, *tullnärer*, were dependent on help, advice and support from *their* superiors. Letters to the head state servant (*kamrer* Johan Jöransson in Stockholm) display bonds of dependence, but also expressions of common interests. The local *tullnär* would sometimes call Johan Jöransson 'my lord', but also 'dear brother'. Johan Jöransson was asked to extend credit and to stand surety for the *tullnär*. When he sent his official reports and letters to Stockholm, the *tullnär* did not hesitate to include private letters, asking Johan Jöransson to have them delivered to the right addressees. Such practices suggest trust and cooperation rather than fear, and were probably extremely important in getting the network of personal relations and, by extension, the state to work.[33]

State servants' dependence on their superiors manifested itself in a particularly tangible manner when, in the eighteenth century, widows of deceased servants applied to the Government for a state pension.[34] Such pensions were hard to come by. Their number was capped, and widows would sometimes even 'stand in line' for a particular pension, waiting for another widow to die. Only those who were deemed worthy stood a chance, and this is where the help of the husband's superiors was so important. It was not uncommon for the deceased husband's former boss to intercede for the widow, vouching for her reputation. A major general, for instance, interceded for the widows of two captains, Appelman and Holm, and the president of the Royal Court of Appeal vouched for the merits of a former employee with a view to helping his widow.[35]

At the beginning of the eighteenth century, most state pensions seem to have been granted to widows of military officers. This is hardly surprising, since Sweden had been through a long period of war, which had had a particular impact on the families of military servants. It was easy to argue the case that these men had made significant contributions to the good of the country and that the state consequently had a duty to care for their families. This kind of argument had been used to improve the conditions of widows in the seventeenth century too, and it continued to be useful in the early nineteenth century.[36]

In the course of the eighteenth century, however, increasing numbers of widows of state servants in the civil sector also applied for state pensions. Widows of men who had worked in the ecclesiastical sphere (clergymen and teachers), in municipal administration (such as mayors) or in the regional state administration likewise tried to avail themselves of such pensions. For instance, the widow of *landskamrer* (regional accountant) Hiohlman in Örebro (deceased in 1757) applied for one, as did the widows of other *landskamrerer*, *landssekreterare* (regional secretaries) and bailiffs in other parts of Sweden.[37] Just like their sisters in the military sector, they emphasised the efforts made by their husbands for the good of the country. They, too, had fought battles worthy of attention and recognition. The widow of the bailiff Bergbohm, for example, argued that her husband had done his utmost to explain and correct the large 'balance' he had accrued in his professional life. The husband had spent some years 'in great trouble and illness', but had eventually managed 'before the end of his life, praise the Lord, [to] account for himself so that the state did not lose anything in the least because of him'. The result, though, had been that the family had had its property sequestered and that the widow now lived in utter misery. She did not claim a pension proper, but humbly asked for a small pecuniary contribution.[38]

For lower state servants in the period 1650 to 1780, however, these options were rarely available. There were simply too many widows and too few pensions to go round. In the absence of pensions, the families of scribes and clerks of various kinds had to make other arrangements and take other precautions. They relied on both horizontal relations – other people and families in the same situation – and vertical relations – individuals and families in somewhat higher positions. Through the vertical relation between the husband and his superior, as well as the more horizontal but still uneven relations between his wife and other wives in the local community, a lower customs official's family was able to survive, albeit precariously. These criss-crossing relationships built early modern states. It was because the state needed people like this to guard its interests in various places across the realm, and because it was unable adequately to fund the new structures, that the families of lower state servants had to rely on many kinds of income-earning opportunities and social contacts. Their dependence, for instance, on the inspectors made them susceptible to control, but it also forced them to forge new social contacts that could be of great value in all walks of life. The uneven alliances between women from different social strata, described in Chapter 3, should also be read in this light. The vulnerability of lower office holders and their families made the work, contacts and reputation of women necessary ingredients, both in their own lives and in the history of state formation.

Control through the courts

Court systems played a central role in the lives of early modern people, in Sweden as in all parts of Europe. People could avail themselves of the possibilities that access to the courts offered, but they could also be reported to a court if they acted against codified or tacit rules.[39] Lower state servants were no exception.[40] In their capacity as private persons, they could both accuse other people and be accused – for instance of stealing. In their capacity as state servants, they could both report people who, for example, tried to evade tax, customs and excise, and be reported themselves for embezzlement or overzealous behaviour. So, while they were certainly similar to most early modern subjects in their reliance upon the court system, their interactions with it were both more frequent and, sometimes, more fraught. The case leading to the dismissal of the searcher Jean Henrik Lemon in 1745 illustrates this point particularly well.

To begin with, the case only concerned two hides intended for the production of shoes. Hans Wittfoth, a local merchant, had tried to smuggle these hides into Örebro, but the cart had been stopped by Lemon at the southern entry point. Wittfoth's legal representative Nils Fries (who would later become mayor and co-owner of the rifle factory)[41] subsequently confronted Lemon in the excise court. Fries argued that the hides had only been used as a covering to protect a load of sugar from Gothenburg, and that it was commonly accepted that one did not have to pay customs on such protective materials. He also denied that Wittfoth had tried to defraud the state of anything; the hides had been clearly visible and he had not tried to conceal them.[42]

At this point, a member of the excise court intervened. Councillor Boman reproached Lemon for what had happened, but Lemon retorted that this was none of Boman's business and that, if Boman considered himself to have an interest in the matter, he should recuse himself. Boman answered that he had no interest whatsoever and that he was entitled to make reproaches in his capacity as a judge, not least since he had often found that searchers did not act according to the rules. Lemon answered – and he was probably quite agitated by now – that the only rule of relevance was that he, Lemon, had to ask all travellers if they had any goods to declare, a task he had faithfully performed on this occasion. As for Boman's words about the importance of following rules, Lemon was sure that such punctiliousness was never seen in the excise court except when searchers had erred. Lemon was reproached for his harsh words; did not he and his colleagues always have the opportunity to appeal, the court asked? But Lemon sniffed at this; when he and his peers asked to see the court records, they were never delivered to them until the time limit for an appeal had passed.[43]

After a heated exchange between Boman and Lemon, all but one of the judges of the excise court found that Lemon should be punished for his disrespectful words. Very probably, Lemon was both exasperated and aggressive at this point, because his brother (also a searcher) intervened, saying: 'Why do you keep on talking, can't you see they are all your enemies and against you[?] [T]here is no point in speaking here.' The only judge who held a different opinion was the customs inspector Hans Wigart. He had not admonished Lemon during the quarrel, and had supported Lemon's claim that it was his duty to ask all travellers if they had anything to declare. As a consequence, Boman accused Wigart of complicity.[44]

On this occasion, the excise court in Örebro did not act in the interests of the searcher. Burghers sat as judges in these courts, and would not necessarily side with the officials, even if some burghers did have financial interests in the customs as such. This could make the officials' situation very difficult, particularly if they were outsiders (like the Lemon brothers, who came from Karlstad), and the support of their local superior was then vital. But even with such support, interaction with state courts involved risks. Both the incident at the entry point to the town and the subsequent court proceedings seem to have involved shouting, anger and very heated feelings, to the point where the searcher was regarded as having overstepped the mark and insulted the court. When Lemon was convicted, the verdict was based on the legal code of 1734, which forbade disrespect of the courts.

For the explicit purpose of putting an end to all the controversy and litigation that ensued from the exaction of customs and excise, the Swedish state had set up the excise courts in the late seventeenth century.[45] This was also the period in which the number of customs officials grew apace.[46] It was the brief of these courts to make sure that subjects paid what was due to the state, but they were also charged with ensuring that customs officials did not exact more than was rightfully theirs. This was a tricky task. Customs officials were supposed to confiscate smuggled goods, and were entitled to a share of their value. But while income from confiscations played a very minor role from a fiscal point of view,[47] it could be vital to the officials' households. Searchers in particular had a very strong personal interest in ferreting out smugglers and excise-evaders. That they might overstep the limit was certainly not inconceivable, and this was clearly what Boman thought searchers often did.

The excise courts were dominated by people from the urban community. As a rule, the only representative of the customs administration was the customs inspector. All the other judges would be burghers, members of the municipal corporations, and they would probably have a greater tendency to see the world from the point of view of their fellow burghers than from that of the searchers, the customs scribes or the customs inspectors, for that matter. As the excise court in Örebro put it in 1755, the court had a responsibility to make sure that 'faithful taxpaying subjects were not troubled by inequitable customs' in a way that would go against the orders of the king.[48] This was a correct description of the court's task, and statute law added that it was incumbent on customs inspectors to ensure that neither Swedish subjects nor 'strangers' were forced to pay more customs and excise than was their lawful duty.[49] This was not, however, the court's only function; it also had a responsibility to safeguard the rights of the state and, consequently, to support the claims of customs officials when these were well founded. But Lemon felt that such punctiliousness was never seen, at least not in the excise court in Örebro. Other customs officials obviously shared his view; the searcher Forsberg, for instance, frankly declared his opinion that the excise court was partial.[50]

Lemon and Forsberg expected the court to be fair, and to support them when they did their jobs. Their interactions with the court in Örebro taught them that fairness could not be taken for granted, but at least Lemon had the support of one of the judges. Not only did Wigart refrain from publicly accusing Lemon, along with the other judges; he even defended him. It is likely that the inspector took a personal interest in helping Lemon after his dismissal. Lemon was transferred south to Skövde, where he was given the job of customs scribe; the former holder of that position was transferred to Lemon's post as a searcher in Örebro. The men obviously changed positions and Lemon was effectively promoted. Hans Wigart used his professional network to make amends to him.[51]

In his dealings with the court, Lemon displayed a striking degree of confidence. It seems clear that he thought he had acted by the rules, and that Boman and the other judges were wrong to accuse him. When he called on Boman to recuse himself, Lemon also demonstrated a basic knowledge of the law: a person who has an interest in a matter is not suitable to judge the case. This kind of confidence and knowledge was linked to his occupational role, and can be found in other customs officials as well. When the customs scribe Hans Prytz, for example, was accused by his superior of being an obstinate and refractory servant, Prytz did not apologise, but insisted that he was right and that customs inspector Strömholm was wrong.

On that occasion a peasant from the adjacent area of Bergslagen had complained to Strömholm about having been forced to pay customs twice, first at home and then on his arrival in Örebro, when he met Prytz. Strömholm ordered Prytz in writing to repay the peasant, but Prytz refused, citing a recent statute saying that the peasants of Bergslagen were to pay customs in their nearest town. Prytz read this as a direct order from the highest level of the state administration and refused to obey his local superior. It was the customs scribe in Bergslagen who ought to repay what he had wrongfully received, Prytz argued. Strömholm asked Prytz what he thought would happen 'if a subordinate refuses to obey the orders of his superior'. No order could be maintained if servants behaved in this way, he pointed out, and it was Prytz's duty simply to follow the written directive he had been given. To this, Prytz answered that he was as capable as anyone else of understanding what his duties were – a dig at the inspector – and that he would therefore not repay the peasant unless a formal court judgment forced him to do so. In the end, the excise court found that Prytz was to repay the peasant, arguing that the statute in question did not mean that peasants were prohibited from paying in Bergslagen. In addition, Prytz was exhorted to defer to his superior in future.[52] That the court found in Strömholm's favour is unsurprising, particularly as Strömholm was himself a member of it; it is more surprising that Prytz claimed the right to interpret the rules himself, questioning in effect the hierarchical order between a customs scribe and a customs inspector.

Since there were specially designated courts dealing with matters of customs and excise, customs officials are particularly visible in their records. Other lower state servants came into contact with other parts of the court system, most prominently the magistracy courts. These interactions subjected them, too, to control. One obvious form of control was when state servants were reprimanded for not having completed their accounts on time. Faced with such criticism, they often defended themselves by referring to their impossibly large workload. This was what Hiohlman, regional accountant in Örebro, did when he was accused of irregularities. As the court well knew, he said, he was

> every day so submerged in arduous work for the state, [and] my papers and old correspondence are in such disorder that I can under no circumstances swiftly produce evidence about what actually happened eleven years ago, and add to this [my problems with] the sprawling correspondence about the new taxation which must take place immediately.[53]

Hiohlman's excuses for not being in court that day were accepted on account of his 'arduous work for the state'. Other state servants expressed themselves in similar or even more outspoken terms. For instance, one eighteenth-century bailiff and his secretary grumbled that 'it is incomprehensible how [the state] can insist on giving new tasks to those in charge of the administration of taxes; even without such extra tasks, we will soon be smothered under the burden of duties that require both assiduity and a sense of responsibility'.[54]

In 1762, the town auditors in Örebro declared that they were unable to complete their control of the accounts for 1760, in spite of the fact that the town clerk Aron Bergström had delivered his books on time and in good order. But this was to little avail since a large number of former town clerks had left their accounts in a mess, and in some cases even had a personal debt to the town. The claims went as far back as 1743.[55] The military administration probably suffered from the same affliction; at any rate, it was pointed out as noteworthy that a particular scribe was industrious and did deliver his accounts in an impeccable manner.[56] Clearly, not everybody was like him. The man who was responsible for the excise court records of 1746 had left town, leaving behind him nothing but a list of 'brief and unintelligible' points from which it would be difficult, the court feared, to construct an accurate record.[57] Courts had to devote much time to these matters.

Another form of court control had to do with preventing state servants from earning extra income in ways that were perceived as encroaching on the exclusive rights of the burgher community. This control was not of course exerted by the state, but by the community, through the magistracy court. Nevertheless, it is relevant to discuss it here, since this was an area in which local communities made the task of the struggling master particularly difficult. As members of municipal communities (*burskapsägande borgare*), male burghers were privileged both politically and economically. They were eligible for municipal offices and had the right to vote on matters of concern to their community. They had officially recognised rights to support themselves in certain ways – for instance as merchants, cordwainers, bakers etc. – and could call on the local courts to protect these rights to burgher occupations (*borgerlig näring*) if anyone encroached upon them. They could have access to town property such as arable fields and pastures. In contrast, people who did not belong to the community were barred from such rights, at least in principle.

Town inhabitants without burgher rights included semi-proletarian residents and temporary visitors, such as war refugees, prisoners of war and, in the case of Örebro, the rifle-producing smiths who had been forced to move to town with their families.[58] This heterogeneous group also included many state servants and their wives. While very different in many respects, a customs scribe, a clerk and a female pedlar were nevertheless similar in their roles as outsiders in the urban environment. In their dealings with the local courts, they were often brought face to face with the fact that they did not belong to an acknowledged estate or corporation.[59] In 1756, for instance, a local burgher questioned the widow Anna Trång's right to hold a piece of land in the town, arguing that neither Anna nor her deceased husband (a searcher) had been members of the burgher corporation and that the land should therefore be given to him instead. The court, however, found in Anna's favour, pointing out that both Anna and her husband were children of local burghers.[60]

While Anna did win the case, it was only because she and her husband had family connections to the burgher community, not because rights of possession were well protected in general. Lower state servants without such connections found it difficult to gain access to land or other benefits that burghers enjoyed.[61] Not even customs inspectors as a rule were allowed into the burgher communities.[62] Since many of these officials, as we have seen, were dependent on extra income, it was a particular disadvantage to be barred from taking up burghers' occupations, and it is likely that many tried to circumvent these prohibitions. The fact that statute law explicitly prohibited customs officials from engaging in such occupations probably suggests that infringements did occur.[63] State servants also tried to become members of the burgher community. For instance, eight customs officials, including customs inspector Wigart, apparently attempted to become members in Örebro, but failed.[64]

The degree to which towns did in fact exclude outsiders from power and material resources is hard to gauge. It is clear that outsiders were, sometimes, granted the right to take up trades and crafts that might just as well have been looked upon as reserved for burghers. Thus, the corporatist system may not have been quite as rigid as one would expect, or as it was in some other parts of Europe. It should also be borne in mind that being an outsider conferred certain advantages, such as freedom from the obligation to pay municipal taxes.[65] It is also possible that being less heavily taxed was one of the few advantages of being a lower state servant.[66]

Still, the power to grant rights and make concessions was in the hands of the municipal authorities or, in other words, the magistracy. When it did grant a right, it could attach conditions; for example, when a rural tailor was allowed to make and sell clothing, even though he was not a member of the tailors' guild, it was on condition that he only catered for the needs of servants. The municipal authorities exercised discretion; when a sword maker and his wife were granted the exceptional right to engage in local trade, this was only because the couple were known to be 'proper and honest people'.[67] So, while the system had a degree of flexibility and provided some space for outsiders, it was not one where everyone enjoyed the same rights regardless of personality and behaviour. The system was flexible, but also arbitrary. As was shown above, many lower state servants and their wives chose to take up tasks that did not fall within the scope of *borgerlig näring* – such as teaching, providing legal advice, doing laundry and providing care – which emphasises how difficult it was to gain access to the forms of work that the burgher community controlled.

Confrontations in court often brought into sharp focus the social, economic and political differences between those who belonged to the burghers' community and those who did not. Lemon's exasperated words bear witness to this, as do the words of other lower state servants. Other outsider groups were less vociferous and less equipped with resources. The verbal skills and legal knowledge of lower state servants explain why the discontent of this group is visible in the sources, but in fact such discontent may have been much more widespread, for instance among women who did not belong to the community. Their need to carve out a living on the margins and with the help of uneven alliances must also be seen in the light of the monopolistic rights of the burgher corporation.[68]

The courts were meeting places and contact zones where people's views of themselves, of 'others' and of society were shaped. Courthouse encounters reminded those who did not belong to the burgher community of their position as outsiders. The more the municipal authorities tried to ensure that their monopolistic rights were not infringed, the more outsiders became aware of the differences that structured town life. Members of the latter group were more likely to spot the differences and inequalities than the burghers, and among them, lower state servants may have been particularly observant, since they were in the paradoxical situation of being both excluded and, at the same time, expected to exercise authority over those who excluded them. People such as the searcher Lemon were hit by the arbitrariness of the excise court, which was dominated by municipal interests, but they were also in a position where they could give voice to a discontent that may have been more widespread.[69]

Fluid boundaries

The work of customs officials required them to be on the move, and their places of work could be almost anywhere. For some, this meant that their places of residence could turn into places of work, while for others their places of work became their homes. Often there were tangible, physical reasons for these patterns. For instance, customs official Johan Andersson in Helsingborg described, in the 1670s, how he had written a customs receipt 'in my winter rooms, where my wife and children and other household members were to keep warm'.[70] Another example is the customs scribe Anders Lybeck, who had permission from his superiors to receive customs and excise in his home during the winter. The most likely explanation for this arrangement is that the customs house was too cold to work in. Rather than insist on customs being received in the official places, which would have triggered demands for more firewood to heat those places, the customs administration was apparently happy to let Lybeck direct his 'customers' to his home instead. Converse examples are the customs scribe Chreiman and the searcher Lundius, who both slept in the customs houses on at least some occasions. In Lundius's case, the fact that he slept there, together with his little daughter (for whom he was evidently responsible at the time), may have reflected the poor quality of his own home, but it may also have had to do with the need to cover this particular entry point. In the latter case, the customs administration would have had little to object to; guarding the entry points was a crucial part of the officials' job.[71] In fact, late-eighteenth-century legislation mentioned in a matter-of-fact way that customs scribes often lived in the customs houses.[72]

The belongings of ordinary domestic servants could be hard to disentangle from those of their master, since they lived on the same premises. In much the same way, the fluid boundaries between workplace and home could confuse the distinction between the property of the state and that of the state servant. Thus, working materials, tools and money often appear to have been kept in the state servant's home. In his role as regional treasurer, Lars Kåhre was in charge of the liquid funds of the regional state administration. In accordance with his brief, he submitted monthly inventories to show that he was keeping track of the state's money. One of these inventories reports in 1698, rather matter-of-factly, that 'one bag' containing 853 *daler* was kept in Kåhre's home. There is little to suggest that this was against the rules, and there are other examples to the same effect.[73] It is likely that people came to Kåhre's home both to pay and to receive their dues, and that he really needed to have cash readily available.[74]

At other times, keeping objects belonging to the state at home provoked unfavourable comment. When customs inspector Hans Wigart failed to locate the customs ledger and had to retrieve it from customs scribe Eliander's residence, he was not pleased. His reaction, though, did not spring from a general disapproval of working from home. Rather, it had to do with the twofold risk of customs evasion and embezzlement. If the ledger was not in its proper place, the official on duty would write down the sum received on a scrap of paper instead. Such pieces of paper were easily and perhaps intentionally 'lost', preventing control of what was due from the official and allowing him and the customs payer to collude. As we have seen, the winter arrangements for Anders Lybeck were in order because, in his case, the whole place of collection, including the ledger, had been moved to his home.[75] On a later occasion, Wigart explicitly urged his officials to leave the ledger in their respective customs houses every night.[76]

In reports on the effects of devastating town fires, it sometimes transpires that state servants had kept important documents at home and, as a result, lost them in the flames. Some of these papers were of course private, but in other cases they had also kept state documents in their houses. Thus, when the state was investigating irregularities in the accounts for Jönköping (1759), a former town clerk reported that he had kept the documents in question in his home, the house had burned down, and they were now irretrievably lost.[77] Clearly, the boundaries between workplace and home were fluid for early modern lower state servants. In this respect, their situation was unlike that of modern civil servants, but like that of early modern domestic servants, who lived and worked in the houses of their masters and were expected to defend the latter's interests and property. Lower state servants did not work in well-defined spaces, but in any place to which their duties took them. They were 'extra-bureaucratic' in the literal sense of the word, since they seldom worked 'im Büro' (in the office), but outside, in a wide range of other places.

If the Swedish state had thought in terms of 'private' and 'professional' spheres, and if it had been convinced that a separation of these was essential to its interests, such a separation would probably have been an important component of its control system; as we have seen, there was certainly no lack of inventiveness when it came to devising mechanisms for control. The distinction was not made because the 'confusion' of private and professional means and spaces served the purposes of the state. It was rational to have people on the spot. The importance attached to presence is evident from the customs maps commissioned by the authorities in the middle of the eighteenth century: it was explained, often in painstaking detail, how the boundaries of the customs area were monitored, and sometimes the maps showed where the customs officials lived. For instance, a map made of Ängelholm in 1733 explicitly mentioned 'the servants' accommodation',[78] as did the maps of Nådendal and Duved.[79] The map of Dalarö, on the main sea approach to Stockholm, showed not only the house of the customs inspector, but also those of the many other customs officials living there.[80] Clearly, the state's presence was more pronounced at Dalarö, where shipments of great value passed every day, than at Duved, situated on the slope of a high mountain and obviously home to just one customs official. Nevertheless, the house of that single official and his household was carefully marked on the map.

These maps reveal the often fluid boundary between state and private property. The map of Strängnäs, for instance, included 'the house of customs scribe Elfving's father-in-law'.[81] Presumably, the father-in-law was better known in town than Elfving and the house was named after him, but this does not explain why it was included on a map made by the customs authorities. Most likely, the house, albeit private, was used by Elfving for the purposes of the state: he may have had his office there and goods may have been stored in it. The situation was the same in other towns: property belonging to the state servant, his family or some other private individual was used for the benefit of the customs authorities. This seems to have been particularly common in wintertime. The customs houses were poorly insulated and officials such as Anders Lybeck in Örebro were granted the right to receive customs in their own homes instead. The situation was the same in Kajana, Finland, where there was 'a private house where the customs are received in winter', and in Nådendal.[82] There was clearly no sharp line of demarcation between state spaces and private spaces, simply because the customs authorities found it of value to have 'strongholds' on the spot, be they state-owned or not.

The customs authorities needed people to live in these strongholds, people on whose faithfulness and vigilance they could rely. The fluidity of town boundaries made every pair of eyes employed by the state important. Towns were surrounded by fences of varying types and quality, but it was impossible to monitor every little corner at all times. The customs maps frequently include explanations as to why certain parts of the town boundaries were unfenced – 'there are bogs on both sides … no fence is necessary' – or assurances that, when needed, guards were put in place – 'lacking a proper fence, this side of the town is guarded at market times'.[83] The areas near the town entry points and the customs houses (if there was a dedicated customs house) were particularly important to supervise, and there had to be people around who could do the job.

Because of this, it made sense to have customs officials and their families living near or even in their offices and other workplaces. The state depended on them to be there and to protect its interests. If the families took advantage of the situation, for instance by using state funds for their own benefit, this was certainly perceived as a problem, but a problem to be weighed against the many advantages of having people on the spot. In this respect too, state servants and their families were similar to domestic servants. Domestic servants also lived and worked in the same place and sometimes availed themselves of the possibility of 'borrowing' their master's property. This was a problem, but not one serious enough to make people stop hiring and relying on servants.

Conclusion

In its efforts to get a grip on society and to control its own servants, the Swedish early modern state had a number of tools and strategies at its disposal. It regulated urban and rural space with a view to controlling the movements of customs payers, and it sought to build a system for the levy of customs and excise that was impossible for customs officials to manipulate. To prevent officials from fraternising with customs payers, the state also devised a policy that meant that they had to move at intervals from town to town. By setting up special courts for matters of customs and excise, and by having specially appointed customs inspectors to control the work of subordinate officials, the state endeavoured to control revenue as efficiently as possible. The control system was comprehensive and far-reaching, but did not include the separation of private space from professional space. Customs officials worked in the customs houses and at town entry points, but they also moved about in the streets and in the countryside, and did some of their work from home. Conversely, they and their family members clearly used state spaces for their own purposes; they could, for instance, sleep in the customs houses. Everything suggests that they did so with the approval of their local superiors and the central authorities. To have people on the spot was regarded as vitally important, be they women or men.

This chapter has given a number of examples of how efforts by the state to force or encourage its servants to behave in certain ways led to unforeseen 'conversations' or 'negotiations'. State servants talked to each other about their jobs and about the limits of their powers, questioned the authority of some of their superiors, forged close bonds with others, and criticised local courts for being unfair. The language of these contacts could be confident and self-assured, but it could also draw upon notions of dependence and help.[84] Examples of the former are the lower state servants who argued that they knew their work better than anyone else and that their local superior and the excise court had no business meddling in their affairs. Examples of the latter are found whenever people in fact needed help, which was evidently quite often. Both men and women argued that they and their families required assistance and support, either from 'Christianly mild' people (such as their local superiors) or from the state. The fact that state servants were outsiders to the urban communities in which they worked could make their need for assistance pressing.

Just as the state exploited lower state servants and their families, these families sometimes exploited the state's resources – not least cash – for their own ends; as we have seen, the lack of separation between private and professional spheres made this possible. But the parties not only exploited, but were also dependent on each other. The state's dependence on these families explains why the restrictive policies of urban communities were perceived to be a problem not only by the people who were excluded from many ways of making a living, but by the central state as well. It was in the interest of the state that its servants could support themselves.

It would be disingenuous to claim that these mutual and even parasitic dependencies made servant families and states each other's equals. Early modern states were infinitely more powerful than each individual family. Nor must these dependencies be allowed to eclipse the intense ambition to establish control over society that is characteristic of early modern governments. Early modern states struggled to be independent of the will of their subjects. In practice, however, these struggles assumed many different forms, none of which completely lacked elements of negotiation and, consequently, dependence. Masters could boss servants around and often did so, but making the early modern state work was a task of such magnitude and complexity that it required more sophisticated instruments and strategies than just discipline and intimidation. Personal loyalty and old notions about what it meant to serve others remained important elements.

But as this chapter has shown, these notions about service were gradually combined with new and meticulously constructed control systems, the purpose of which was to control both servants and subjects. Thus, the idea that service of the state was about extending personal help and assistance to a master was undermined. Instead, it was replaced by the idea that a state servant was a person who followed impersonal rules.

Notes

1 ULA, Örebro Accisrätt, A, Vol. I, 317, 25 January 1747; box '1744–49'.

2 ULA, Örebro Accisrätt, A, Vol. I, 46–7; KB, Kart- och bildsektionen, General-tull-arrende-societetens svenska tullatlas, map no. 81.

3 Wittrock, *Regering och allmoge*, 216; RA, Kammarkollegiet, Tull- och licentkontoret, F I, Vol. VIII, instruktion för inspektorerna över småtullarna och acciserna, 9 March 1675, item 1.

4 *Kongl. Maj:ts Reglemente för Landt-Tulls- och Accis-Kamrarne i Riket, 17 December 1756*, §18; *Kongl. Maj:ts Landt-Tulls och Accis-Ordning, 17 December 1756*, Chapter 1, §10, item 4, Chapter 8, §16; *Kongl. Maj:ts förnyade Land-Tulls och Accis Stadga, 19 September 1776*, Chapter 14, Chapter 19, §3. For complaints about poor fencing, see also ULA, Örebro Rådhusrätt och magistrat, court record, 15 January 1655.

5 KB, Kart- och bildsektionen, General-tull-arrende-societetens svenska tullatlas, map no. 54.

6 For disputes about roads taken, see ULA, Örebro Accisrätt, A, Vol. I, 450–1, 709, 812, 827–8; A, Vol. II, 21 January, 22 September 1779; 16 January 1782.

7 Örebro Accisrätt, A, Vol. I, 8 December 1743.

8 See Chapter 1.

9 ULA, Örebro Rådhusrätt och magistrat, court records, 2 April 1649, 20 December 1654 and 12 September 1692. Örebro Accisrätt, A, Vol. I, 858–9.

10 *Kongl. Maj:ts Landt-Tulls och Accis-Ordning, 17 December 1756*, Chapter 1, §10, Chapter 2, §§3, 4. See also, for example, ULA, Örebro Accisrätt, A, Vol. I, 752, concerning the use of the chests and the receipts.

11 *Kongl. Maj:ts Reglemente för Landt-Tulls- och Accis-Kamrarne i Riket, 17 December 1756*, §§ 20, 21.

12 *Kongl. Maj:ts förnyade Land-Tulls och Accis Stadga, 19 September 1776*, Chapter 13. See also ULA, Örebro Accisrätt, A, Vol. I, 513; A, Vol. II, 6 and 25 August 1778, 11 April 1782, 23 January 1784.

13 Smith, *Studier i svensk tulladministration*, Part I, 169–70, 175–8; Nilsson, '1634 års regeringsform', 202.

14 *Kongl. Maj:ts Reglemente för Landt-Tulls- och Accis-Kamrarne i Riket, 17 December 1756*, §17.

15 *Kongl. Maj:ts Landt-Tulls och Accis-Ordning, 17 December 1756*, Chapter 5, §9, Chapter 7, §4.

16 *Ibid.*, Chapter 2. On the dissemination of information via churches, see also E. Reutersward, *Ett massmedium för folket: studier i de allmänna kungörelsernas funktion i 1700-talets samhälle* (Lund: Historiska institutionen, Lunds universitet, 2001).

17 ULA, Örebro Accisrätt, A, Vol. I, 342, 450–1.

18 E.g. ULA, Örebro Accisrätt, A, Vol. I, 811, 820: Berglind reports Wingström.

19 ULA, Örebro Accisrätt, A, Vol. II, 22 December 1783. See also ULA, Örebro Accisrätt, A, Vol. I, 369–70, 545–6 (29 March 1764).

20 See Chapter 2, 37.

21 ULA, Örebro Accisrätt, A, Vol. I, 822–3. Customs officials were entitled to carry loaded rifles according to *Kongl. Maj:ts förnyade Land-Tulls och Accis Stadga, 19 September 1776*, Chapter 20, §3.

22 Smith, *Studier i svensk tulladministration*, Part I, 150–5. See also Brewer, *Sinews*, 109–12 for a similar policy in Britain.

23 RA, Överdirektörens för landtullen arkiv, Personella berättelser 1748, Örebro; ULA, Örebro Nicolai, Husförhörslängder A 1, Vol. III (1750–64).

24 RA, Överdirektörens för landtullen arkiv, Personella berättelser 1773, Ladugårdslandet.

25 *Kongl. Maj:ts Reglemente för Landt-Tulls- och Accis-Kamrarne i Riket, 17 December 1756*, §7. That important documents could be lost in this way is shown in Örebro Accisrätt, box '1695–1810', letter of 20 March 1735 to Magnus Lundqvist, letter of 22 October 1735 to Örebro excise court.

26 The building in question was no. 167 south. ULA, Örebro Rådhusrätt och magistrat, K 2 A, Vol. III, Mantals- och boskapslängd över Örebro stad för år 1761; Örebro Nicolai, Husförhörslängder A 1, Vol. III (1750–64).

27 ULA, Örebro Kämnärsrätt, 24 February 1764.

28 GLA, Ulricehamns församling, födelse- och dopbok 1688–89, 137. Thanks to Dag Lindström for drawing my attention to this source.

29 KB, Kart- och bildsektionen, General-tull-arrende-societetens svenska tullatlas, map no. 20.

30 ULA, Örebro Accisrätt, A, Vol. I, 536–7.

31 ULA, Örebro Accisrätt, A, Vol. I, 327, 366; 11 April 1755.

32 ULA, Örebro Accisrätt, A, Vol. I, 534–5; 25 October 1743, 66. Also 369–70.

33 Smith, *Studier i svensk tulladministration*, Part II, 64–5, 106, 126–8, 184, 289–93.

34 'Kungl. Maj:t' (The Royal Majesty) is a term referring to the Government as such, not to the monarch in person. Petitions to Kungl. Maj:t were routinely transferred to Statskontoret, a central administrative agency. See Chapter 5, 130, for a discussion of the sources.

35 RA, Statskontorets arkiv, E 1 D, Vol. I, Aminoff, Ökenström: both women referred to the death of other widows who had enjoyed a state pension; Vol. VI, Funck; Vol. XII, Appelman, Holm; Vol. XVI, Malmyn: the employer interceded for the widows; Crusebjörn: the mother wanted to 'inherit' the pension of her deceased daughter (both mother and daughter had been married to state servants).

36 M. E. Ailes, 'Wars, widows, and state formation in 17th-century Sweden', *Scandinavian Journal of History*, 31 (2006), 17–34; C. Prytz, *Familjen i kronans tjänst: donationspraxis, förhandling och statsformering under svenskt 1600-tal* (Uppsala: Historiska institutionen, Uppsala universitet, 2013); E. Larsson, *Från adlig uppfostran till borgerlig utbildning: kungl. krigsakademien mellan åren 1792 och 1866* (Uppsala: Historiska institutionen, Uppsala universitet, 2005).

37 RA, Statskontorets arkiv, E 1 D, Vol. VI, landssekreterare Browall; Vol. XII, landskamrer Kröger and landssekreterare Bursell.

38 RA, Statskontorets arkiv, E 1 D, Vol. I, kronofogde Bergbohm.

39 Hunt, *Women in Eighteenth-Century Europe*, 5.

40 Hardwick, *Practice of Patriarchy*, 25 on the ways in which the French state tried to control notaries.

41 Klingnéus, *Bönder blir vapensmeder*, 59–60.

42 ULA, Örebro Accisrätt, A, Vol. I, 163, 165, 186 (6 November 1745).

43 *Ibid.*

44 *Ibid.*

45 'Kongl. Maytz förordning och stadga öfwer acciis rätterne', 2 May 1672.
46 Smith, *Studier i svensk tulladministration*, Part I, 271.
47 Åmark, *Sveriges statsfinanser*, 566.
48 ULA, Örebro Accisrätt, box '1752–1819', 31 October 1755: 'På det rikets trogne och skattskyldige undersåtar emot vår nådige och höga överhets allernådigste befallningar icke med oskälig tull måge bliva besvärade'.
49 *Kongl. Maj:ts Reglemente för Landt-Tulls- och Accis-Kamrarne i Riket, 17 December 1756*, appendix 2, 'Denna Ed aflägga alla Tull- och Accis-Betjente'.
50 ULA, Örebro Accisrätt, A, Vol. I, 25 October 1743: Forsberg said, 'iag ber och hr. rådman at betienterne skier den rätt som wederbör'.
51 RA, Överdirektörens för landtullen arkiv, Personella berättelser 1748, Skövde. The name of the customs inspector in Skövde was Petter Wigart but, curiously, he does not seem to have been related to Hans Wigart. The author extends her thanks to Theresa Johnsson, who helped clarify the matter.
52 ULA, Örebro Accisrätt, box '1752–1819', 31 October 1755. Prytz invoked Kammar- och Kommerskollegiet's resolution of 2 November 1749. His words were: 'nog positivt lät förmärcka sig så wähl som någon annan förstå sin sysla, och therföre, utom dom, icke finner sig wara befogad at restituera Anders Pärsson någon tull'.
53 Örebro Kämnärsrätt, 1745 (my translation). The record can be found in ULA, Örebro Accisrätt, A, Vol. I, 108.
54 Quoted in Frohnert, *Kronans skatter*, 124 (my translation).
55 ULA, Örebro Rådhusrätt och magistrat, court records, 15 February and 25 May 1762.
56 ULA, Örebro Kämnärsrätt, A I, Vol. XIV, n. pag., letter of recommendation for Lars Christian Bagge, 1764.
57 ULA, Örebro Accisrätt, A, Vol. I, 491.
58 Stadin, *Småstäder, småborgare*, 41; Chapter 1 in this book.
59 See e.g. ULA, Örebro Rådhusrätt och magistrat, court records, 8 August 1653; 5 November 1655; 14 April 1656; 19 September 1692; 15 March 1756; 31 May 1756.
60 ULA, Örebro Rådhusrätt och magistrat, court records, 6 and 20 September 1756.
61 ULA, Örebro Accisrätt, A, Vol. I, 231: customs scribe Eliander was criticised for having gained access to information that only burghers were entitled to see.
62 Stadin, *Småstäder, småborgare*, 47, 91, 126–9. Contrariwise, it did happen that members of the community took up the job of customs official, at least for a period of time. Westling, *Småstadens dynamik*, 173.
63 *Kongl. Maj:ts Landt-Tulls och Accis-Ordning, 17 December 1756*, Chapter 11, §4, item 3.
64 ULA, Örebro Rådhusrätt och magistrat, F 9 B:1, odaterad förteckning över herrar och innevånare i Örebro som icke vunnit burskap.
65 Smith, *Studier i svensk tulladministration*, Part II, 287. See e.g. Örebro Rådhusrätt och magistrat, court record, 11 October 1756: a 70-year-old bricklayer no longer wanted to be a burgher, as the taxes were too onerous.
66 E.g. ULA, Örebro Rådhusrätt och magistrat, court records, 9 July and 3 September 1649: the postmaster and the bell-founder were exempt from certain taxes. Örebro Accisrätt, A, Vol. I, 1, 1743: the executioner Johan Ekerot (who was a state employee) argued that he ought to be exempt from excise.

67 ULA, Örebro Rådhusrätt och magistrat, court records, 14 July 1762 and 27 September 1762.

68 Cf. Stadin, *Småstäder, småborgare*, 51: 'Single women who lacked membership in the municipal community had few chances of supporting themselves' (my translation). See also Vainio-Korhonen, 'Handicrafts' on the relative flexibility in Turku around 1800; and Ogilvie, *Bitter Living* on the very harsh system in early modern Württemberg.

69 Discussion inspired by M.L. Pratt, 'Arts of the Contact Zone', *Profession* 1991, 33–40.

70 RA, Äldre kommissioner 167, skrivelse från Johan Andersson till kommissarierna om Sören Christenssons attest.

71 ULA, Örebro Accisrätt, A, Vol. I, 340, 342, 353–4.

72 *Kongl. Maj:ts förnyade Land-Tulls och Accis Stadga, 19 September 1776*, Chapter 19, §14.

73 For other examples, see e.g. ULA, Örebro Rådhusrätt och magistrat, court record, 1 October 1656: Peder Joensson kept tax money at home. Smith, *Studier i svensk tull-administration*, Part II, 45: the official stamp was to be kept in the customs house, but apparently this was not always what happened.

74 ULA, Örebro Länsstyrelses Arkiv, Landskontoret, F V, Vol. I, Kassainventarium, August 1698.

75 ULA, Örebro Accisrätt, A, Vol. I, 8 December 1743.

76 ULA, Örebro Accisrätt, A, Vol. I, 369–70. (probably 1746).

77 RA, Äldre Kommissioner 139, Vol. II, Jönköpings län 1759.

78 KB, Kart- och bildsektionen, General-tull-arrende-societetens svenska tullatlas, map no. 23, 'Betjänternes logementer'.

79 KB, Kart- och bildsektionen, General-tull-arrende-societetens svenska tullatlas, maps nos. 50 and 21.

80 KB, Kart- och bildsektionen, General-tull-arrende-societetens svenska tullatlas, map no. 20.

81 KB, Kart- och bildsektionen, General-tull-arrende-societetens svenska tullatlas, map no. 61.

82 KB, Kart- och bildsektionen, General-tull-arrende-societetens svenska tullatlas, maps nos. 11 and 50.

83 KB, Kart- och bildsektionen, General-tull-arrende-societetens svenska tullatlas, maps nos. 22 and 106.

84 See also Hallenberg, 'Hapless heroes', who makes the same point about how lower state servants' presentations of themselves varied depending on the intended audience.

5

His role and hers

Based as they were on ideals of spousal cooperation, the households of lower state servants only functioned to the extent that such ideals were everyday realities. Through their various 'jobs', wives contributed income to the household, and their social contacts were helpful in integrating the family into the urban community, since state servants were not normally members of the burgher estate. What is more, wives shared with their husbands the quotidian responsibility for the state office, as the state itself acknowledged; this even went so far as to involve the women in the core tasks of customs administration. Wives were their husbands' 'helpmates'. The first half of this chapter shows that we must be cautious not to read the households of early modern lower state servants in the light of nineteenth-century bureaucracy and its reliance on the male-breadwinner model. Early modern state administration relied, rather, on a two-supporter model.

However, in spite of their working together for the state, husbands' and wives' identities were not similarly affected. The state addressed husbands in other ways than wives, faced husbands with other challenges, and eventually expected husbands to change their behaviour in ways that wives did not have to. Working for the state also allowed husbands to make acquaintances and develop homosocial networks from which wives were partly excluded. State servants were sometimes enjoined by their master to act as each other's helpmates. The semi-military character of customs officials' work makes these processes of gender differentiation particularly clear, but such differentiation also took place in state administration in general. At the same time, state servants as a group were themselves gradually differentiated along lines of class, as some state servant households were able to avail themselves of privileges others could not have, and in this process new ideals about the duty of (some) men to maintain their families emerged. The second half of the chapter analyses identity formation among state servants and suggests that it explains why bureaucracy would eventually be gendered as unquestionably masculine.

Positions of authority

In the 1780s, Eric Jakob Låstreng was accused of illegally selling aquavit. Summoned to court, Låstreng testified how on the evening in question he and his friends – three lower customs officials – had been peacefully drinking beer and playing cards in the western customs house in Örebro. Presumably, his friends could provide him with an alibi, but to prove his innocence further, Låstreng said: 'I believe it to be common knowledge that, being an unmarried person without household and property, I am not in a position to engage in any form of trade and that all suspicions of [my] acquiring or storing aquavit must therefore disappear as of themselves.'[1]

Låstreng's words point to the importance attached to household position in early modern society. Men who were heads of households could, as a matter of course, engage in trade, while those who lacked that status could not. Låstreng presented this as a well-known and uncontested fact. There was a radical difference between married and unmarried men, just as there was a 'gulf' between what married and unmarried women could do. Not being in an independent position, men such as Låstreng probably had even less economic agency than many married women. Similar examples have been found in English sources, suggesting that this was a common experience of early modern bachelors. One Thomas Page of Suffolk, for instance, was prosecuted for selling butter and cheese, 'beinge a man unmarried'.[2]

Marriage brought status, authority and resources to both men and women, in early modern Sweden and elsewhere. The activity patterns of Swedish women clearly show that marriage was a decisive factor for their agency. Married women were conspicuously more active in commerce, in managerial work and in everyday administration than unmarried women, all of these being activities that presupposed access to property, other people's labour and de facto authority.[3] If summoned to court on a charge of illicit selling of aquavit, a married woman could not have credibly argued that, like Låstreng, she lacked the necessary resources. What both wife and husband could, and often did, do was to invoke her allegedly limited awareness of what the law prescribed. Through such strategies, the couple could stretch the argument about women's assumed cognitive shortcomings to the utmost, and it would sometimes be in their interests to do so. But what married women actually did, not least in the commercial sector, suggests that they could and did act with authority and as legitimate representatives of their households. Acting in this way was important. In Bernard Capp's words, a passive wife was a liability and 'beyond a certain point wifely submissiveness was against the interests even of the husband'.[4] Kekke Stadin has shown that, while female obedience was emphasised in the much-used Lutheran *Table of Duties*, obedience was seldom described as a virtue in Swedish funeral sermons referring to women.[5] Wives had to protect and assert the rights of their households, and they could not do so if they were too meek. This circumstance has wide implications for state formation. If the husband's job consisted in protecting the rights of the state, and if it was difficult for him to do this by himself, the state, too, had a keen interest in active and vigilant wives.

Unsurprisingly, therefore, previous research has shown that early modern state service was to a large extent handled as a de facto joint enterprise, and that both higher and lower state servants' wives acted with self-reliance for their husbands and, indirectly, for the state.[6] When in 1698 an official in Linde was unable to deliver his moneys to the regional administration on time, his wife travelled to Örebro, where she visited her husband's guarantor and some other friends. She more or less forced them to borrow the required sum in the town and deliver it on behalf of her husband. Clearly, she was acting in the interests of her household, but her assertiveness also meant that the state received its income on time.[7] In a similar way, the wife of a customs inspector in Gothenburg actively pursued her absent husband's interests in a complex dispute with the magistracy that erupted in the 1630s. In so doing, she not only asserted the interests of her husband and her household; she also acted in the interests of the state.[8] In both cases, the married woman's authority was an asset to both the household and the state for which it worked.

The need for an active wife was particularly obvious in customs officials' families. Monitoring the boundaries of a town was a complicated task, and every extra pair of eyes was crucial. As these families often lived in close proximity to the customs houses, the wives were at or near their husbands' workplaces and ideally placed to assist and stand in for them. Customs scribe Edberg's wife Catharina Wiberg had for example been in or near the customs house on the day when a certain peasant had tried to smuggle textiles into town, as she told the excise court in 1783. Catharina Forsberg, another customs scribe's wife, had observed in 1743 how a consignment of grain was delivered to the customs house one evening. Emerentia Klen, the wife of a third customs scribe, had noticed how in

1755 a searcher had been at his post on a certain day. A fourth, anonymous wife was in the customs house when two travellers came in to have their papers signed, and she proceeded to wake up her husband, who was asleep at his post in the same building.[9] Clearly, these four women's daily chores meant that they were near the customs houses and noticed what went on there.

Other evidence can also be marshalled to show that wives and other household members took part in the work of lower state servants. Statutory law regulated the work of customs officials in detail, including how confiscated goods were to be dealt with. Such goods were later to be resold, unless the owner eventually turned up to pay the duty, and it was important that their value be preserved intact. Court cases illustrate how angry people could become if their seized property was mishandled or destroyed.[10] The laws did not spell out exactly how the care of confiscated goods was to be organised, but as such goods could include living animals, keeping their value intact meant feeding them. It is likely that wives, children and other household members could make themselves useful by tending confiscated cows and horses, and there are examples of this happening. Margareta Ström, the wife of an Örebro customs official, mentioned in court on one occasion that she had come to the customs house to look for fodder for a confiscated horse. Since she was accused at the time of having stolen from some peasants, we must assume that everything she said was intended to portray her as an honest and upright person. Consequently, looking for fodder for confiscated horses was most probably an honourable activity that customs officials' wives were expected to engage in.[11]

It would be a mistake to read these examples as wives occasionally assisting their husbands when the latter had too much to do. Lower customs officials always had too much to do and the areas they had to monitor were too large for them; therefore, it was always necessary to involve other household members. Notions of occasional assistance obscure the extent to which spousal cooperation was fundamental to the way these households worked. They also obscure how spousal cooperation was crucial to making customs administration and, by extension, the state as a whole work. This was true not only of Sweden, but of the Dutch Republic and the German-speaking area as well. Many offices required spousal cooperation, and some of the work was done by the wife, even if the office was in the husband's name.[12]

Wives did not just happen to notice what went on near the customs houses; they were expected to do so. When customs inspector Wigart was investigating the reasons why a traveller had been able to drive into town without being properly searched, he asked customs scribe Prytz what had happened. It turned out that Prytz had been on leave that day to attend a funeral, but the searcher Funck had been ordered to take his place. Wigart asked Prytz whether, on his return from the funeral, his wife and the rest of his household had not informed him about what had happened. Prytz responded that they had indeed confirmed that Funck had been at his post, in spite of not being well. The way Wigart saw it, Prytz and his family were jointly responsible for making sure the entry point to the town was properly monitored. Prytz and his wife did not have to be there in person, but they had to make sure the job was properly done. If the searcher had left his post, the wife ought to have reported this to her husband.[13] Prytz's answer reveals that he and his family accepted this view.

A core task of customs officials' households was to levy customs and excise and subsequently record the sums collected. There is no doubt that lists of tax, customs and excise received were as a rule signed by men, but this does not mean that their wives never played an active part in this work. Moreover, when they did stand in for their husbands, it does not seem to have caused any dissatisfaction at the central state level. The story of how the searcher Lars Wingström was dismissed from office makes this clear.

Accused of embezzling excise, Wingström had been dismissed by the excise court of Örebro in 1780. He did not accept the decision, however, but appealed to the *Kammarkollegium* (the Court of Chamber). The ensuing investigation revealed that customs official Berglind had ordered Wingström to write an excise receipt for a wigmaker's fourteen-year-old apprentice 'because of his neat handwriting'. Contrary to the rules, the sum in question had not been noted in the ledger, which was the cause of the excise court's suspicions. Had Wingström taken the excise money himself? Wingström answered that customs scribe Roth had been temporarily absent and had never transferred responsibility for the ledger to him. The money had been received by Roth's wife, and she admitted to having received it. Somewhat surprisingly, she also admitted to having taken one-third of the sum for herself; the rest she had given to Wingström and Berglind (something they denied). Her husband, the customs scribe, claimed to have been away on a legitimate errand for no more than thirty minutes and said that he had asked Wingström to 'take care of the customs' while he was away.[14]

Instead of Roth receiving the money, noting it in the ledger and writing the receipt, Wingström had written the receipt, Roth's wife had taken charge of the money, and nothing had been recorded in the ledger. A number of errors had been committed, but according to the

Kammarkollegium, the key issue was whether or not responsibility for the ledger had been duly transferred to Wingström. If not, the excise court had had no grounds for dismissing him, since the responsibility remained with the customs scribe. It was never an issue that the wife had received the money instead of the husband. The husband's colleagues were implicated by her claim that they had all shared the money in an unlawful manner, and it would not have been surprising if they had tried to blame her for meddling in business that was her husband's. But they never used this argument. Nor did the *Kammarkollegium* regard her involvement in receiving excise money as irregular; evidently, it considered husband and wife to be jointly responsible for the office. Just like Wigart, it accepted that the couple could have others do the actual job, but if they wanted to transfer their responsibility this had to be duly documented. Merely to ask Wingström to 'take care of the customs' was not sufficient.

It is telling that the *Kammarkollegium* did not require the husband to delegate responsibility to his wife in the same way as he was supposed to delegate it to his colleague. In view of how much attention the customs administration normally devoted to whether or not formal responsibility had been transferred from one official to another – eighteenth-century excise court records often refer to the issue – this speaks to the tacit understanding that couples shared responsibility for the husband's office, even though the wives do not seem to have sworn the professional oath together with their husbands.

When early modern women have been assumed to have been barred from certain types of work, lack of advanced education has often been adduced as a reason. It is true that skills in reading, writing and arithmetic were important in handling customs and excise, and wives who completely lacked these skills did not fulfil all the requirements placed on the households to which they belonged. However, three things must be borne in mind here. First, the acquisition of such skills did not require a university education, but could be achieved in other ways. Literacy levels were high among both men and women in late-seventeenth-century Sweden, as a consequence of widespread teaching in families or local schools. Men probably acquired the necessary skills in these ways, and women may have been taught them too. For noblewomen, keeping accounts was described as a crucial and typically female skill.[15] Second, both men and women could hire other people to write and add up numbers for them. The use of such substitutes was not a problem, as long as it remained clear who was ultimately responsible for the accounts. Men holding relatively high positions in the regional administration used substitutes in this way. In Örebro, regional treasurer Broström had an accountant in 1756 and a scribe in 1761 (the latter living with him), none of whom were mentioned in the regional state budget. Broström, whose salary was 200 silver *daler*, must therefore have paid these men out of his own pocket. The town secretary Johan Erik Bergström had a 'scribe boy' living with him.[16] Both men and women were regarded as capable of employing and governing others, as long as they were married and of good repute. Third, although reading, writing and arithmetic were important parts of a customs official's work, it also involved other tasks, such as keeping one's eyes open, policing borders and guarding doors and gates. Not least, it included the assertion of rights, both in social encounters and in court. This did not require formal education, so much as the authority to make people listen and defer to you.

The assumed impropriety of working in public has also been regarded as a reason for women's exclusion from certain types of work. The work of lower state servants often took place outdoors, but in fact this does not seem to have prevented wives being actively involved. In the Dutch Republic, women could hold offices such as those of doorkeepers, bridge operators, weighing assistants at public scales, carriers and measurers, all of which involved acting in public. In the German-speaking area, women were active as gatekeepers, fence keepers and toll collectors. They weighed grain at the public scales and operated warehouses.[17] The situation was the same in Sweden. Women monitoring public space was clearly seen as perfectly acceptable.

Married women were expected to act on behalf of their household and to do so with authority and assertiveness. In the kind of communities that early modern towns and cities were, the never-ceasing social encounters and the ever-present risk of being dragged to court made it necessary for husbands and wives to be alert, vigilant and active, rather than submissive, meek and passive. This was especially important for those whose job it was to protect the rights and interests of the state. State offices were joint enterprises, and both spouses had to be able to wield authority in order to manage the office satisfactorily. Therefore, the fact that wives had less formal legal capacity than husbands does not explain why they were given a different role in relation to the state than their husbands. The reasons for this have to be sought elsewhere.

State servant identities

In situations where lower state employees became embroiled in conflicts, they often described themselves as servants of the king and, consequently, as unassailable. In 1655, for instance, two soldiers who were displeased at not having received their wages on time shouted at the man they held responsible: 'Pay us, if you do not want the devil to have you; we are servants of the Crown – and let us have some beer!' When customs official Erik Kraft reported in 1678 that he had suffered disrespect and intimidation while simply 'exercising his office', he added that the incident had set a dangerous example: a large group of onlookers had seen 'that customs officials are so mistreated in the service of the Crown'. When the confiscation of a horse by customs officials triggered a minor riot in 1779, involving townspeople, visitors to the town and customs officials, one of the officials was later reported to have cried out to the hostile crowd during the turmoil: 'Do not touch me, I am a man who represents the Crown!'[18]

Note how these state employees talked about themselves. The soldiers called themselves 'servants of the Crown', and the customs officials pointed out that they exercised their office 'in the service of the Crown', invoking the protection to which those who represented the Crown were entitled. Other state employees used similar language. Customs official Johan Andersson Brunnberg described himself as a 'servant of the Crown' whose working situation was made intolerable by the machinations of the local mayor. While the mayor was said to be a profit seeker, Brunnberg described himself as a poor but educated man, honourable and willing (though unworthy) to serve the Crown. He pointed out that right-thinking people – a category that did not include the mayor – usually respected the decisions of customs officials, because otherwise it would be impossible to serve the king.[19]

The most likely explanation for the frequent references to these men's status as servants of the Crown is that they were repeatedly addressed in such terms. Soldiers, customs officials and other lower state servants were constantly instructed, criticised, monitored, punished, supported and praised in their capacities as state servants. Their superiors and peers addressed them as such, legal discourse described them as such, and taxpayers detested them as such. Their day-to-day practices and interactions made them susceptible to a message that underlined their status as servants of the Crown, even when the point of that message was that they had acted as unfaithful servants. The more they were addressed as servants of the king, the more they identified themselves as his servants, particularly in situations where they had little else to cling to than the supposed unassailability of their positions. Even if historians are unable to demonstrate this mechanism in detail, there was probably a 'looping effect': once the label of state servant had been attached to these men, it started to affect their thinking about themselves.

In this context, the oaths that all state servants had to swear take on a special meaning. They emphasised their relationship to the Swedish king and, after 1721, to the four-estates Parliament, as well as their responsibility to defend the interests of king, country and, post-1721, the constitution. This was a general oath of fidelity, sworn with God as witness and stressing the subordinate position of the servant. Customs officials made additional promises relevant to their particular office. In the late seventeenth century, a customs inspector swore that he would take responsibility for his office and follow all regulations and instructions, as well as whatever his *fullmakt* bound him to do. He also promised to present two people who would stand surety for him.[20] In the eighteenth century, customs inspectors swore an oath never to 'introduce, assist or promote royal absolutism', but to combat it in every way and to report if they heard any news of its reintroduction in Sweden; this, it must be remembered, was just a few decades after the death of King Charles XII.

Eighteenth-century customs inspectors pledged, moreover, to protect the rights of king and Crown to customs and excise, to respect the provincial laws and royal statutes, to be fair, to deliver money and accounts on time, to obey their superiors and never to accept bribes. In addition, since their office involved being a member of an excise court, inspectors swore a judge's oath. Customs scribes and searchers also swore to treat subjects with courtesy and not to accept bribes, and searchers promised to be sober. It was deemed important that all officials swear these oaths, and they were usually administered at a local court, even in periods when the customs administration was run by a private company.[21] Such oaths helped instil a sense of professional identity in state servants at all levels, but may have been particularly important for lower officials. They emphasised that the man in question was especially chosen for his office. He had been selected for the job, and for this reason he had special rights and responsibilities. In general terms, these responsibilities had to do with serving the interests of king and Crown, but after the demise of royal absolutism, they also meant serving common interests symbolised by the four-estates Parliament.[22]

The built environment also served to inculcate a sense of selection and identity in state servants. In Örebro, the men who worked under the regional governor had their offices in the four-storey castle, behind thick granite walls. The holders of municipal offices worked in the town hall – less impressive, with only two storeys, but a stone building nonetheless. Customs officials, by contrast, had only the red-painted wooden customs houses and the excise chamber if they wanted to take shelter. Searchers had to be more or less constantly on the move – in town or in the vicinity of the town – so they could rarely hide inside buildings at all.[23] Clearly, the ways in which state servants were allotted space and material protection in the form of walls set many of them apart from other subjects.

Thus, the process of inculcating a professional identity in male state servants relied on a number of subtle mechanisms. Through the ways in which they were addressed, promises of royal protection, requirements to take oaths and the built environment in which they operated, these men were singled out from the rest of the population. And, while the promise of royal protection did include state servants' entire households, it was usually the husbands who had to deal with angry taxpayers, had reason to describe themselves as the king's men and needed to invoke unassailability. Moreover, the professional oaths were sworn by the men, not by the couple, even though the wives' involvement was both accepted and expected.[24] Clearly, these small differences in how the male and the female half of a state servant's household were treated mattered. What also mattered was the support and solidarity the husbands could receive from within their peer group. Several examples from Örebro bear witness to this.

To cope with the large influx of people on the occasion of the Henriksmäss fair, customs officials from other towns and cities were temporarily posted in Örebro. In 1746, two of these helpers came from Stockholm. During the fair they confiscated some textiles, but evidently they had to leave before their claims for payment were dealt with by the Örebro excise court. In this situation, customs scribe Hans Pihlgren represented the two searchers and helped them to assert their rights. It is hard to know what his reasons were. They may have been personal friends of his, but it is equally possible that customs officials stuck together and helped each other simply because they were colleagues. Pihlgren acted in the same way for a former colleague.[25] In other cases, it is clear that customs officials acted out of a sense of collegial solidarity. In 1784, complaints were levelled against customs scribe Lars Moberg by his superior accusing him, among other things, of being drunk, losing passports (deposited in the customs house) and failing to transfer responsibility for the ledger. Not least, the sums collected did not add up to those recorded in the ledger. In his defence, Moberg cited illness and lack of time. The missing funds, he said, had been lent to inhabitants of the town, and it had been his intention to recover and deliver them as soon as possible. The excise court questioned several other customs officials, who admitted that Moberg's behaviour had not been impeccable; yet they claimed that he had done his job until the previous day. Customs scribe Gyllenspetz said he had asked him about his health and Moberg had answered that he had a headache. The case suggests that Moberg's colleagues thought there had been extenuating circumstances and that they were unwilling to portray him as an unfaithful servant.[26]

Solidarity among peers presupposes notions of mutual obligation and willingness to assist one another. At times, state servants did demonstrate such a willingness to help. The eighteenth-century state encouraged this by actively enjoining its employees to assist each other. This was part of an ambition to make different parts of the state administration work smoothly together, which in turn had to do with enhancing efficiency. The language in which this ambition was framed included concepts of help, assistance and support, all of which had a personal ring. Thus, in customs statutes from the mid-eighteenth century, the legislator referred to the need to 'lend one another a helping hand' (*handräckning*). This was how cooperation between customs officials in port and inland towns was described. It was also how the statutes described the support that customs officials were supposed to receive from governors and regional state administrations. When fairs were arranged that were too large for the regular staff to handle, it was incumbent on the local customs administration to 'call for help' from a neighbouring town. Soldiers could also be called upon to lend customs officials a helping hand.[27] State administration was built on notions of service to a master and further buttressed by a requirement of mutual help among state servants. As men's work for the state could be described in terms of help, 'help' was not in itself coded exclusively as female work. Men's helping each other was something that reinforced them as a peer group.

Solidarity within peer groups was therefore another mechanism that helped create a state servant identity. Servants of the state were colleagues and comrades, linked to each other through both professional and family networks. Even male relatives who did not belong to the profession could show a sense of belonging and solidarity with members of the state servant group. When a man called Lemon, a tavern keeper from Lerbäck, appeared in court as a witness, for example, he said that while customs official Carl Öman was not a personal friend of his, Lemon had nevertheless shown hospitality to him and his wife (who was later accused of stealing) because they were customs officials and several of Lemon's relatives worked for the customs administration.[28] Networks could also extend beyond relatives in the narrow sense of the word. Hans Wigart, a customs inspector in Örebro in the 1740s, was the son of a Saxon prisoner of war, who was probably something of an outsider in Västervik where Hans was born. When Hans was baptised, however, the witnesses included Sven Hoffer and his wife Apollonia Henricsdotter. Sven Hoffer was a customs official and may have helped Hans secure a career in the customs administration.[29]

Too much emphasis should not, though, be placed on male networks. First, just as there are examples of solidarity among male peers, there are also examples of competition and deceit. The levy of customs and excise was organised in a way that encouraged officials to inform on each other. And this certainly happened: the searcher Zakris Wikman, for instance, was accused by his fellow officials Carl Wallgren and Petter Lindstedt of embezzling state money. As a consequence, he lost his job and had to become a garrison soldier instead.[30] Second, state servants' wives were not entirely excluded from all aspects of these fraternal networks. Casual references suggest that the men did not always socialise on their own, but that the families knew each other too. When customs official Jonas Höijer wrote to inspector Bergman on official business, he ended his letter by sending 'humble greetings to your amiable wife and the mademoiselles [*sic*]'.[31] Wives sometimes identified as the spouses of state servants, claiming the social prestige that was associated with this professional group. On one occasion in 1663, a customs official's wife scorned the wife of an artist, claiming a better place in church on the grounds that, while her husband wielded power over state property, her adversary's husband wielded power over little else than his 'stinking paint pots'.[32] Another wife claimed in 1764 to be an honest and upright seller of textiles, buttressing the claim with the argument that she was married to a searcher.[33] Thus, women did tap into notions of social difference and prestige deriving from their husbands' employment.

But state service as such was nevertheless associated with manhood. This cannot be explained with reference to royal protection, oath taking, the built environment and male collegiality alone. It was the distinctively military character of much of the work of lower state servants that marked it as a job for men. As Alexandra Shepard has shown, early modern manhood was closely linked to volatile notions about the legitimate and illegitimate use of violence. Nowhere are the use of violence and the question of its legitimacy more central than in the state sphere. States claim a monopoly on the legitimate use of violence in society, as exercised by judiciaries and police forces. They also claim responsibility for the defence of their territories and make men engage in their defence, endorsing broad use of violence as long as the purpose is to protect territory and people.[34] Historically, the distinctions among meting out justice, upholding internal order and defending the polity against attack have been blurred, often because these tasks, which seem so different from each other to the modern mind, have the deployment of violence in common and were carried out by the same group of men: servants of the state.[35]

Swedish bailiffs of the early modern period have been compared to common soldiers. Sixteenth-century depictions of bailiffs and their entourage show men in armour waving their swords intimidatingly at peasants proffering their taxes. In their letters, bailiffs described themselves as soldiers and hard men (but also as wretched subjects in need of help).[36] Customs officials, in turn, had much in common with bailiffs, and it is unsurprising that they too were associated with soldiers. They were often embroiled in disputes that involved the use of violence and were equipped with tools that could be used as weapons. Searchers were easily recognised by the long, spear-like tool they used to probe the contents of vehicles, and they could, and sometimes did, use these spears to threaten customs payers and colleagues. When accused, searcher Lundius had to admit that he had lost his temper one day and dashed out of the customs house, waving his spear at postmaster Löthman who had annoyed him.[37] There are also examples of customs officials carrying proper weapons while on duty. In 1779, customs inspector Fineman had discovered that peasants trading in oxen were able to reach the market place south of Örebro clandestinely by taking a road through the forest, thus avoiding paying customs duty. Fineman ordered his men to watch the road at night and told them to carry loaded rifles. Despite being thus equipped with weapons and authority, though, they were unable to prevent the peasants from using the road. On another occasion, customs officials in Örebro were reported to have used sabres, rapiers and whips against a group of townspeople who were incensed by the customs administration's confiscation of a horse.[38]

These examples are from the end of the period under discussion, but there is evidence of military connotations in the sixteenth and seventeenth centuries too. A lower customs official was at that time often referred to as a *tullknekt*, a word that can be translated as customs servant. *Knecht* is the common German word for a male rural servant, signalling the man's subordinate position, and *knekt* could be used in the same way in early modern Swedish. Like all servants, *knektar* had a master who could use them for his own purposes. But *tullknekt* can also be translated as customs soldier, because *knekt* was often used for a foot soldier. Common soldiers were referred to as 'gemena knechtar' and often mentioned together with ordinary seamen. Like them, *tullknektar* were clearly distinguished from officers.[39] More comparable to officers in rank were those customs officials who patrolled the coastline by boat; they were called captains or lieutenants (*jaktlöjtnant*), titles that also underline the military character of customs officials' work.[40] The ways in which people talked about officials of the customs administration also suggest that the officials were associated with the military sector, as when some customs officials in Helsingborg were described as 'worse than the enemies of the realm'.[41] Whether such statements accurately reflect people's views of these officials is of course a matter of debate; drawing parallels with enemies of the realm may have been something people did in the heat of the moment. However, there was no lack of alternative nicknames if the aim was simply to insult them – they were referred to as snoopers, sharks, dogs and rats – so when the inhabitants of Helsingborg chose to compare them precisely to enemies of the realm, it probably tells us that, on this occasion, it was their military and violent associations that loomed large in people's minds.

The military taint of customs officials' work did not wear off with time. In fact, at the end of the period covered by this book, the oaths the officials swore were phrased in terms that strongly emphasised the military connotations of their office. When customs official Mattias Åkerberg swore his oath at the excise court of Örebro in about 1777, he promised to protect the monarchy and the four estates from conspiracies and to do so with his own 'life and blood'. Five other customs officials pledged to offer their lives for their master in the same way.[42] The sacrifice of life and blood was the soldier's ultimate way of serving his master and showing him fidelity.

In the Dutch Republic, lower public offices could be held by women as well as men, but there was a clear gender division of labour. As in Sweden, there was a link between manhood and offices with connotations of violence, danger and military pursuits. Offices reserved for men were typically in the areas of public order and safety: the night watch, the fire brigade, the civic militia.[43] In Sweden, England and the Dutch Republic, the use of violence was linked to manhood. Jobs typically involving it would therefore be gendered as male.

Social differences

In the seventeenth century, the word *betjänte* (servants) could still be used of all customs officials. Searchers belonged to this group, but so too did chief inspector Ehrentahl and the customs inspector at Blockhusudden, who was responsible for duty to a value of 60,000 silver *daler*. They were all His Majesty's servants and were referred to as *betjänte*.[44] With time, however, perceived and constructed differences among customs officials grew, as the oaths they took show. In the mid-eighteenth century, customs inspectors had an over-arching responsibility to protect a number of crucial state rights, and they also promised to defend the country against reactionary *coups d'état*. Their drinking behaviour was not mentioned at all in their oath. By contrast, searchers were bound not to become inebriated while on duty. The oaths the men took addressed them in different ways, and distinctions such as these underlined the differences between an inspector and a searcher. Such distinctions affected male identities and also intersected with emerging notions of (some) men's responsibility to support their families.

Notions of difference were linked to privileges. There were appealing sides to being employed by the early modern state. It was possible to pursue a career in ways that peasants could not, and to ameliorate one's family's standard of living. Just like 'ordinary' masters, the state could offer protection and other good things, making the job of a state servant more attractive. This was what some lower state servants discovered: they could improve their lot in life if they behaved according to a certain standard and enjoyed the support of their superiors. Some customs scribes were promoted to inspectors, and some inspectors even became chief inspectors, in certain cases with an annual salary of 600 silver *daler*. Many searchers were promoted to customs scribes.[45] There was, of course, also a risk of going down in the world. Having been a customs scribe in Skövde, Nils Lundius became a searcher in Örebro. He pitied himself and his bad luck: 'that he, who had been a customs scribe, now has to serve in poverty and misery as a searcher'.[46] Lower customs officials could experience drudgery and criticism, rather than glory and appreciation. But others were more successful. They grasped the importance of having certain skills, such as arithmetic and accounting, and of drawing them to their employer's attention. Chief inspector Forsman in Västerås described, obviously with some pride, how he had set up the customs administration in Mariefred from scratch, and chief inspector Hagert detailed his diligent studies and his wide-ranging professional experience.[47] They fashioned themselves as good and reliable servants and were able to build better lives for themselves and the next generation.[48]

In their dealings with state institutions, some state servants' families learnt to emphasise how much they depended on the husband/father and his income-earning capacity. The husbands had given valuable service to the state and now the state had to care, at least temporarily, for their widows and fatherless children. Some customs officials' families also took part in such conversations. In the early 1690s, the widow of Erik Lyding, a customs official in Vyborg, petitioned the government and was granted half of her husband's annual salary (175 silver *daler*). Sigrid Gyllenkrok had been married to the inspector of maritime customs for Finland and petitioned for temporary relief in 1693. These women had been married to higher customs officials. But the widow of Anders Cedergreen, who had been a mere *strandridare* (customs patrolman) in his lifetime, also petitioned the Crown with the help of Cedergreen's successor in 1694, with a modest request for one month's salary.[49]

Such arguing strategies are often found in petitions for pensions submitted to government bodies. These petitions are emphatically *not* a reliable source when it comes to charting the capacity of women to make economic contributions to their households, since they reflect exactly what the state asked for: evidence of need and lack of means to support oneself.[50] Petitions do not say anything about the widow's actual ability to work, nor do they tell us anything about the gender division of labour between the spouses while they were both alive. What they do reveal, though, is a dialogic process through which notions of gender, work and a duty to provide were shaped. In this process, ideas about the differing responsibilities of men and women were articulated and nurtured.

A sample of mid-eighteenth-century petitions for state pensions provides an ambivalent picture of women's working capacity.[51] In one case, a widow produced a letter from the local court asserting that she was unable to support herself and her children because she was blind. The tacit assumption was evidently that, had she been able to see, she would have supported the family herself. In another case, the widow described how she had at first provided for herself and her children through manual work, but was now too old to do so. A third widow emphasised that she had no other means of providing for herself than by spinning. In cases such as these, the idea was clearly that adult women would *normally* support themselves and their children. Only when poor health, disability or old age prevented them from doing so would they ask for support from someone else.[52] Even in situations where it would not have been in their interests to mention that they could work and support themselves, women nevertheless said that they normally did so.[53] In fact, in one case the petitioner explicitly attacked the idea that manual work was demeaning for a woman. But she added that, unfortunately, she was now too old to work.[54]

In other cases, however, widows' petitions were based on the idea of 'seemly' or 'fitting' (*anständig*) provision and upbringing.[55] One woman, whose husband had been a military officer, referred to letters certifying that she was unable to support herself 'with her own means and the benefits accruing to her from her two deceased husbands' and that she could not ensure 'fitting provision and education' for her eight children.[56] Another woman argued that she lacked seemly provision, adding a reference to the Bible, where a shrewd estate manager said: 'poverty is difficult for people of all estates, but when it befalls a person who is not strong enough to dig and is ashamed to beg, then it becomes an odious burden, accompanied by scorn'.[57] Manual work was not, to her, a fitting source of income, since it might expose her to scorn and contempt. As her husband had now died, she claimed, the state had to step in and grant her a pension. It was of some importance, no doubt, that this woman was of high noble extraction.[58]

What these arguments about decent and seemly provision tell us is that state institutions must sometimes have been responsive to them – otherwise they would not have been put forward. It seems that, for some women, arguments about seemly provision were seen as valid, even though they were *not* old or suffering from a disability. The Swedish state did accept that it had to take over the financial responsibilities of (some of) its former servants; it was an argument that worked in certain contexts.[59] But once people realised that there was a chance of extracting money from the state, they adapted their arguments accordingly, stating – or exaggerating – the responsibility of the deceased men and rhetorically diminishing the women's capacity to perform incoming-earning work themselves. A discourse about the state's responsibility to provide the widows of former servants, military officers not least, with an equitable living was seized on and exploited by broader groups. This happened at the same time as other women were arguing, vociferously, for their capacity and *right* to support themselves and their families.[60]

In these dialogues between state institutions and some state servants' families, both parties were affected. On the one hand, the dialogues presupposed that husbands had responsibilities for their families. On the other, they constructed and validated ideas about the responsibilities of the state. These two claims were interlinked, as it was the husband's alleged responsibilities for his wife and family that the state was asked to take over. Sometimes, the widow's family of origin had assisted her temporarily, but it was assumed that such arrangements could not last and that the state therefore had to step in.[61] Notions about the state's and husbands' responsibilities did not arise as an automatic effect of families being economically dependent on the husband's state salary. In fact, most state servants' families lived precarious lives and depended, as we have seen, on sources of income beyond the husband's salary. Their economies were predicated on a two-supporter rather than a male-breadwinner model. They can hardly have expected to live on the husband's salary alone, nor can they have expected the state to give the widow support that would enable her to lead a 'decent' life, 'fitting' to her status. To the extent that notions about a husband's responsibility to support his family existed and began to expand in the eighteenth century, they did not grow in a mechanical way out of material realities, but rather were shaped discursively in the zones of contact between state institutions and state servants' families. The importance of such zones has been observed in other European countries as well.[62] As not all state servants' families were able to draw on these notions and benefit materially from them, their articulation emphasised differences among servants of the state.

Another notion nurtured in contacts between state institutions and state servants' widows was that of 'equal treatment'. Many women petitioning for a state pension argued that they knew that other women in their social group and in the same situation had received a certain level of support from the state. Consequently, they wanted to be assisted in the same way as their 'equals' (*vederlikar*). Maria Elenna von Seth, whose husband had fought in the battle of Poltava, described how she had been ill and had incurred expenses for medical care. As a consequence, her resources had been depleted so that they no longer sufficed to ensure 'necessary and reasonably decent provision' for her. She asked to be given a pension the same size as those granted to her equals.[63] Similarly, Brita Christina Behmer, in 1755, petitioned for the same sort of support as her 'vederlikar'. She apparently had a pension of 30 silver *daler* a year, but asked to have the sum raised to 100, since this, she claimed, was what her equals enjoyed.[64]

The propensity to use arguments about equal treatment should be seen in the light of how petitions for pensions were processed in the state administration.[65] For such a petition to be successful, the woman had to muster the support of both the local clergy and the local court. The vicar and a representative of the court had to attest, in writing, that she was indeed a good Christian and that she lacked the means and the capacity to support herself and her children (if she had any). These papers were then submitted to the central state authorities together with the petition itself. By seeking support in the local community in this way, the woman would have made it publicly known that she was attempting to secure a pension or some other form of pecuniary help. It is unlikely that this knowledge would have remained with the vicar and the court representative; it is far more likely that the rumour would have spread more widely. How else can we account for the fact that many women knew how much their equals were receiving, and pointed out to the authorities that the demise of another woman had effectively created a vacant pension? People must have talked about these things.

These conceptions and ideas of fairness and equality had their roots in the administrative procedures that wove state and local communities together. The petitioners based their cases on traditional claims of individual hardship (illness, disability, large families) and appealed to traditional notions of benevolence, charity, grace and merit. But they also referred to advantages that some of their peers enjoyed and, in doing so, tapped into ideas about fairness. Was it fair that, other things being equal, they should be given less than some of their peers evidently received? Was it fair that, as everybody could see, some people should receive more than their social equals?

Despite this discourse about equality and fairness, however, society was far from equal. The Swedish society of estates, like so many other early modern societies, was marked by stark social differences. While all members of society, in principle, had the right to submit petitions, the sources suggest that it was more common for families of military officers and other higher state servants to ask for state pensions and be successful. It was also in these social groups that new notions about a husband's responsibility to support his family could gain a foothold.[66] This does not mean that customs scribes and searchers never used these notions to buttress their claims for better salaries. They argued that their wives and children would suffer if their employer did not increase their pay, and this was of course an implicit way of saying that the families were dependent on the men's salaries. Searcher Lindstedt pointed out that he had spent the best part of his life working for the customs administration, suggesting that he had made sacrifices in his service of the state. But such claims were put forward in situations where the men had been criticised for some form of misdemeanour (too much drinking, tardiness in delivering accounts) and cannot be taken as genuine expressions of how they looked upon their role as head of household.[67] In order to defend themselves, they tried to tap into notions about the breadwinning husband and the responsibilities of employers. For most customs officials' families, however, the ideal of a breadwinning father was unrealistic. What the widow of an ordinary customs official could hope for was, at best, to keep half her husband's salary for a year.[68]

Conclusion

The seventeenth-century Swedish bishop Jesper Svedberg expressed concern at one point that the distinction between a clergyman's office and that of his wife might be blurred. The wife could and should assist her husband in various ways, but there were after all some core tasks, such as writing sermons, with which she must not interfere. While spousal cooperation was necessary, Svedberg maintained that there had to be a clear dividing line between the husband's role and that of his wife.[69] The fact that Svedberg found reason to comment on the matter suggests that in everyday life this line was frequently ignored, since the clerical office was a joint responsibility of the spouses. Marriage and headship of a household conferred status, authority and resources on both husband and wife, and as early modern state offices were in effect placed in the care of married couples, it was difficult and not always desirable to uphold the distinction between his role and hers.

Yet it would be disingenuous to claim that the notion of the state office being a male task was completely lacking in early modern society. There was such a notion, but it was not as strong and pervasive as it would become in the nineteenth century; and more importantly, the reasons for it were different from those that would apply in a fully fledged nineteenth-century bureaucracy. As previous chapters have shown, the classic criteria of state bureaucracy simply do not apply to early modern Swedish state administration. State servants were not specialists, but people who by necessity engaged in multiple employments; they did not always have formal training, but relied on more generic skills and street-smartness; there was no clear separation of their private and professional lives, as the frequent confusion of money and space shows. Together, these facts go a long way towards accounting for the very active role played by state servants' wives. They do not, however, explain why state service was, after all, conceived of as a job for men.

As suggested in this chapter, the jobs of bailiffs and customs officials had strong military connotations. If we think of these men as modern bureaucrats, we will miss the point. Instead, we should think of them as servants, and not so much civil servants as military servants. Bailiffs and customs officials were not soldiers, but the conditions under which they carried out their work were very similar to those of common foot soldiers. They had to confront ordinary people in ways that caused offence and exposed them to physical and verbal violence. Military service has often been gendered as male, and the association of the tasks of bailiffs and customs officials with the military sphere provides one explanation for the partial exclusion of women from early modern state service. Women did accompany men on military campaigns, but the fighting was primarily thought of as the men's job.

Another explanation has to do with the ways in which the master treated its servants. As this chapter has shown, the men were addressed by their master in a number of ways that the women were not. They were called servants of the king and were repeatedly treated as such. Even when rebuked and punished as unfaithful, they were rebuked as the king's servants. Their oaths reminded them of their duties (similar to those of soldiers), and the built environment in which they took precarious shelter also reminded them of who they and their master were. They belonged to family groups and their wives were arguably their most important fellow workers, but they also belonged to peer groups and had male colleagues. These mechanisms set the men apart from the women and created a sense of male professional identity. By treating the men as state servants, the state made them into state servants. By making up new categories of state servants, the state 'made up' the men, since social categories and people tend to interact with each other. People respond to the categories in which they are placed.[70]

As wives and widows of state servants, women were not placed in a specific category. Nevertheless, some wives and widows also responded to the ways in which they were addressed by the state. If the state asked for evidence of their husbands' prowess and fidelity, they provided such evidence. If it asked for the local community's assurance that a widow needed financial help, the widow saw to it that such assurances were forthcoming. If the state promised to assist those who had worked hard, widows assured it that they and their husbands had done just that. Families adapted their rhetoric and their strategies to what they saw worked. In these interactions with the state, ideas about women's and men's roles were shaped and reshaped. Notions of difference between women and men were nurtured – but so too were notions of difference among men.

Notes

1 ULA, Örebro Accisrätt, A, Vol. I, 859.

2 Shepard, *Meanings of Manhood*, 208. On the gulf between married and single women, see Gowing, 'Ordering the body'.

3 Stadin, *Stånd och genus*, 83 points out that the status of unmarried people in Sweden was lower than that of married people. On the patterns of married women's activities in Sweden, see Ågren, *Making a Living*, Chapter 3. For claims that married women were unaware of what the law said, see many examples in ULA, Örebro Accisrätt. For similar claims in England, see B. Capp, 'Separate domains? Women and authority in early modern England', in P. Griffiths, A. Fox and S. Hindle (eds), *The Experience of Authority in Early Modern England* (Basingstoke: Macmillan; New York: St Martin's Press, 1996), 117–45 (121–2).

4 Capp, 'Separate domains?', 127.

5 Stadin, *Stånd och genus*, 65.

6 Vanja, 'Auf Geheiß der Vögtin', 77; Norrhem, *Kvinnor vid maktens sida*, 61–2, 158–9; B. Harnesk, 'Everyday resistance and the hidden transcript in seventeenth-century Sweden', in P. Karonen (ed.), *Hopes and Fears for the Future in Early Modern Sweden, 1500–1800* (Helsinki: Finnish Literature Society, 2009), 250–61 (259).

7 ULA, Örebro Kämnärsrätt, A I, Vol. VII, January 1698.

8 Smith, *Studier i svensk tulladministration*, Part II, 171–4.

9 ULA, Örebro Accisrätt, A, Vol. I, 57, 419–20; Örebro Accisrätt, box '1752–1819', 11 April 1755; A, Vol. II, 20 February 1783.

10 ULA, Örebro Accisrätt, A, Vol. I, 63–4.

11 *Kongl. Maj:ts förnyade Land-Tulls och Accis Stadga, 19 September 1776*; Örebro Accisrätt, A, Vol. I, 541–5, 1 February 1764; Örebro Kämnärsrätt, 1764.

12 Heijden and Schmidt, 'Public services', 368, 378; Vanja, 'Auf Geheiß der Vögtin'.

13 ULA, Örebro Accisrätt, box '1752–1819', 11 April 1755.

14 ULA, Örebro Accisrätt, A, Vol. I, 820; A, Vol. II, 19 July 1781.

15 Stadin, *Stånd och genus*, 147–50, 254; W. Pursche, *Borgmästare Erland Svensson: en storköpman i Vadstena 1632–1657* (Vadstena: Föreningen Gamla Vadstena, 1983), 25, 28–30 n. 59; Chapter 1 in this book.

16 ULA, Örebro Rådhusrätt och magistrat, court records, 5 July 1756 and 17 November 1762; Länsstyrelsen Örebro, Landskontoret, mantalslängd 1761, landsstat 1761.

17 Heijden and Schmidt, 'Public services', 381; M. E. Wiesner, *Working Women in Renaissance Germany* (New Brunswick, NJ: Rutgers University Press, 1986), 76.

18 ULA, Örebro Rådhusrätt och magistrat, court record, 18 December 1655, 151; Örebro Accisrätt, Inkomna skrivelser 1695–1755, no. 1; Örebro Accisrätt, A, Vol. II, 27 January 1779.

19 RA, Äldre kommissioner 167, letters from Johan Andersson, 22 January 1674 and 11 March 1674.

20 RA, Överdirektörens vid småtullarna och accisen arkiv, E 1, Vol. VI, kaution for Anders Lenström, Linköping, 1693.

21 *Kongl. Maj:ts Reglemente för Landt-Tulls- och Accis-Kamrarne i Riket, 17 December 1756*, 4257–61. See also Smith, *Studier i svensk tulladministration*, Part I, 274, concerning late-seventeenth-century oaths. In addition, see ULA, Örebro Accisrätt, A, Vol. I, 58 (1743).

22 Cavallin, *I kungens och folkets tjänst*, 73.

23 See maps from 1652 and 1785, the former in Lantmäteriet, Historiska kartor, akt 1880K-D3, the latter in K. F. Karlsson, *Blad ur Örebro skolas historia*, Part I (Örebro, 1871). That customs houses were made of wood and painted red can be seen from ULA, Örebro Kämnärsrätt, 8 September 1757.

24 Cf. Wiesner, *Working Women*, 76; Vanja, 'Auf Geheiß der Vögtin', 84.

25 ULA, Örebro Accisrätt, A, Vol. I, 483–9, 450–1.

26 ULA, Örebro Accisrätt, A, Vol. II, 23 January, 4 March and 16 September 1784.

27 *Kongl. Maj:ts Reglemente för Landt-Tulls- och Accis-Kamrarne i Riket, 17 December 1756*, 4220, 4222, 4225, 4247; *Kongl. Maj:ts Landt-Tulls och Accis-Ordning, 17 December 1756*, 4353; *Kongl. Maj:ts förnyade Land-Tulls och Accis Stadga, 19 September 1776*, 700.

28 ULA, Örebro Kämnärsrätt, 21 February 1764.

29 Arkiv Digital, Västervik C:2 (1697–1724), 23, 29, 199; Västervik C:3 (1724–45), no. 42, p. 101. The author extends her thanks to Theresa Johnsson for providing this information.
30 ULA, Örebro Accisrätt, A, Vol. I, 342, 450–1.
31 ULA, Örebro Accisrätt, A, Vol. I, 656.
32 Smith, *Studier i svensk tulladministration*, Part II, 288.
33 ULA, Örebro Kämnärsrätt, A 1, no. 14, 21 February 1764.
34 Shepard, *Meanings of Manhood*, Chapter 4.
35 Cf. Tilly, *Coercion*, 75.
36 Hallenberg, 'Hapless heroes'.
37 ULA, Örebro Accisrätt, A, Vol. I, 324–54.
38 ULA, Örebro Accisrätt, A, Vol. II, 27 January 1779, 22 September 1779. See also Örebro Accisrätt, A, Vol. I, 822–3.
39 *SAOB*, 'knekt', senses 1 and 2.
40 Wikberg, *Alla dessa tullar*, 52–3.
41 RA, Äldre Kommissioner 167.
42 ULA, Örebro Accisrätt, A, Vol. I, 712, 714, 731, 741, 743, 764.
43 Heijden and Schmidt, 'Public services', 376.
44 RA, Kammarkollegiet, Tull- och licentkontoret, F I, Vol. IX, cautioners beskaffenhet; Vol. X, dödsattester.
45 *Kongl. Maj:ts Reglemente för Landt-Tulls- och Accis-Kamrarne i Riket, 17 December 1756*, 4267.
46 ULA, Örebro Accisrätt, A, Vol. I, 324–54. Lundius was the man who had to change positions with Jean Henrik Lemon (see Chapter 4).
47 RA, Överdirektörens för landtullen arkiv, Personella berättelser, 1748.
48 See Smith, *Studier i svensk tulladministration*, Part II, 37, 187, on the careers of customs officials' children.
49 RA, Kammarkollegiet, Tull- och licentkontoret, F XVI, Vol. V.
50 In 1739, rules on applying for state pensions were laid down. On petitions in general, see L. H. van Voss, 'Introduction', *International Review of Social History*, 46 (2001), Supplement, 1–10.
51 The sample consists of 101 eighteenth-century petitions found in Statskontorets arkiv, E 1 D, Vols 1, 6, 11, 12, 16.
52 See also Ailes, 'Wars, widows', 25.
53 RA, Statskontorets arkiv, E 1 D, Vol. VI, Maria Molenia, Vol. XVI, Salonius; Sommar.
54 RA, Statskontorets arkiv, E 1 D, Vol. XVI, Skarff.
55 The word *anständig* entered the Swedish language in the late seventeenth century. Its basic meaning was 'fitting' for someone/something, or 'corresponding to somebody's character, status or position'. It was often used in the sense 'seemly', 'decent' or 'equitable' (often relating to education, income or a funeral). In the nineteenth century, it could refer to a respectable relationship between the sexes (*oanständig* meaning indecent or shameful), but not, it seems, in the eighteenth century. *SAOB*, 'anständig', sense 2.

56 RA, Statskontorets arkiv, E 1 D, Vol. I, Reenstråhle.

57 RA, Statskontorets arkiv, E 1 D, Vol. XVI, Rehbinder. See also Luke 16, the parable of the shrewd manager. Thanks to Sofia Ling who pointed this out.

58 She was a *friherrinna* (baroness), but her husband had been a mere lieutenant.

59 Prytz, *Familjen i kronans tjänst*; Ailes, 'Wars, widows'.

60 Ling, *Konsten att försörja sig*.

61 RA, Statskontorets arkiv, E 1 D, Vol. XVI, Sahlefelt; Schröder.

62 Hanley, 'Engendering the state'; Hunt, 'Women and the fiscal-imperial state'; M. Schmidt Blaine, 'The power of petitions: Women and the New Hampshire provincial government, 1695–1770', *International Review of Social History*, 46 (2001), Supplement, 57–77.

63 RA, Statskontorets arkiv, E 1 D, Vol. I, Seth.

64 RA, Statskontorets arkiv, E 1 D, Vol. XI, Behmer. For other examples, see Vol. I, Rhydell; Vol. VI, Westerling; Vol. XVI, Humble.

65 Cf. M. Wottle, *Det lilla ägandet: korporativ formering och sociala relationer inom Stockholms minuthandel 1720–1810* (Stockholm: Stads- och kommunhistoriska institutet, 2000), 210.

66 Stadin, *Stånd och genus*, 260–3; Vanja, 'Auf Geheiß der Vögtin', 91.

67 ULA, Örebro Accisrätt, A, Vol. I, 366 (Lindstedt), 557–8 (Letin, Fernström, Dahlberg).

68 *Kongl. Maj:ts Reglemente för Landt-Tulls- och Accis-Kamrarne i Riket, 17 December 1756*, section 'Marknads och reseomkostnad', §14.

69 Stadin, *Stånd och genus*, 202–3.

70 Florén, 'Nya roller, nya krav'; I. Hacking, 'Making up people', in I. Hacking, *Historical Ontology* (Cambridge, MA, London: Harvard University Press, 2002), 99–114.

Conclusion: Service, gender and the early modern state

To build something new, one needs something with which to begin. This book has argued that old and widely accepted notions of service to others provided the cultural template for early modern Swedish governments as they mustered new resources to expand their spheres of influence. This expansion is generally referred to as the process of state formation and has often been discussed from a macrosociological perspective, in which Max Weber's views on bureaucratisation have loomed large. The focus of this book has instead been microhistorical: charting social tensions and how they were dealt with in everyday life, the book unpicks the detailed mechanisms of state formation. Once uncovered, these mechanisms do, however, speak to a broad range of scholarly issues, including macrosociological concerns.

To build something new, one needs something with which to begin. Throughout this period, ideas about what service to others meant coloured early modern states, their administrations and the conditions of the people who embodied them. Like other servants, state servants were expected to be faithful and to put their master's interests before their own. Like other servants, state servants were used as instruments of their master and had to carry out arduous and unappealing tasks. Like other servants, state servants represented their master in public and were expected to defend and assert the rights of the one they served. And, like other servants, state servants sometimes failed to live up to these lofty ideals: they 'borrowed' from their master's funds, they slept at their posts instead of protecting their master's rights, and they behaved in ways that undermined their master's position in the eyes of others.

The literature on early modern state formation has identified efficiency, finance and legitimacy as problems that confronted many early modern European states. These problems manifested themselves on the ground as riots, protests, smuggling, embezzlement, tax evasion, military defeat, defection, corruption, lack of cash, lack of credit, lack of compliance, and so on. The solutions varied across Europe, and scholars have used this variation as a basis for state typologies, but whether we are looking at patrimonial, bureaucratic, absolutist or constitutional states,[1] the problems generally manifested themselves on the ground: in local contexts, where local representatives of the state had to handle them. The obstacles that these representatives – state servants – had to overcome explain why state formation was protracted and not always successful. State servants were learning by doing and the various ways in which they dealt with the obstacles suggest why developments were not the same everywhere.

Service was not the only cultural template used by early modern Swedish governments; the household, with its gendered division of work, was another. In this period, Swedish society was based on the ideal and the practical reality of the two-supporter model. Both husband and wife were expected to contribute in various ways to the household, and this was true of all strata in society. Consequently, there was nothing exceptional about families being engaged in state administration. State offices were acknowledged to be the responsibility of married couples rather than individual men, and it is patently clear that state formation benefited from this accepting attitude. Some tasks, however, were regarded as more fitting for men than for women and were gendered as male. As this book has shown, the military connotations of early modern state service account for its original connections to manhood. Even jobs that seem peaceful and unobtrusive to the modern mind – like that of customs officials – had clear military connotations during this period. In the longer term, however, such work was transformed, involving both the reconceptualisation of state service as civil service and the gradual exclusion of women. This, however, was a protracted and convoluted set of developments.

Women's work

The early modern Swedish state harnessed ordinary men and women to the huge endeavour of becoming one of Europe's strongest nations. What this meant to peasant communities whose resources of men were depleted during the great wars is well known: women, old men and boys had to take over the tasks of men in their prime.[2] This book has added another important dimension to this picture by clarifying the ways in which women married to lower state servants contributed to state formation.

In Weber's account of rational bureaucracy, adequate salaries for state servants are regarded as important disincentives to corruption. While this may be true, the argument is based on the implicit and problematic assumption that men's incomes are the only ones that matter. In societies where a two-supporter model prevails, however, families rely on at least two sources of income. The importance of all forms of income needs to be recognised, and by acknowledging the earnings of women, histories of bureaucratisation become more gender-sensitive and more historically true. By working to support their families, the wives of lower state servants in fact subsidised state formation. Without their economic contributions, the state would have had to raise their husbands' salaries, or else see them move on to other jobs. Without their contributions, the state would have had to accept men taking up other employments besides their state office and resorting to bribe-taking and other corrupt behaviours. All these alternatives were unattractive to the state, and while some men did of course demand more pay, resign from their offices, engage in other pursuits and act corruptly, such phenomena would have been even more pronounced had it not been for the wives. This argument is of course counterfactual, since we have no possibility of checking what would have happened if circumstances had been different. It is clear, however, that Swedish governments were aware of the importance of wives' economic contributions and effectively endorsed them. As Marie Lennersand and Maria Sjöberg have shown, high government officials explicitly prescribed that wives should support their state-employed husbands during slack seasons. This was exactly what they did.[3] Wives also supported state-employed husbands by posting security and, as we have seen, the state actively encouraged or demanded such contributions.

Finding a legal source of income was not easy for those who did not belong to a socio-political estate. In Swedish towns and cities, failure to gain membership of the burgher estate made it considerably more difficult to make a lawful living. Such excluding mechanisms account for many of the financial difficulties people could run into. They also explain why it can be time-consuming for the historian to find information on these people's daily practices of work, not least the women's. Naming practices further complicate the task of linking husbands and wives to each other. Nevertheless, this book has shown how the wives of lower state servants earned income through various commercial and other pursuits: they baked bread, cooked, made and sold beer and liquor, did laundry, looked after children and animals, arranged funerals, ran errands, engaged in trade in textiles, and extended credit. While these tasks are all familiar to historians of gender and work in urban contexts, the ways in which they were linked to the process of state formation have rarely been spotted and discussed. Seen in a larger perspective, these practices on the ground make clear how commercialisation and state formation were closely entangled in the daily lives of lower state servants and their wives.

By building social ties and managing social relations in their local communities, these women also relieved some of the tensions that their husbands' work could at times give rise to. Customs officials were often detested by local people, who called them thieves, dogs, snoopers, sharks and rats. Their employer's efforts to minimise collusion and embezzlement by having them move from one place to another did not make it easier for them to be integrated in communities. Officials had to rely primarily on the social support they could receive from kinsmen, colleagues and superiors. Seen in this light, it is clear that wives' work for other women in town could be a way of establishing social connections that were of great value. As this book has shown, even when women were linked to one another in alliances that were socially very uneven, such alliances were nevertheless precious, not least to outsiders such as lower state servants and their families. Moreover, these alliances could be valuable to the state as well. Building legitimacy was a vital concern of early modern states, and until all or most hostility towards state servants had been overcome, state formation remained incomplete. To the extent that wives managed to reduce people's hostility to their husbands, they indirectly created legitimacy for the state.

The core task of all state servants was to assert the rights of their master. It was a task that required both vigilance and assertiveness. A servant of the state could not sleep at his post, either literally or in a more metaphorical sense, nor could he fulfil his master's expectations if he was afraid to step forward and expose himself to aggression. A state servant and his spouse were expected to take joint responsibility for his office, and even if this did not necessarily mean that husband and wife did exactly the same things on the state's behalf, it is very clear that it would not have been in the interests of the state to have state servants' wives who were meek rather than assertive, who hid inside their houses, who were reluctant to appear in public and who hesitated to speak up. While historians of gender are familiar with the notion of wives as 'deputy husbands', the ways in which early modern states benefited from the assertive and self-confident behaviour of married women have rarely been pointed out as a factor for success in state formation.

Women married to lower state servants thus subsidised early modern states, contributed to their legitimacy, and protected and asserted rights and interests of central importance to them. Many of these contributions were acknowledged at the time, as was the two-supporter model. With time, however, these realities were lost from view. The ideal of the individual male civil servant triumphed, so much so that when women began to be employed by the state around 1900 this was, erroneously, seen as a radical break with the past. It is not possible here to pinpoint exactly when and how consciousness of married women's earlier contributions to the state began to wane. An analysis of how the notion of service changed will, however, provide some clues.

Service

When you take an existing phenomenon and use it to build something new, it will be transformed. In the early modern period, the notion of service did retain many of its old meanings and connotations, but it also underwent a process of semantic bifurcation. The ways in which men's and women's work were entangled with state formation and commercialisation go some way towards explaining this change.

In many contexts today, women's work is conceptualised as help, assistance, service or work for others in general. The *Oxford English Dictionary* (*OED*) points out that 'service', in the sense of 'the condition of being a servant', now usually means 'domestic service'. The dictionary then goes on to list examples of this usage where the serving person is a woman: 'putting one's daughters into service' and 'a maid [that] has been at service'.[4] On the other hand, 'service' can also denote service for the state and, in the latter case, it very often refers to military service. 'To take service' means to enlist under a military commander or join a fighting force, and 'the service' frequently refers to the army or the navy. Here, the gendering of service is the opposite of that of domestic service: the examples in the *OED* refer to clergymen and to military officers, office holders who until the twentieth century were male.[5] The Swedish counterpart to the *OED* conveys a similar distinction. 'Service' (*tjänst*) denotes a position or employment, either clearly subordinate or permanent and well-regulated in character (such as salaried public employment). The latter meaning covers, for instance, service of the state, the Church or the town, and has historically been associated with men. The former meaning is somewhat gendered as female even though 'tjänstefolk' (servants) can refer to both men and women.[6]

In modern-day linguistic usage, it would seem, the sense of 'service' is bifurcated and often clearly gendered. There are some types of service that are mostly performed by men and others that are mainly performed by women. Moreover, while men's service is often linked to prestige, women's service is not. The meanings of 'service' and the tasks associated with it are not at all the same: today, it is almost absurd to put women's low-paid provision of care and men's highly respected enactment of state authority under the same heading.

In the early modern period, this was not so. Male servants were frequently described as being 'in service', and the tasks associated with male service were similar to the ones carried out by female servants: they consisted in farm work and domestic work. In Richard Lucas's *The Duty of Servants* (1685), 'the servant' is regularly referred to as 'he' and the servant's duty to *his* master and mistress is emphasised.[7] In a similar way, Swedish *tjänst* and *tjäna* were not clearly gendered at this time, as these words could refer to the work of both male farmhands and maidservants. An example from 1676 mentions a son of seventeen who was 'away in service' and a daughter of thirteen who was 'at home with her mother'. Another example, from 1603, mentions a male farmhand who had been 'in service' of a man called Pär Olsson.[8] Historically, domestic service has not been strictly gendered as female.

The literature on state formation often mentions, though merely in passing, that medieval state servants were actually the domestic servants of the ruler. In the early modern period, lower state servants were still modelled on domestic servants and the service they performed could be described as 'help' or 'assistance', just as the work of their wives was so described. The state itself used a paternalistic language of service and help: it exhorted its servants to lend each other a helping hand, it granted some families financial support labelled 'funeral help', and it euphemistically used the word 'help' to refer to certain forms of tax.[9] When the state tried to reform the behaviour of customs officials with a propensity for heavy drinking and violence, it underlined the importance of being 'friendly and benevolent' and of giving speedy *help* to customs payers. In a wider perspective, notions of social inequality and difference were coupled with ideals of reciprocity and help. Subjects were expected to defer to the powers that be, but the latter were expected to help those in need.

Much of Swedish early modern discourse and social life was conceptualised in personal terms, making the notions of help and service to others useful for talking about many kinds of social relations that we might not describe in those terms today. And while it is true that some tasks assigned to state servants were more often linked to men and others to women, 'service' was a powerful semantic field that both men and women, and individuals and institutions alike, could use to make sense of what they were doing and how they were linked to each other. Help and service to others were key concepts in early modern Christian society. They were broad notions, applicable in many contexts and available to all. They could be used both to describe relationships between peers and to talk about relationships of subordination. And they clearly included both women and men.

By the nineteenth century, however, a process of bifurcation was clearly under way. In the middle of that century, the bishop Carl Adolph Agardh wrote an ambitious statistical work on Swedish society, in which no little attention was devoted to the social and economic conditions of women. They were, Agardh claimed, seriously disadvantaged in the labour market, where no other options were available to them but to go into domestic service. For men, by contrast, there was a wide spectrum of occupations, of which service of the state was one. Agardh noted: 'When a man gets a position ['tjenst'] it means that he gets a state office; when a woman gets a position it means that she becomes a domestic servant in a private house.'[10]

Living not so long after the end point of this book, Agardh noticed the incongruity and gender-specificity of the two semantic lines that had by then developed. 'Service' meant different things for men and women. Moreover, men's service work was more precisely defined, whereas women's service consisted in 'doing everything that needs to be done'.[11] Clearly, Agardh's exposition shows that in Sweden, as in England, a process of bifurcation would eventually occur.

Some of the reasons for this process can be identified. First, the relationship between the state as master and its servant became more impersonal with time. While state service had its origins in domestic service in the ruler's household, the life of seventeenth- and eighteenth-century servants of the state must have been very different from that of their medieval predecessors. They did not live in their master's house and, for good or ill, they were not included in the domestic intimacy that was central to the ordinary master–servant relationship. In fact, social and spatial distance was at the heart of the relationship, and assertions that the king would extend his protection to his servants and their people were perhaps a poor substitute for being physically close to a master and mistress.

This lack of proximity and intimacy transformed the relationship. An early modern proverb taught that 'lords have servants so that they do not have to do everything themselves'.[12] The words remind us of Agardh's image of the female servant as someone who is always at her master's beck and call to carry out whatever tasks the master, or mistress, needs to have done. While this image partly tallies with the work of early modern state servants, it is nevertheless important to note that, in that context, master and servant were seldom face to face. As direct interaction was rare, it had to be replaced with other arrangements for giving orders: the master's directions had to be relayed in writing, by letters dealing with specific issues, or by general laws and regulations that had a wider application. Searchers and customs scribes acted on rules proclaimed by the state and passed on by people authorised to speak for it, such as judges, customs inspectors and regional governors. The connection between searchers and customs scribes on the one hand and king and Parliament on the other was there, but it was tenuous. It was also marked by the state's ambition to control its employees and their movements. Consequently, the idea that service of the state was about extending personal help and assistance to a master, who would in turn protect his servants, was gradually undermined and replaced by the idea that a state servant was an individual who followed impersonal rules.

But the shift from a personal to an impersonal relationship was slow and was not completed within the chronological limits of this study. Moreover, as the study makes clear, the personal elements of the master–servant relationship could offer significant advantages to the expanding early modern state. The lack of a strict dividing line between the servant's private space and the space occupied by the state allowed the latter better to monitor the many places where state order had to be upheld and state taxes levied. The sometimes unclear line between servants' own funds and those of the state was a source of concern, but this should not eclipse the fact that the state could benefit from 'lending' to and 'borrowing' from its employees. The widespread use of sureties (*borgen*, *kautioner*) bears witness to this: people's private money was used to guarantee state revenues. In certain respects, then, early modern state administration was different from the Weberian ideal type, but this does not make it irrational.

A second factor of importance in this context is that, over long swathes of time, state service has been linked to manhood. The link was not, however, the same in the early modern period and in the nineteenth century. In the sixteenth and seventeenth centuries, tasks involved in work for the state had clear military connotations, whether they were performed in the army and navy or in sectors that would nowadays be classified as part of the civil service. Bailiffs and customs officials were often described in ways that emphasised their similarity to soldiers, and their everyday work practices show that they had to handle situations of assault and defence, aggression and violence. The distinction between military and civil service was not at all as marked as it would later become.

Now, as that distinction became sharper, one might have expected work in the civil service to have become more available to the female halves of households. If the work of a customs official ceased to be a matter of handling violence, why did it remain a man's job? It is obvious that we cannot account for the situation Agardh described simply by pointing to tradition and the legacy of the past. Instead, the focus should be on the process by which the state sought to inculcate a new type of behaviour in lower state servants. Unruliness, inebriation, disobedience and excessive violence in this group of men were perceived to be problems that had to be resolved, because otherwise the legitimacy of the state would be seriously endangered. Lower state servants had to be taught to behave in polite rather than impolite ways. They had to be, in the words of a Swedish statute, 'friendly and benevolent, attentive and fair'. A civil servant was now not only the opposite of a military servant; he also had to be the opposite of an uncivil servant.

The project of instilling more palatable behaviour in lower state servants was not directed at the couple. It targeted individual men only. Men were the ones who were expected to be sober, agreeable, and conscientious followers of rules. As this book has argued, these men's identities were shaped by such expectations and by the ways in which they were treated and addressed by their employer. Their self-images must have been affected, but so too must general notions in society of the typical state servant.

Thus, while state service had in practice been a joint responsibility of couples in the early modern period, it was gradually transformed into a responsibility of individual men. The process of change was driven by the state's concerns about controlling its servants, who were often far away from their employer. It was also driven by concerns about maintaining and increasing legitimacy in the eyes of subjects. As side effects of this process, lower state servants became less similar to ordinary servants and the central role of wives was eclipsed. Once state formation had advanced beyond a certain point, two of its original cultural templates – service to others and the two-supporter model – were discarded.

The state as master

State formation did not begin in the early modern period. Medieval polities were based partly on the existence of monarchical states, and people accepted states in the Middle Ages, not least because of the responsibility of kings to uphold peace and justice.[13] But from the sixteenth century state formation accelerated apace, putting strong pressure on rulers. How could the responsibility for upholding peace be squared with active engagement in warfare? How could it be squared with the many unpleasant consequences that war had for societies? Previous scholarship has emphasised these dilemmas of legitimacy, and Charles Tilly in particular has stressed that they created spaces for negotiation between states and subjects: 'bargaining over the state's extractive claims produced rights … that had not previously existed'. Tilly has also pointed out that there was a direct relationship between governments and taxpayers in Sweden long before such a relationship was created in other European polities, the implication being that Swedes, who suffered a heavy burden of warfare, were also among those who could reap the greatest political benefits from that suffering.[14]

In a similar way, I have argued that it is useful to think of early modern states as dependent on their populations, rather than so strong that they were completely absolved from any social or political considerations. My focus has not, however, been so much on those who could benefit politically from this situation – that is, people who belonged to the socio-political estates and were represented in Parliament. Rather, the protagonists of this book are the households that embodied 'the state's extractive claims' in local communities. The mundane work of these men and women and the ways in which they adapted to concrete situations are an important yet little observed part of the grand narratives. Swedish historians have pointed out that the early modern Swedish nobility was unwilling to man all the new positions created by the expanding state, as well as far too small; the job of a customs inspector would have held little appeal for a member of the lesser nobility and would have been completely unacceptable to an aristocrat. Consequently, other men and their wives had to step in instead. Because of their humble backgrounds, these people had to learn how to be state servants. Their master, in turn, had to learn how to strike a balance between controlling and supporting them.[15]

The fiscal-military state created new jobs and new investment opportunities for elite groups in many parts of Europe.[16] In Sweden, it also offered jobs to people lower down the social ladder and involved them in networks of credit and mutual help. Both men and women could support themselves in these new ways, and society was knit together by these criss-crossing relationships. State formation brought people into contact with one another: professionally, commercially and socially. Linking state and markets through their daily practices, lower state servants' households were in the front line. They helped make the Leviathan stronger.

Notes

1 Ertman, *Birth of the Leviathan*, *passim*.

2 J. Lindegren, *Utskrivning och utsugning: produktion och reproduktion i Bygdeå 1620–1640* (Uppsala: Historiska institutionen, Uppsala universitet, 1980), *passim*.

3 M. Sjöberg, *Kvinnor i fält 1550–1850* (Möklinta: Gidlunds, 2008); M. Lennersand, J. Mispelaere, C. Pihl and M. Ågren, 'Gender, work and the fiscal-military state', in Ågren, *Making a Living*, 178–203.

4 *Oxford English Dictionary*, 'service', n. 1, I.1a.

5 *Ibid.*, 'service', n. 1, I.4a, c.5b.

6 *Svenska Akademiens Ordboks* Arkiv, Lund, 'tjäna', sense 1.

7 Lucas, *The Duty of Servants*, 32, 47, 64, 67, 91, 108.

8 *Svenska Akademiens Ordboks* Arkiv, Lund: 'tjäna'. The examples are from a probate inventory from Stockholm, 26 October 1676, and from a court record of 1603, also from Stockholm. See also 'tjänst', 'tjänare'.

9 K. Ågren, *Adelns bönder och kronans: skatter och besvär i Uppland 1650–1680* (Uppsala: Historiska institutionen, Uppsala universitet, 1964), 78.

10 C. A. Agardh and C. E. Ljungberg, *Försök till en statsekonomisk statistik öfver Sverige: den statsekonomiska afdelningen*, Part II, Book I (Carlstad, 1854), 285: 'Att en man får en tjenst betyder att han får ett embete i staten, att en qvinna får en tjenst betyder att hon blir ett legohjon i ett enskilt hus.'

11 *Ibid.*

12 P. E. Wahlund, *Osed och ordsed: det är 1234 oemotsägliga ordspråk och kärnfulla talesätt, hämtade ur sal. hr Christopher L. Grubbs Penu proverbiale och här ånyo återgivna med förklaringar, kommentarer, ordlista samt andra gagneliga bihang*, 4th edn (Stockholm: Natur och kultur, 1990), based on C. L. Grubb, *Penu proverbiale* (1665), no. 734.

13 J. R. Strayer, *On the Medieval Origins of the Modern State* (Princeton: Princeton University Press, 1970); see also Chapter 2 in this book.

14 Tilly, *Coercion*, 25, 27, 103.

15 See also Lennersand, *Rättvisans och allmogens beskyddare*.

16 Brewer, *Sinews*, 182–90.

Appendix

To group the verb phrases describing sustenance activities, the same categories were used as in Ågren, *Making a Living.*

Of the 139 activities, 61 (44 per cent) were culled from the excise court records. This explains why trade in meat, beer and liquor are mentioned so often, as well as the many references to servants being sent to pay excise or deliver malt.

In the category 'Administration and justice', the first eight observations concern women who acted as deputy husbands or as public servants in their own right (e.g. 'be in charge of public scales', 'work as town guard'). The following observations concern women who did 'everyday administration' – that is, they acted as representatives of their households at court or in similar contexts.

In the category 'Trade', activities of both buying and selling have been included. While it is probably obvious why selling is a sustenance activity, it may be less evident in the case of buying. It is, however, difficult and often impossible to tell if the person who bought something did so with the intention of consuming it or of reselling with a profit. In cases where the amount is clearly stated it may be easier to tell (e.g. 'order combs in large quantities'), but even small quantities could be bought with a view to later reselling (e.g. 'sell wine in small quantities').

Because of naming practices, it has not been possible to ascertain with absolute certainty and in every case that the woman who performed the activity was married to a particular public servant. It is, however, certain in most cases and likely in the remaining ones. 'Public servant' refers both to men in state service and to people holding municipal offices.

Sustenance activities among women associated with public servants in Örebro, Sweden, mid-seventeenth and mid-eighteenth centuries (total 139)

Category	Activity
Administration and justice	act as representative of town at auction
	be in charge of public scales
	deliver money to regional administration
	demand repayment of debt
	dispute debt (2)
	pay deceased husband's debts to bailiff
	report someone for trade in meat
	take back excise money from customs official
	work as town guard
Agriculture, forestry	gather in hay
	keep pigs
	rake
	slaughter cow (2)
Care	organise funeral
	prepare rooms for funeral
	take care of mortally ill person
Crafts, construction	sew sack
	sew shirts to order
	spin cotton
	spin yarn
Credit	act as intermediary in credit market
	borrow silver bowl to use as surety
	borrow with pawn as surety
	extend credit (9)
	lend hops to someone
	stand surety (2)
Food, accommodation	bake and sell bread (2)
	bake bread in neighbour's house
	brew
	produce liquor (4)
	provide short-term lodgings
	provide sweets and sweet bread
	rent out rooms (4)

(cont.)

(*cont.*)

Category	Activity
	run tavern (5)
	take care of lodgers
	work as housekeeper for regional governor
Hunting, fishing	—
Managerial work	have calf slaughtered (2)
	have fabric dyed
	have female servant sell tar
	have peasants deliver iron
	have sleigh blanket sewn
	have someone grind (3)
	have steak sent to someone
	have wallpapers sent from Stockholm
	order female servant to go to mill
	order female servant to report cow at customs house
	send boy to pay excise
	send day labourer on errand
	send female servant with excise money
	send female servant with fabric
	send girl to pay excise
	send peasants with firewood
	send servants to mill
	supervise servants
Teaching	—
Theft, misappropriation	steal candlestick, spoon, clothing
	steal from peasant's wagon
	steal goose
Trade	buy and sell pillow case
	buy cow (2)
	buy fabric
	buy oxen
	buy rye in small quantities
	buy stolen apron
	buy woollen fabric
	commission someone to sell something (2)
	demand payment (2)
	demand payment for beer
	demand payment for iron
	have others sell on commission
	have shop (3)

(*cont.*)

Category	Activity
	make financial transactions (2)
	man shop
	order combs in large quantities
	order malt
	order textiles from Stockholm
	order wine from Stockholm
	purchase goods in market place
	purchase timber
	sell beer
	sell beer illegally
	sell black cloth
	sell clothing (2)
	sell clothing and kitchen utensils
	sell cotton skirt
	sell gloves and linen
	sell handkerchiefs on commission
	sell hen on commission
	sell meat
	sell silk on commission
	sell skin rug
	sell tar
	sell textiles on commission
	sell wine in small quantities
	sell woollen fabric
	trade in bills of exchange
	trade in fish
Trade in real estate	rent out land and house
Transport	carry meat on commission
	carry veal steak
	transport lemons
	transport malt to mill
Other specified work	own ship
Unspecified work	—

Sources: ULA, Örebro Rådhusrätt och magistrat, F 2, Vol. IV (1721–32), Vol. V (1733–38), Vol. VI (1737–40), Vol. VIII (1748–55), Vol. IX (1756–60), Vol. XII (1772–77) [probate inventories]; Örebro Rådshusrätt och magistrat, A 1 a, Vol. VII (1652–56), Vol. XV (1688–90), Vol. XVI (1691–93), Vol. LX (1756–59), Örebro Accisrätt, Örebro Kämnärsrätt, A 1, Vol. VI (1684–89), Vol. VII (1653–1700), Vol. XIV (1757–64), Örebro Hall och Manufakturrätt [court records]; Örebro Rådhusrätt och magistrat, K 1 b, Vol. VI (Krono- och stadsräkenskaper) [town accounts]; Örebro Rådhusrätt och magistrat, F 9 c, Vols I–IX; Karlsson, *Blad ur Örebro skolas äldsta historia.*

Bibliography

Archival sources

Kungliga Biblioteket, Stockholm (KB)

Kart- och bildsektionen
  General-tull-arrende-societetens svenska tullatlas

Landsarkivet, Göteborg (GLA)

Ulricehamns församling, födelse- och dopbok 1688–89

Landsarkivet, Uppsala (ULA)

Länsstyrelsen i Kopparbergs län
  Landskansliet
Länsstyrelsen i Örebro län
  Landskontoret
Örebro Accisrätt
Örebro Kämnärsrätt
Örebro Nicolai
  Husförhörslängder
Örebro Rådhusrätt och magistrat
  Domböcker [court records]
  Bouppteckningar [probate inventories]
  Mantalslängder [tax lists]

Lantmäteriet, Gävle

Historiska kartor

Riksarkivet, Marieberg, Stockholm (RA)

Äldre Kommissioner
Kammarkollegiet, Kansliet

Kammarkollegiet, Tull- och licentkontoret
Överdirektörens för landtullen arkiv
  Huvudarkivet, Inkomna handlingar
    Personella berättelser

Överdirektörens vid småtullarna och accisen arkiv
Statskontoret

Svenska Akademiens Ordboks arkiv, Lund

Published primary sources

Agardh, C. A. and Ljungberg, C. E., *Försök till en statsekonomisk statistik öfver Sverige: den statsekonomiska afdelningen*, Part II, Book I (Carlstad, 1854).

Anon., *Tankar om husbönders och tjenstehjons borgerliga rätt* (Stockholm, 1779).

Arkiv Digital, Västervik C:2 (1697–1724), C:3 (1724–45).

Elgenstierna, G., *Den introducerade svenska adelns ättartavlor, med tillägg och rättelser* (Stockholm: Norstedt, 1925–36).

GaW Database, Uppsala University (www.gaw.hist.uu.se).

Historisk statistik för Sverige: D. 1, Befolkning 1720–1967, 2nd edn (Örebro: Statistiska Centralbyrån (SCB), 1969).

Holmbäck, Å. and Wessén, E., *Magnus Erikssons landslag* (Stockholm: Nord. bokh. (distr.), 1962).

Höppener, J., *Bonde-Cur för den sjuka Riks-kroppen inom hus* (Stockholm, 1774).

Journal för Litteraturen och Theatern (Stockholm 1809).

Karlsson, K. F., *Blad ur Örebro skolas historia*, Part I (Örebro, 1871).

Karlsson, K. F., *Blad ur Örebro skolas historia*, Part II (Örebro, 1872).

Karlsson, K. F., *Blad ur Örebro skolas historia*, Part III (Örebro, 1875).

Karlsson, K. F., *Blad ur Örebro skolas historia*, Part IV (Örebro, 1899).

Kongl. Maj:ts förnyade Land-Tulls och Accis Stadga, 19 September 1776, in R. G. Modée, *Utdrag utur alle ifrån den 7. decemb. 1718–1791 utkomne publique handlingar*, (Stockholm, 1742–1829), Part X, 662–706.

Kongl. Maj:ts Landt-Tulls och Accis-Ordning, 17 December 1756, in R. G. Modée, *Utdrag utur alle ifrån den 7. decemb. 1718–1791 utkomne publique handlingar* (Stockholm, 1742–1829), Part VI, 4272–354.

Kongl. Maj:ts Reglemente för Landt-Tulls- och Accis-Kamrarne i Riket, 17 December 1756, in R. G. Modée, *Utdrag utur alle ifrån den 7. decemb. 1718–1791 utkomne publique handlingar* (Stockholm, 1742–1829), Part VI, 4212–71.

Kryger, J. F., *Tankar wid lediga stunder*, Part I (Stockholm, 1761).

Lucas, R., *The Duty of Servants* (London, 1685).

Machiavelli, N., *The Prince*, trans. W. K. Marriott (Ancona: Ancona Media, 2015).

Modée, R. G., *Utdrag utur alle ifrån den 7. decemb. 1718–1791 utkomne publique handlingar*. 15 parts (Stockholm: 1742–1829).

Möller, J., *Oförgripliga tankar om barnamord, til desz orsaker och anledningar, samt de medel och utwägar, som böra anwändas til desz förekommande* (Stockholm, 1796).

Ordbok över svenska språket [*SAOB*] (Lund: Gleerupska univ.-bokh. [distributör], 1893–).

Otter, S. von, 'Landshöfdingen Salomon von Otters Lefwernes Beskrifning'. In C. C. Gjörwell, *Det swenska biblioteket*, Part III (Stockholm: Nyström & Stolpe, 1759).

Oxford English Dictionary.

Reuterholm, N., *Nils Reuterholms Journal* (Stockholm: P. A. Norstedt & Söner, 1957).

Schmedeman, J. (ed.), *Kongl. stadgar, förordningar, bref och resolutioner, ifrån åhr 1528. in til 1701 angående justitiæ och executions- ährender, med een förteckning på stadgarne främst, och ett fulkommeligit orda-register efterst wid wercket öfwer thes: innehåld;*

uppå hans kongl. may:tz allernådigste befalning och privilegier, til thet almänne bästas tienst, och hwars och ens särskilte nytto, sålunda med flijt samlade, och genom trycket i dagzliuset befordrade, Part I, Åhr 1706 (Stockholm, 1706).

Stiernman, A. A. von, *Samling Utaf Kongl. Bref, Stadgar och Förordningar &c. Angående Sweriges Rikes Commerce, Politie och Oeconomie Uti Gemen, Ifrån Åhr 1523. In til när-warande tid. Uppå Hans Kongl. Maj:ts Nådigesta Befallning*, Parts I–VII (Stockholm, 1747–75).

Svenskt biografiskt lexikon (Stockholm: *Svenskt biografiskt lexikon*, 1918–).

Sveriges rikes lag: gillad och antagen på riksdagen år 1734. Facsimile of version printed in 1780 (Stockholm: Inst. för rättshistorisk forskning, 1984) [1734 Act].

Wahlund, P. E., *Osed och ordsed: det är 1234 oemotsägliga ordspråk och kärnfulla talesätt, hämtade ur sal. hr Christopher L. Grubbs Penu proverbiale och här ånyo återgivna med förklaringar, kommentarer, ordlista samt andra gagneliga bihang*, 4th edn (Stockholm: Natur och kultur, 1990).

Secondary sources

Ågren, K., *Adelns bönder och kronans: skatter och besvär i Uppland 1650–1680* (Uppsala: Historiska institutionen, Uppsala universitet, 1964).

Ågren, M., 'Another process of state formation: Swedish customs officials, their work and households', *Cultural and Social History*, 11 (2014), 31–49.

Ågren, M., *Domestic Secrets: Women and Property in Sweden, 1600–1857* (Chapel Hill: University of North Carolina Press, 2009).

Ågren, M., 'Emissaries, allies, accomplices and enemies: Married women's work in eighteenth-century urban Sweden', *Urban History*, 41 (2014), 394–414.

Ågren, M. (ed.), *Making a Living, Making a Difference: Gender and Work in Early Modern European Society* (New York, London: Oxford University Press, 2017).

Ailes, M. E., 'Wars, widows, and state formation in 17th-century Sweden', *Scandinavian Journal of History*, 31 (2006), 17–34.

Åmark, K., *Sveriges statsfinanser 1719–1809* (Stockholm: Norstedt, 1961).

Amussen, S. D., *An Ordered Society: Gender and Class in Early Modern England* (Oxford: Basil Blackwell, 1988).

Asker, B., *I konungens stad och ställe: länsstyrelser i arbete 1635–1735* (Uppsala: Stiftelsen för utgivande av arkivvetenskapliga studier, 2004).

Asker, B., *Hur riket styrdes: förvaltning, politik och arkiv 1520–1920* (Stockholm: Riksarkivet, 2007).

Beik, W., *Urban Protest in Seventeenth-Century France: The Culture of Retribution* (Cambridge: Cambridge University Press, 1997).

Bengtsson, R., *Bland smugglare, kapare och obstinata köpmän: Göteborg genom tiderna ur ett tullperspektiv* (Stockholm: Carlsson, 2006).

Bengtsson, R., 'Eric Ohlsson Pelbergh i Malmö: en accismästares vedermödor under de första svenskåren', *Argus* (1990), 34–8.

Bennett, J., '"History that stands still": Women's work in the European past', *Feminist Studies*, 14 (1988), 269–83.

Bodell, K., *Stad, bondebygd och bergslag vid mitten av 1600-talet: varuutbytet i Örebro och dess omland enligt tullängdernas vittnesbörd* (Stockholm: Almqvist & Wiksell, 1970).

Boydston, J., 'Gender as a question of historical analysis', *Gender and History*, 20:3 (2008), 558–83.

Braddick, M. J., *State Formation in Early Modern England, c. 1550–1700* (Cambridge: Cambridge University Press, 2000).

Braut, E., *Frå spinnelin til lerret: kvinnearbeid i Stavanger ca 1700–1775* (Oslo: Tingbokprosjektet, 1994).

Bredekamp, H., 'Hobbes's visual strategy', in P. Springborg (ed.), *The Cambridge Companion to Hobbes's "Leviathan"* (Cambridge: Cambridge University Press, 2007), 29–60.

Brewer, J., *The Sinews of Power: War, Money and the English State, 1688–1783* (London: Unwin Hyman, 1989).

Bruijn, J. R., 'States and their navies from the late sixteenth to the end of the eighteenth century', in P. Contamine (ed.), *War and Competition between States* (Oxford: Clarendon Press, 2000), 69–98.

Capp, B., 'Separate domains? Women and authority in early modern England', in P. Griffiths, A. Fox and S. Hindle (eds), *The Experience of Authority in Early Modern England* (Basingstoke: Macmillan; New York: St Martin's Press, 1996), 117–45.

Carlsson, S., *Ståndssamhälle och ståndspersoner 1700–1865: studier rörande det svenska ståndssamhällets upplösning*, 2nd rev. edn (Lund: Gleerup, 1973 [1949]).

Cavallin, M., *I kungens och folkets tjänst: synen på den svenske ämbetsmannen 1750–1780* (Göteborg: Historiska institutionen, Göteborgs universitet, 2003).

Christensen, J., *Bönder och herrar: bondeståndet i 1840-talets liberala representationsdebatt. Exemplen Gustaf Hierta och J. P. Thorell* (Göteborg: Historiska institutionen, Göteborgs universitet, 1997).

Clark, A., *Working Life of Women in the Seventeenth Century* (London: Routledge, 1992 [1919]).

Contamine, P., 'Introduction', in P. Contamine (ed.), *War and Competition between States* (Oxford: Clarendon Press, 2000), 1–7.

Corfield, P. J., *Power and the Professions in Britain 1700–1850* (London: Routledge, 1995).

Denys, C., 'The development of police forces in urban Europe in the eighteenth century', *Journal of Urban History*, 36:3 (2010), 332–44.

Earle, P., 'The female labour market in London in the late seventeenth and early eighteenth centuries', *The Economic History Review*, 42 (1989), 328–53.

Eibach, J., 'Das offene Haus: kommunikative Praxis im sozialen Nahraum der europäischen Frühen Neuzeit', *Zeitschrift für historische Forschung*, 38 (2011), 621–64.

Elmroth, I., *För kung och fosterland: studier i den svenska adelns demografi och offentliga funktioner 1600–1900* (Lund: Liber Läromedel/Gleerup, 1981).

Erickson, A. L., 'Married women's occupations in eighteenth-century London', *Continuity and Change*, 23 (2008), 267–307.

Ericsson, B., 'Nordisk stadsadministration vid 1700-talets mitt i komparativt perspektiv', in B. Ericsson *et al.* (eds), *Stadsadministration i Norden på 1700-talet* (Oslo, Bergen, Tromsø: Universitetsforlaget, 1982), 343–76.

Ertman, T., *Birth of the Leviathan: Building States and Regimes in Medieval and Early Modern Europe* (Cambridge: Cambridge University Press, 1997).

Fahlbeck, E., 'Ämbets- och tjänstemän', in *Statsvetenskapliga studier till Statsvetenskapliga föreningens i Uppsala tjugufemårsdag 7/11 1944* (Uppsala, Stockholm: Almqvist & Wiksell, 1944).

Falk, E., *Verbala förolämpningar i 1630-talets Uppsala: en historisk talaktsanalys* (Uppsala: Institutionen för nordiska språk, Uppsala universitet, 2011).

Fällström, A.-M. and Mäntylä, I., 'Stadsadministrationen i Sverige-Finland under frihetstiden', in B. Ericsson *et al.* (eds), *Stadsadministration i Norden på 1700-talet* (Oslo, Bergen, Tromsø: Universitetsforlaget, 1982), 173–286.

Fiebranz, R., Lindberg, E., Lindström, J. and Ågren, M., 'Making verbs count: The research project "Gender and Work" and its methodology', *Scandinavian Economic History Review*, 59 (2011), 273–93.

Florén, A., 'Nya roller, nya krav: några drag i den svenska nationalstatens formering', *Historisk tidskrift*, 107 (1987), 505–29.

Frohnert, P., *Kronans skatter och bondens bröd: den lokala förvaltningen och bönderna i Sverige 1719–1775* (Stockholm: Institutet för rättshistorisk forskning, 1993).

Gaughan, J. P. and Ferman, L. A., 'Toward an understanding of the informal economy', *The Annals of the American Academy of Political and Social Science*, 493:1 (1987), 15–25.

Gowing, L., 'The manner of submission: Gender and demeanour in seventeenth-century London', *Cultural and Social History*, 10:1 (2013), 25–45.

Gowing, L., 'Ordering the body: Illegitimacy and female authority in seventeenth-century England', in M. J. Braddick and J. Walter (eds), *Negotiating Power in Early Modern Society: Order, Hierarchy and Subordination in Britain and Ireland* (Cambridge: Cambridge University Press, 2001), 44–62.

Gustafsson, S., *Leverantörer och profitörer: olika geografiska områdens och sociala gruppers handel med fästningsbygget Sveaborg under den första byggnadsperioden 1748–1756* (Helsingfors: Finska Vetenskaps-Societeten, 2015).

Hacking, I., 'Making up people', in I. Hacking, *Historical Ontology* (Cambridge, MA, London: Harvard University Press, 2002), 99–114.

Hallenberg, M., 'The golden age of the aggressive male? Violence, masculinity and the state in sixteenth-century Sweden', *Gender and History*, 25 (2013), 132–49.

Hallenberg, M., 'Hapless heroes: Two discourses of royal service in sixteenth-century Sweden', in P. Karonen (ed.), *Hopes and Fears for the Future in Early Modern Sweden, 1500–1800* (Helsinki: Finnish Literature Society, 2009), 35–54.

Hallenberg, M., *Kungen, fogdarna och riket: lokalförvaltning och statsbyggande under tidig Vasatid* (Eslöv: Symposion, 2001).

Hallenberg, M., *Statsmakt till salu: arrendesystemet och privatiseringen av skatteuppbörden i det svenska riket 1618–1635* (Lund: Nordic Academic Press, 2008).

Hanley, S., 'Engendering the state: Family formation and state building in early modern France', *French Historical Studies*, 16:1 (1989), 4–27.

Hardwick, J., *Family Business: Litigation and the Political Economies of Daily Life in Early Modern France* (Oxford: Oxford University Press, 2009).

Hardwick, J., *The Practice of Patriarchy: Gender and the Politics of Household Authority in Early Modern France* (University Park: Pennsylvania State University Press, 1998).

Harnesk, B., 'Everyday resistance and the hidden transcript in seventeenth-century Sweden', in P. Karonen (ed.), *Hopes and Fears for the Future in Early Modern Sweden, 1500–1800* (Helsinki: Finnish Literature Society, 2009), 250–61.

Harnesk, B., *Legofolk: Drängar, pigor och bönder i 1700- och 1800-talens Sverige* (Umeå: Umeå universitet, 1990).

Hay, D. and Craven, P. (eds), *Masters, Servants, and Magistrates in Britain and the Empire, 1562–1955* (Chapel Hill: University of North Carolina Press, 2004).

Hedlund, R., *Västerås befolkning vid slutet av 1600-talet: en socialhistorisk studie* (Västerås: Västerås kulturnämnd, 1980).

Heijden, M. van der and Schmidt, A., 'Public services and women's work in early modern Dutch towns', *Journal of Urban History*, 36:3 (2010), 368–85.

Howard, S., 'Investigating responses to theft in early modern Wales: Communities, thieves and the courts', *Continuity and Change*, 19:3 (2004), 409–30.

Hoyman, M., 'Female participation in the informal economy: A neglected issue', *The Annals of the American Academy of Political and Social Science*, 493:1 (1987), 64–82.

Hunt, M. R., *The Middling Sort: Commerce, Gender, and the Family in England 1680–1780* (Berkeley: University of California Press, 1996).

Hunt, M. R., 'Women and the fiscal-imperial state in the late seventeenth and early eighteenth centuries', in K. Wilson (ed.), *A New Imperial History: Culture, Identity and Modernity in Britain and the Empire, 1660–1840* (New York: Cambridge University Press, 2004), 29–47.

Hunt, M. R., *Women in Eighteenth-Century Europe* (New York: Pearson Longman, 2009).

Jansson, K. H., *Kvinnofrid: synen på våldtäkt och konstruktionen av kön i Sverige 1600–1800* (Uppsala: Historiska institutionen, Uppsala universitet, 2002).

Jansson, K. H, '(O)rättfärdigt våld: fejdkultur i 1500-talets rättsliga och militära gränsland', in M. Sjöberg (ed.), *Sammanflätat: civilt och militärt i det tidigmoderna Sverige* (Uppsala: Historiska institutionen, Uppsala universitet, 2009), 85–100.

Jansson, K. H., 'Våldsgärning, illgärning, ogärning: könskodat språkbruk och föreställningar om våld i den medeltida landslagen', in E. Österberg and M. Lindstedt Cronberg (eds), *Våld: representation och verklighet* (Lund: Nordic Academic Press, 2006), 145–65.

Jansson, K. H., 'Våld som aggression eller kommunikation? Hemfridsbrott 1550–1650', *Historisk tidskrift*, 126 (2006), 429–52.

Karlsson, Å., *Den jämlike undersåten: Karl XII:s förmögenhetsbeskattning 1713* (Uppsala: Historiska institutionen, Uppsala universitet, 1994).

Karonen, P., *'Raastuvassa tavataan': Suomen kaupunkien hallinto- ja oikeuslaitoksen toimintaa ja virkamiehiä suurvalta-aikana* (Jyväskylä: Jyväskylän yliopisto, 1995).

Klingnéus, S., *Bönder blir vapensmeder: protoindustriell tillverkning i Närke under 1600- och 1700-talen* (Uppsala: Historiska institutionen, Uppsala universitet, 1997).

Korda, N., *Labors Lost: Women's Work and the Early Modern English Stage* (Philadelphia: University of Pennsylvania Press, 2011).

Kotkas, T., *Royal Police Ordinances in Early Modern Sweden: The Emergence of Voluntaristic Understanding of Law* (Leiden: Brill, 2013).

Kroener, B. R., 'The modern state and military society in the eighteenth century', in P. Contamine (ed.), *War and Competition between States* (Oxford: Clarendon Press, 2000), 195–220.

Landberg, H., *Det kontinentala krigets ekonomi: studier i krigsfinansiering under svensk stormaktstid* (Stockholm: Läromedelsförlagen, 1971).

Larsson, E., *Från adlig uppfostran till borgerlig utbildning: Kungl. Krigsakademien mellan åren 1792 och 1866* (Uppsala: Historiska institutionen, Uppsala universitet, 2005).

Lennersand, M., *Rättvisans och allmogens beskyddare: den absoluta staten, kommissionerna och tjänstemännen, ca 1680–1730* (Uppsala: Historiska institutionen, Uppsala universitet, 1999).

Lennersand, M., Mispelaere, J., Pihl, C. and Ågren, M., 'Gender, work and the fiscal-military state', in M. Ågren (ed.), *Making a Living, Making a Difference: Gender and Work in Early Modern European Society* (New York: Oxford University Press, 2017), 178–203.

Lilja, S. and Nilsson, L., *Historisk tätortsstatistik del 2: städernas folkmängd och tillväxt. Sverige (med Finland) ca 1570-tal till 1810-tal* (Stockholm: Stads- och kommunhistoriska institutet, 1996).

Lind, P., *'Strunt alt hvad du orerar': Carl Michael Bellman, ordensretoriken och Bacchi Orden* (Uppsala: Litteraturvetenskapliga institutionen, Uppsala universitet, 2014).

Linde, M., 'Envåldskungens makt och ämbetsmännens: ämbetsmannakontroll och maktlegitimering i Karl XII:s Sverige', in *Karolinska förbundets årsbok* (Stockholm: Karolinska förbundet, 1997), 43–103.

Lindegren, J., 'Men, money and means', in P. Contamine (ed.), *War and Competition between States* (Oxford: Clarendon Press, 2000), 129–62.

Lindegren, J., *Utskrivning och utsugning: produktion och reproduktion i Bygdeå 1620–1640* (Uppsala: Historiska institutionen, Uppsala universitet, 1980).

Lindström, D., *Skrå, stad och stat: Stockholm, Malmö och Bergen ca 1350–1622* (Uppsala: Historiska institutionen, Uppsala universitet, 1991).

Ling, S., *Konsten att försörja sig: kvinnors arbete i Stockholm 1650–1750* (Stockholm: Stockholmia förlag, 2016).

Lövgren, A.-B., *Handläggning och inflytande: beredning, föredragning och kontrasignering under Karl XI:s envälde* (Lund: Historiska institutionen, Lunds universitet, 1980).

Lundgren, B., 'Det äro många postmästaränkor som sitta vid tjänsterna efter männen ...', *Historisk tidskrift*, 1 (1987), 23–34.

MacKay, L., 'Why they stole: Women in the Old Bailey, 1779–1789', *Journal of Social History*, 32:3 (1999), 623–39.

Maza, S., *Servants and Masters in Eighteenth-Century France: The Uses of Loyalty* (Princeton: Princeton University Press, 1983).

Meldrum, T., *Domestic Service and Gender, 1660–1750: Life and Work in the London Household* (Harlow: Longman, 2000).

Montenach, A., 'Legal trade and black markets: Food trades in Lyon in the late seventeenth and early eighteenth centuries', in D. Simonton and A. Montenach (eds), *Female Agency in the Urban Economy: Gender in European Towns, 1640–1830* (New York: Routledge, 2013), 17–34.

Myrdal, J., *Det svenska jordbrukets historia*, Vol. II: *Jordbruket under feodalismen: 1000–1700* (Stockholm: Natur och Kultur, 1999).

Neale, M., 'Making crime pay in late eighteenth-century Bristol: Stolen goods, the informal economy and the negotiation of risk', *Continuity and Change*, 26:3 (2011), 439–59.

Nilsson, S. A., '1634 års regeringsform i det svenska statssystemet', in S. A. Nilsson, *De stora krigens tid: om Sverige som militärstat och bondesamhälle* (Uppsala: Historiska institutionen, Uppsala universitet, 1990), 199–225.

Nilsson, S. A., 'Den karolinska militärstaten: fredens problem och krigets', in S. A. Nilsson, *De stora krigens tid: om Sverige som militärstat och bondesamhälle* (Uppsala: Historiska institutionen, Uppsala universitet, 1990), 245–70.

Norrhem, S., *Kvinnor vid maktens sida: 1632–1772* (Lund: Nordic Academic Press, 2007).

Norrhem, S. *Uppkomlingarna: kanslitjänstemännen i 1600-talets Sverige och Europa* (Umeå: Umeå universitet, 1993).

Ogborn, M., 'The capacities of the state: Charles Davenant and the management of the excise, 1683–1698', *Journal of Historical Geography*, 24:3 (1998), 289–312.

Ogilvie, S. C., *A Bitter Living: Women, Markets, and Social Capital in Early Modern Germany* (Oxford: Oxford University Press, 2003).

Oja, L., 'Childcare and gender in Sweden *c.* 1600–1800', *Gender and History*, 27 (2015), 77–111.

Ojala, K., 'Opportunity or compulsion? Domestic servants in urban communities in the eighteenth century', in P. Karonen (ed.), *Hopes and Fears for the Future in Early Modern Sweden, 1500–1800* (Helsinki: Finnish Literature Society, 2009), 206–22.

Østhus, H., *Contested Authority: Master and Servant in Copenhagen and Christiania, 1750–1850* (Florence: European University Institute, 2013).

Parker, G., 'Warfare', in P. Burke (ed.), *The New Cambridge Modern History*, Vol. XIII (Cambridge: Cambridge University Press, 1979), 201–19.

Peterson, C., *Peter the Great's Administrative and Judicial Reforms: Swedish Antecedents and the Process of Reception* (Stockholm: Institutet för rättshistorisk forskning, 1979).

Pihl, C., *Arbete: skillnadsskapande och försörjning i 1500-talets Sverige* (Uppsala: Historiska institutionen, Uppsala universitet, 2012).

Pratt, M. L., 'Arts of the Contact Zone', *Profession* 1991, 33–40.

Prytz, C., *Familjen i kronans tjänst: donationspraxis, förhandling och statsformering under svenskt 1600-tal* (Uppsala: Historiska institutionen, Uppsala universitet, 2013).

Pursche, W., *Borgmästare Erland Svensson: en storköpman i Vadstena 1632–1657* (Vadstena: Föreningen Gamla Vadstena, 1983).

Raeff, M., *The Well-Ordered Police State: Social and Institutional Change through Law in the Germanies and Russia, 1600–1800* (New Haven: Yale University Press, 1983).

Reuterswärd, E., *Ett massmedium för folket: studier i de allmänna kungörelsernas funktion i 1700-talets samhälle* (Lund: Historiska institutionen, Lunds universitet, 2001).

Runefelt, L., 'Att springa bort sin dag för en hare: lättja, egennytta och rörlighet i retorik om allmogen 1750–1850', in M. Wallenberg Bondesson, O. Husz, J. Myrdal and M. Tydén (eds), *Människans kunskap och kunskapen om människan: en gränslös historia* (Lund: Sekel Bokförlag, 2012), 96–112.

Sabean, D. W., *Property, Production, and Family in Neckarhausen, 1700–1870* (Cambridge: Cambridge University Press, 1990).

Schmidt Blaine, M., 'The power of petitions: Women and the New Hampshire provincial government, 1695–1770', *International Review of Social History*, 46 (2001), Supplement, 57–77.

Scott, J. C., *The Art of Not Being Governed: An Anarchist History of Upland Southeast Asia* (New Haven: Yale University Press, 2009).

Scott, J. C., *Seeing like a State: How Certain Schemes to Improve the Human Condition Have Failed* (New Haven: Yale University Press, 1998).

Shepard, A., *Meanings of Manhood in Early Modern England* (Oxford: Oxford University Press, 2003).

Simonton, D., *A History of European Women's Work: 1700 to the Present* (London: Routledge, 1998).

Sjöberg, M., *Kvinnor i fält 1550–1850* (Möklinta: Gidlunds, 2008).

Skuncke, M.-C., *Carl Peter Thunberg: Botanist and Physician. Career-Building across the Oceans in the Eighteenth Century* (Uppsala: Swedish Collegium for Advanced Study, 2014).

Smith, W., *Studier i svensk tulladministration,* Part I: *Från äldsta tid till omkring 1718.* Sveriges allmänna tulltjänstemannaförenings skriftserie, 3 (Stockholm: Sveriges allmänna tulltjänstemannaförenings skrfiftserie, 1956).

Smith, W., *Studier i svensk tulladministration,* Part II: *Tulltjänsten i landsorten på Kristinas tid.* Sveriges allmänna tulltjänstemannaförenings skriftserie, 4 (Stockholm: Sveriges allmänna tulltjänstemannaförenings skriftserie, 1955).

Söderberg, T., *Den namnlösa medelklassen: socialgrupp två i det gamla svenska samhället intill 1770-talet* (Stockholm: Bonnier, 1956).

Sörndal, O., *Den svenska länsstyrelsen: uppkomst, organisation och allmän maktställning* (Lund: Lunds universitet, 1937).

Spence, C., *Women, Credit and Debt in Early Modern Scotland* (Manchester: Manchester University Press, 2016).

Stadin, K., *Småstäder, småborgare och stora samhällsförändringar: borgarnas sociala struktur i Arboga, Enköping och Västervik under perioden efter 1680* (Uppsala: Historiska institutionen, Uppsala universitet, 1979).

Stadin, K., *Stånd och genus i stormaktstidens Sverige* (Lund: Nordic Academic Press, 2004).

Strayer, J. R., *On the Medieval Origins of the Modern State* (Princeton: Princeton University Press, 1970).

Stretton, T., *Women Waging Law in Elizabethan England* (Cambridge: Cambridge University Press, 1998).

Stuart, K., *Defiled Trades and Social Outcasts: Honor and Ritual Pollution in Early Modern Germany* (Cambridge: Cambridge University Press, 1999).

Styles, J., 'Clothing the north: The supply of non-élite clothing in the eighteenth-century north of England', *Textile History*, 25:2 (1994), 139–66.

Thisner, F., *Indelta inkomster: en studie av det militära löneindelningsverket 1721–1833* (Uppsala: Historiska institutionen, Uppsala universitet, 2014).

Thisner, F., *Militärstatens arvegods: officerstjänstens socialreproduktiva funktion i Sverige och Danmark, ca 1720–1800* (Uppsala: Historiska institutionen, Uppsala universitet, 2007).

Thunander, R., *Hovrätt i funktion: Göta hovrätt och brottmålen, 1635–1699.* (Stockholm: Institutet för rättshistorisk forskning, 1993).

Tilly, C., *Coercion, Capital, and European States, AD 990–1990* (Oxford: Blackwell, 1990).

Tin-bor Hui, V., *War and State Formation in Ancient China and Early Modern Europe* (Cambridge: Cambridge University Press, 2005).

Tralau, J., 'Leviathan, the beast of myth: Medusa, Dionysos, and the riddle of Hobbes's sovereign monster', in P. Springborg (ed.), *The Cambridge Companion to Hobbes's "Leviathan"* (Cambridge: Cambridge University Press, 2007), 61–81.

Vainio-Korhonen, K., 'Handicrafts as professions and sources of income in late eighteenth- and early nineteenth-century Turku (Åbo): A gender viewpoint to economic history', *Scandinavian Economic History Review*, 48:1 (2000), 40–63.

Vanja, C., 'Auf Geheiß der Vögtin: Amtsfrauen in hessischen Hospitälern der Frühen Neuzeit', in H. Wunder and C. Vanja (eds), *Weiber, Menschen, Frauenzimmer: Frauen in der ländlichen Gesellschaft 1500–1800* (Göttingen: Vandenhoeck und Ruprecht, 1996), 77–95.

Vanja, C., 'Zwischen Verdrängung und Expansion, Kontrolle und Befreiung: Frauenarbeit im 18. Jahrhundert im deutschsprachigen Raum', *Vierteljahrschrift für Sozial- und Wirtschaftsgeschichte*, 79:4 (1992), 457–82.

Voss, L. H. van., 'Introduction', *International Review of Social History*, 46 (2001), Supplement, 1–10.

Walker, G., *Crime, Gender and Social Order in Early Modern England* (Cambridge: Cambridge University Press, 2008).

Weber, M., *Wirtschaft und Gesellschaft: Grundriss der Verstehenden Soziologie*, 5th rev. edn (Tübingen: J. C. B. Mohr (Paul Siebeck), 1972).

Westling, C., *Småstadens dynamik: Skänninges och Vadstenas befolkning och kontaktfält ca 1630–1660* (Linköping: Historiska institutionen, Linköpings universitet, 2003).

Whittle, J., 'Servants in rural England *c.*1450–1650: Hired work as a means of accumulating wealth and skills before marriage', in M. Ågren and A. L. Erickson (eds), *The Marital Economy in Scandinavia and Britain, 1400–1900* (Burlington, VT: Ashgate, 2005), 89–107.

Wiesner, M. E., *Working Women in Renaissance Germany* (New Brunswick, NJ: Rutgers University Press, 1986).

Wikberg, K., *Alla dessa tullar – en arkivguide: vägledning till tullarkiv och tullhandlingar i Riksarkivet* (Stockholm: Riksarkivet, 2006).

Wirilander, K., *Herrskapsfolk: ståndspersoner i Finland 1721–1870* (Stockholm: Nordiska museet, 1982).

Wittrock, G., *Regering och allmoge under Kristinas egen styrelse: riksdagen 1650* (Uppsala: Skrifter utgivna av K. Humanistiska Vetenskapssamfundet i Uppsala, 1953).

Wottle, M., *Det lilla ägandet: korporativ formering och sociala relationer inom Stockholms minuthandel 1720–1810* (Stockholm: Stads- och kommunhistoriska institutet, 2000).

Unpublished source

Karlsson, J. '"God! Let me not waste a moment of this year": An intersectional perspective on the practices of time-use in gentry women's households in Sweden 1793 to 1839', master's thesis (Uppsala University, 2013).

Index

Italic page numbers refer to tables.

EU authorised representative for GPSR:
Easy Access System Europe, Mustamäe tee 50,
10621 Tallinn, Estonia
gpsr.requests@easproject.com

www.ingramcontent.com/pod-product-compliance
Ingram Content Group UK Ltd.
Pitfield, Milton Keynes, MK11 3LW, UK
UKHW021833100926
8556IPUK00004B/320
* 9 7 8 1 5 2 6 1 0 0 6 4 1 *